Nelson's AMAZING Bible Trivia
BOOK ONE

Brad Densmore

THOMAS NELSON PUBLISHERS
Nashville

Printed in Nashville, Tennessee, by Thomas Nelson, Inc.

Unless otherwise indicated, all Scripture quotations are from the New King James Version, copyright © 1979, 1980, 1982 by Thomas Nelson, Inc.

Thomas Nelson Publishers wishes to acknowledge Mr. Matt Lehman, www.newhumor.com, www.csv.warwick.ac.uk, suabk/lighter/jokes/, and Just 4 Fun: Christian Jokes for their contributions to the humor in this book.

Densmore, Brad, 1955–
    Nelson's amazing Bible trivia / Brad Densmore
        p. cm.
    ISBN 0-7852-4259-7
    1. Bible—Miscellanea I. Title

Printed in the United States of America
3 4 5 — 02 01 00

TA LE OF CONTE TS

PART ONE
Old Testament

1. Genesis 3
2. Exodus 17
3. Leviticus 29
4. Numbers 41
5. Deuteronomy 57
6. Joshua 75
7. Judges 89
8. Ruth 103
9. First Samuel 107
10. Second Samuel 123
11. First Kings 137
12. Second Kings 151
13. First Chronicles 165
14. Second Chronicles 175
15. Ezra 189
16. Nehemiah 195
17. Esther 203
18. Job 209
19. Psalms 219
20. Proverbs 231
21. Ecclesiastes 239
22. Song of Solomon 247
23. Isaiah 251
24. Jeremiah 265

25. Lamentations 279
26. Ezekiel 283
27. Daniel 295
28. Hosea 303
29. Joel 307
30. Amos 311
31. Obadiah 315
32. Jonah 319
33. Micah 323
34. Nahum 327
35. Habakkuk 331
36. Zephaniah 335
37. Haggai 339
38. Zechariah 343
39. Malachi 349

PART TWO
New Testament

1. Matthew 355
2. Mark 365
3. Luke 373
4. John 383
5. Acts 391
6. Romans 403
7. First Corinthians 411
8. Second Corinthians 417
9. Galatians 423
10. Ephesians 427
11. Philippians 431

12. Colossians 435
13. First and Second Thessalonians 439
14. First and Second Timothy 443
15. Titus 447
16. Philemon 451
17. Hebrews 455
18. James 461
19. First and Second Peter 465
20. First, Second and Third John 469
21. Jude 473
22. Revelation 477

12. Group . . . .
13. Because . . . .
14. Grand . . . .
15. . . . .
16. . . . .
17. . . . .
18. . . . .
19. . . . .
20. . . . .
21. . . . .
22. . . . .

FOREWORD

The Bible is full of fascinating information. We have discovered this as we have pored over the many questions that make up this book. We take the Bible very seriously, as the inspired Word of God, and have worked very hard to ensure that this book is as accurate as possible. All references are to the New King James Version of the Bible; each question and answer has been examined to make sure the interpretation is accurate and treated with the utmost respect.

Be intrigued with the information you will discover! Not only do you hold in your hands a thousand questions about the Bible, but you are also given bits of information about the times during which each book of the Bible was written. We find these bits of information to be especially helpful, as they help you to place the events of the Bible with those of the secular world. They somehow make the Bible events seem more real.

As you go through the book, you will no doubt be surprised, shocked, and even humored by the facts you will uncover. Laugh! Enjoy the Scriptures that God has given us. Nurture your sense of humor. Remember: Solomon, renowned for his wisdom, said, "There is . . . a time to laugh!" (Eccl. 3:4).

Finally, let's encourage one another with the knowledge and experience of the Bible. It is full of practical ideas for happiness and purpose in this life, as well as promises for the life eternal. Share it with friends and family. We hope to help and to add some curiosity to your study of the Bible through your enjoyment of *Nelson's Amazing Bible Trivia!*

PREFACE

Hi, and welcome to *Nelson's Amazing Bible Trivia!* When the fine people at Thomas Nelson Publishers approached me about writing this book, we established three ground rules from the very beginning:

It had to be biblically based

It had to be packed with usable, helpful information

It had to be **funny!**

I have to admit, it was the latter that interested me the most. You see, I'm a firm believer that if you can make people smile, chuckle, or "laugh 'til they cry," then you have a much better opportunity to help them retain the message. And the Bible's message is one that surely merits retaining!

While we're sure you'll enjoy the humor and entertainment packed in these pages, please don't overlook the potential of *Nelson's Amazing Bible Trivia* as a reference book as well. We've taken steps to make it user-friendly for everything from Sunday morning services to youth groups and Sunday school classes.

It's arranged sequentially to parallel the Bible. For instance, if your group is studying the book of Luke, you can turn right to that section, without having to hunt or consult an index. The answers are at the end of each chapter. (Hey, did we think of everything or what!)

There are questions for every single book of the Bible! Simply because some are only a page or two is no reason to overlook them! (Actually, I'm somewhat short myself, so I can relate!)

The "Top Ten Lists," jokes, songs, and other humorous selections make great ice-breakers for all kinds of groups. If you're looking for new material to get your tribe alive, feel free to give this a shot!

We're hoping that *Nelson's Amazing Bible Trivia* not only encourages and heals you with laughter, but builds upon your Bible knowledge and becomes an indispensable part of your library. Happy reading . . . and **THANK YOU!**

—BRAD DENSMORE

ACKNOWLEDGMENTS

Some *Amazing* people . . .

My nephew, Jeff Kiersey, whose computer acumen made it possible for me to survive (without ulcers!) a major technological upgrade, right in the middle of this project! Jeff is one of those rare people who has lots of intelligence and an equal dose of humility. Thanks also to his wife, my niece, Kelly, for loaning him out!

My editors, Teri Wilhelms and Kate Anderson, and all the professional, courteous, and helpful people at Thomas Nelson Publishers.

My three-year-old grandson, Marshal J. Since I can't quite think of myself as a grandfather, this great kid will see to it that I get younger with each passing day.

My speech and writing students at Jackson Community College, who manage to keep me on my toes. I love you guys!

Finally, my wife, Cathy, who has this passé, whimsical idea that if she keeps kissing me, I'll eventually turn into a handsome prince. One of these days, I suppose, I should tell her the truth.

THE
OLD
TESTAMENT

~GENESIS~

(c. 1950–1550 B.C.)

1. **According to Genesis, what was the first thing God said?**
   A. "Let the land produce living creatures."
   B. "Let there be light."
   C. "Let the waters be gathered into one place."
   D. "Now where did I lay my glasses?"

2. **What were the first things in creation God saw as "good"?**
   A. Land and seas
   B. Video games
   C. Sky and clouds
   D. Trees and plants
   E. Night and day

3. **On which day of creation did God bring about humans?**
   A. The second day
   B. Humans were actually made by Mattel, and God quickly decided they were bad news.
   C. The sixth day
   D. None of the above
   E. The morning of the fourth day

4. **What did God say would happen to the man if he ate from the forbidden tree?**
   A. He would die.
   B. He would realize he was naked.

C. He would have no TV for a week.
D. He would be doomed to till the ground forever.
E. He would be cast out of Eden.

5. **What happened just prior to God's creation of Eve?**
   A. The serpent appeared to Adam.
   B. An angel appeared to Adam.
   C. Adam named the animals.
   D. Adam tasted the forbidden fruit.

6. **Which of the following were NOT part of God's curse for Adam and Eve's disobedience?**
   A. Athlete's foot
   B. The death of Cain
   C. Banishment from Eden
   D. The cursing of the ground
   E. Pain in childbirth

Noah's Top Ten Excuses for Building an Ark

10. 500-foot-long Chris Craft was too expensive
9. Figured it would make a nice restaurant if it didn't rain
8. Pontoon shortage
7. Animals too reckless with jet skis
6. Gophers carved him a great deal on wood
5. Had to show up his neighbors who had the really smooth yacht
4. Hoped to ride the popularity coattails of *Titanic*
3. Was trying to make it into *Guiness Book of World Records*
2. Started out building a deck but just got carried away
1. For a three-hour tour

7. **Why did God put a mark on Cain?**
   A. So that everyone would know he was the son of sinful parents
   B. So he could reenter Eden without having to pay again
   C. To protect him from injury by others
   D. To signify him as "holy unto God"
   E. To remind everyone he came in contact with that he was a murderer

8. **How old was Adam when his third son, Seth, was born?**
   A. 130 years
   B. 865 years
   C. 417 years
   D. 58 years

9. **This man walked with God, and one day God simply "took him."**
   A. Enoch
   B. Methuselah
   C. Jared
   D. Seth
   E. Abel

> **SUPER CHALLENGE #1**
>
> *This man was said to be a ". . . mighty one on the earth. The beginning of his kingdom was Babylon, Erech, Akkad, and Calneh in Shinar. From that land he went to Assyria, and built Nineveh, Rehoboth Ir, Calah and Resen . . ."*
>
> **Can you name him?**

10. **Genesis alluded to a race of giants which existed before the Great Flood. What were they called?**
    A. Nazarites
    B. Centaurs
    C. Troglodytes
    D. Mighty men of old
    E. Philistines

11. **Although Noah's ark was measured in cubits, about how many feet long was it?**
    A. 450
    B. 260

C. 892

D. 1660

12. According to Genesis Chapter 7, how long did the flood waters cover the earth?

   A. 40 days and nights

   B. 100 days

   C. 360 days

   D. Just one weekend when they had planned a family picnic

   E. 150 days

13. What two birds did Noah use to measure the flood-waters?

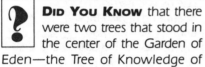

DID YOU KNOW that there were two trees that stood in the center of the Garden of Eden—the Tree of Knowledge of Good and Evil **and** the Tree of Life?

   A. A sparrow and a raven

   B. A pterodactyl and a hummingbird

   C. A pigeon and a crow

   D. A hawk and a dove

   E. A raven and a dove

14. How old was Noah when the flood ended?

   A. 601 years

   B. 825 years

   C. 257 years

   D. 400 years

15. What did God tell Noah would be the sign of His covenant to never flood the earth again?

   A. The sunshine

   B. A secret handshake

   C. A rainbow

   D. The proliferation of animals

16. Which of Noah's sons was cursed for seeing his father's nakedness?

A. Shem
B. Ham
C. Japeth
D. Peeping Tom
E. Canaan

17. **What TWO reasons did men give for constructing the city and Tower of Babel?**
    A. To control their enemies and their flocks
    B. To reach into the heavens and be as gods
    C. To make a name for themselves and not be scattered abroad over the face of the earth
    D. To keep watch over the fertile plains and keep the tribes of God together

18. **When Abram (Abraham) and Sarai (Sarah), his wife, went down to Egypt to escape a famine, what did they tell the Egyptians?**
    A. That Abram was a leper
    B. That they were actually brother and sister
    C. That God had sent them to punish Egypt
    D. That Sarai was pregnant

19. **The first example of tithing appears in Genesis 14, when Abram gives a tenth of his "battle winnings" to this High Priest:**
    A. Uncle Sam
    B. Melchizedek
    C. Chedorlaomer
    D. Birsha
    E. Eliezer of Damascus

Hammurabi's code now official!
(*c.* 1800 B.C.)

20. **God told Abram that his descendants would be enslaved and mistreated for how long?**

A. "Many years"
B. "Two generations"
C. "A thousand years"
D. "Four hundred years"
E. "Until they repent"

21. **Which of the following was true concerning Abraham's family:**
    A. He had a daughter named Hagar with his wife Sarah and an illegitimate son named Isaac with an unnamed woman.
    B. He had a son named Isaac with Hagar and a son named Ishmael with his wife Sarah.
    C. He had a son named Isaac with his wife Sarah and a son named Ishmael with his wife's servant Hagar.
    D. Sarah, his wife, had Ishmael when she was very old and thought herself barren.

22. **How many righteous people did God initially require for Sodom to be spared; what was His final requirement after Abraham argued with Him?**
    A. One hundred; seven
    B. Eighty; twenty
    C. Fifty; ten
    D. Seventy; five

> **SUPER CHALLENGE #2**
> *During a famine, Isaac and Rebekah stayed in a place called Gerar. The Philistine King issued a decree that anyone who molested them would be put to death.*
>
> **Can you name this king?**

23. **After God knew Abraham was willing to sacrifice his son Isaac, an angel stopped him. Abraham sacrificed what instead?**
    A. A ram that was trapped nearby
    B. His nosy neighbor, Mr. Kravitz
    C. A small lamb he had brought along
    D. A dove

24. **To whom did God say, "Two nations are in your womb, and two peoples shall be separated from your body."**
   A. Hagar
   B. Keturah
   C. Sarah
   D. Rebekah

25. **What did Isaac and the Herdsmen of Gerar quarrel over in the Valley of Gerar?**
   A. Servants
   B. Water
   C. Foreign women
   D. Sheep and oxen
   E. Tickets to a NASCAR race at Beersheba

26. **Who helped Jacob "steal" his father's blessing which was intended for Esau?**
   A. Esau
   B. Esau's wife, Judith
   C. Rebekah, Jacob's mother
   D. An angel of the Lord
   E. The ghost of Abraham

   A good man, but has a problematic wife. He and his wife enjoy walking nude in the woods.

   ADAM

27. **During Jacob's dream about a ladder reaching into Heaven, what did God tell him his descendants would be compared to?**
   A. The dust of the earth
   B. The grains of the sand of the sea
   C. The stars of the heavens
   D. Drops of water in the ocean
   E. Flies in a barnyard

28. **Which of the following statements was true concerning Jacob's wives and children?**

A. His father-in-law tricked him by making him marry Rachel first, when he was actually in love with Leah.

B. Leah never produced any children, while Rachel had several children with Jacob.

C. Neither Rachel nor Leah bore children for Jacob, so they gave him their maidservants, and both bore him children.

D. Eventually Jacob had children by both Leah, Rachel, and their maidservants.

E. Jacob practiced celibacy and never fathered children.

29. **What was the new name given to Jacob by the man (angel) he wrestled with?**
    A. Kareem Abdul-Jabbar
    B. Israel
    C. Saul
    D. Abraham
    E. Judah

30. **What were Joseph's brothers planning to blame his death on after they killed him?**
    A. Thieves who robbed then murdered him
    B. Thirst/heat exhaustion
    C. Drowning while watering cattle
    D. A wild animal attack

31. **He slept with his daughter-in-law, whom he mistook for a prostitute. As a result, she had twins. Who was this man?**
    A. Hirah
    B. Reuben
    C. Judah
    D. Benjamin

32. **Which two officials offended the pharaoh of Egypt and found themselves in prison with Joseph?**

A. The astrologer and the cupbearer
B. The vineyard keeper and the chief consul
C. The press secretary and the lobbyist
D. The chief butler and the chief baker
E. The diviner and the chief musician

33. What dream did Joseph interpret for Pharaoh that ultimately led to his being put in charge of all the land in Egypt?

A. A dream in which Pharaoh thought he ate a five pound marshmallow, then awakened to discover his pillow was missing
B. A dream about grapevine branches, with the grapes being squeezed into Pharaoh's cup
C. A dream about seven healthy cows being eaten by seven sickly cows
D. A dream about an army marching on Egypt, made up of skeleton-like soldiers
E. A dream about the death of Potiphar's wife

34. **What did Joseph have his servant put in Benjamin's sack, as if Benjamin had stolen it?**
    A. A silver cup
    B. A gold ring
    C. A red jewel
    D. His Nike sweatband
    E. A letter from Pharaoh

35. **What was Pharaoh's response when he heard Joseph had invited his family to Egypt?**
    A. He was enraged and sent Joseph away, threatening to have him killed if he ever returned.
    B. He was extremely saddened and lowered Joseph's rank.
    C. He offered no response.

Top Ten Reasons Jacob Wrestled with an Angel

10. Jesse "The Body" Ventura was busy serving as governor.
9. Screaming fans didn't realize it was all fake.
8. He knew he wouldn't have a chance against Hulk Hogan.
7. He knew he could tag his partner Samson whenever he got tired.
6. Wings made it easier to get a pin.
5. Esau that he had no chance.
4. The angel was a featherweight.
3. Once in a headlock, the halo could be unscrewed.
2. He had to choose between an angel and Jackie Chan.
1. He was tired of the angel harping on him all the time.

D. He was pleased and offered the best of Egypt to them.

36. **What did Israel (Jacob) say to Joseph (whom he thought long dead) upon meeting him in Goshen?**
   A. "I will punish your brothers for their great evil."
   B. "Am I seeing a ghost?"
   C. "Now I can die peacefully, since I know you are alive."
   D. "Your dreams as a youth have come true."
   E. "Hot diggedy dog! I feel like I just won a million shekels!"

37. **Why did Joseph become displeased with his father, Jacob, just prior to his death?**
   A. Because Jacob had defamed Pharaoh
   B. Because he blessed Joseph's younger son over the older one
   C. Because he asked Joseph to forgive his brothers for selling him into slavery
   D. Because his father accused him of taking advantage of the Hebrews during the famine

38. **Whom did Jacob request that he be buried with?**
   A. Adam and Eve
   B. Abraham and Sarah
   C. Isaac, Rebekah and Leah
   D. Elvis
   E. A & B only
   F. B & C only
   G. A & D only

39. **The book of Genesis ended with what event?**
   A. The renewal of Egypt after the great famine
   B. God's anointing of Moses

C. A chili cook-off

D. The rise of a new pharaoh who disliked the Hebrews

E. The death of Joseph

Q. What answer did Adam give his children as to why they no longer lived in Eden?

A. Your mother ate us out of house and home.

ANSWERS TO GENESIS QUESTIONS

#	ANS	REF	#	ANS	REF
1.	B	1:3	24.	D	25:21–23
2.	E	1:4,5	25.	B	26:20
3.	C	1:27–31	26.	C	27:5–10
4.	A	2:17	27.	A	28:14
5.	C	2:20	28.	D	30:4, 9–12,
6.	A,B	3:14–19			22–24
7.	C	4:15	29.	B	32:28
8.	A	5:3	30.	D	37:20
9.	A	5:24	31.	C	38:15, 27
10.	D	6:4	32.	D	40:1–3
11.	A	6:15	33.	C	41:1–4
12.	E	7:24	34.	A	44:2
13.	D	8:7–8	35.	D	45:16–20
14.	A	8:13	36.	C	46:30
15.	C	9:13–17	37.	B	48:17–19
16.	B	9:22–25	38.	F	49:29–32
17.	C	11:4	39.	E	50:26
18.	B	12:11–13			
19.	B	14:18–20			
20.	D	15:13		Super Challenges:	
21.	C	16:15; 21:3		#1: Nimrod (10:8–12)	
22.	C	18:26, 32		#2: Abimelech (26:11)	
23.	A	22:13			

~EXODUS~

(c. 1500–1400 B.C.)

1. **Historians believe that the Israelite race in Egypt numbered as many as three million people prior to the Exodus. How many of Jacob's descendants originally went to Egypt?**
   A. 144
   B. 1000 men, plus women and children
   C. 70
   D. The Bible doesn't specifically say.

2. **What was the primary reason the Egyptians disliked the Israelites?**
   A. They didn't accept the Israelites' God.
   B. They feared them because the Israelites were so numerous.
   C. Their skin color was noticeably different.
   D. They had a fundamental disagreement regarding the NBA strike.
   E. They saw the Israelites as a draining force on their resources.

3. **What two plans did Pharaoh attempt to implement in order to begin destroying the Israelites?**
   A. Drowning all the children; letting the sick die
   B. Having midwives kill all the babies born; working the older Israelites to death
   C. Throwing all the male children under age three into the Nile; threatening death to women who became pregnant
   D. Having the midwives kill all male children born; throwing all male babies into the Nile

4. **How old was Moses when his mother put him in a basket and hid him among the reeds on the Nile?**
   A. About fourteen years, just when he was starting to get a little obnoxious
   B. Three months
   C. Fourteen months
   D. Two weeks

5. **Why did Moses kill an Egyptian, according to Exodus 2:11?**
   A. The Egyptian had raped his sister.
   B. The Egyptian blasphemed the Hebrew God.
   C. Moses saw him beating a Hebrew.
   D. Moses had just lost a bundle in a pyramid scheme, and was in a rotten mood.
   E. The Egyptian threatened to kill him.

Moses' Top Ten Excuses as to Why He Would Be a Poor Leader

10. He was a late sleeper.
9. His wardrobe was out-of-date.
8. He was computer illiterate.
7. He had no last name.
6. He was afraid of snakes.
5. His driver's license was expired.
4. He had a fondness for pyramids.
3. He preferred to be on a committee.
2. He had tired blood.
1. He was allergic to sand.

6. **What was Moses' father-in-law's name and occupation?**
   A. His name was Jethro, and he was a priest.
   B. His name was Vinnie, and he was a lounge singer.
   C. His name was Midian, and he was a farmer.
   D. His name was Marah, and he was an artisan.
   E. His name was Gershom, and he was a tender of flocks.

7. **When God called Moses from the burning bush, He told Moses that these people would listen to him.**
   A. All of His people
   B. The new generations (youth)
   C. The angels of Heaven
   D. The elders and Pharaoh

8. **Which of the following were NOT among the miracles God showed Moses at his calling?**
   A. A flaming sword
   B. A disease-like transformation of Moses' hand
   C. A vision of the Egyptian Moses killed
   D. A rod that became a serpent
   E. A dancing bear

9. **Which of the following were among the plagues God brought on Egypt?**
   A. Frogs
   B. Blindness
   C. Leprosy
   D. Obvious tan lines
   E. Death of livestock
   F. Boils
   G. Lice

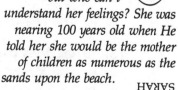

She laughed in the face of God, and was punished for it, but who can't understand her feelings? She was nearing 100 years old when He told her she would be the mother of children as numerous as the sands upon the beach. SARAH

10. **Which of the following did Moses take with him as the Israelites left Egypt?**

A. The body of Pharaoh's son
B. The mummified body of Jacob
C. His cell phone
D. Blank tablets on which God would later inscribe the Ten Commandments
E. The bones of Joseph

11. **What did God do to the Egyptian army just prior to drowning them in the Red Sea?**

SUPER CHALLENGE #1 *God told the Israelites that they were to keep Passover as a feast throughout the generations to come. What specific item were they to remove from their houses on the first day of this holy time?*

A. Forced them to eat brussel sprouts
B. Took the wheels off their chariots
C. Burned half of the army in a pillar of fire
D. Caused many of the Egyptian soldiers to fall asleep
E. Made their horses ill

12. **What did Moses do at Marah in order to make the "bitter" water drinkable and "sweet"?**
A. Touched the water with his rod
B. Tossed in two halazone tablets
C. Knelt by the water and praised God
D. Sacrificed a young goat, and put the blood in the water
E. Threw a tree into the water

13. **What does the Bible say manna tasted like?**
A. Like a cake, with a flavor of pomegranates
B. Like raisins
C. Like unleavened bread, with a sweetness of lemon
D. Like wafers made with honey
E. Like strawberries, only crunchy

14. **When the Amalekites attacked the Israelites at Reph-idim, what was the Israelite victory dependent upon?**
   A. Moses raising his hands
   B. The sword belonging to the angel of the Lord
   C. A serpent on a pole
   D. Aaron's rod raised before the Israelite army
   E. The Israelite's uncanny ability to throw hand-grenades

15. **What important advice did Moses' father-in-law give him, which he followed?**
   A. "Those who disobey God should be put to death."
   B. "Take two more wives for yourself."
   C. "Appoint others to help settle disputes."
   D. "Go to Sinai and wait for God's instructions."

Great Pyramid built at Giza!
(c. 2500 B.C.)

16. **Which of the following were part of the consecration of the people, prior to receiving the Ten Commandments?**
   A. Fasting
   B. Abstaining from sexual relations
   C. Women covering their heads
   D. Prostrating themselves at the foot of the mountain
   E. Washing their clothes

17. **What was the sixth commandment?**
   A. Honor your father and your mother.
   B. You shall not murder.
   C. You shall not commit adultery.
   D. You shall not steal.
   E. You shall not bear false testimony against your neighbor.

18. According to Exodus 21 and 22, which of the following transgressions did God say should result in the death penalty:
   A. Striking and killing another
   B. Cursing one's father or mother
   C. Owning a bull that gores a human to death, but only if you knew it had done so in the past and failed to keep it properly penned
   D. Being a sorceress
   E. All of the above

19. Which four men went up to see God, along with seventy elders?
   A. Moses, Jethro, Joshua, and Hur
   B. Moses, Joshua, Zipporah, and Gershom
   C. Moses, Ithamar, Hur, and Nadab
   D. Moses, Aaron, Nadab, and Abihu

20. How long did Moses stay on the mountain?
   A. Forty days and forty nights
   B. Seven days
   C. As far as anyone knows, he's STILL up there
   D. Eighty-five days and eighty-five nights
   E. Two weeks

21. God ordered other items specifically built at the same time as the ark of the covenant (testimony). What were they?
   A. A table, lampstand, and curtains
   B. A throne, a footstool, and a ring
   C. A crown, a table, and a chariot
   D. A condo, a Cadillac, and a jacuzzi
   E. An altar, a statue of a seraphim, and a crown

22. According to God's order, who was to receive "holy garments"?

A. Moses
B. Doctors
C. Aaron
D. Joshua
E. The High Priest

23. **God told Moses that when he took a census of the people, he should also do what?**
   A. Discern the needs of the widows
   B. Circumcise all male children
   C. Collect money from the adults so that no plague will come upon them
   D. Make certain they have made no idols

24. **What did the Lord tell Moses the punishment was for working on the Sabbath?**
   A. Giving up their heritage as Hebrews
   B. Being put to death
   C. Being sent back to Egypt
   D. A good "talking to"
   E. Manna would be withheld from them and their family

   > **DID YOU KNOW** that Noah's sons' names were Ham, Shem and Japeth? Ancient Jewish tradition holds that the priest Melchizedek is actually Shem! Check out the lifespan of Shem in the genealogies, it could be true!

25. **What instructions did Moses give to the Levites who supported his call to return to God's righteousness?**
   A. "Repent of your idolatry and you will know the true God."
   B. "Today you will enter the promised land with me."
   C. "Destroy the golden calf and all who worshiped it and Jehovah shall be your God."
   D. "Go throughout the camp—let every man kill his brother, companion, and neighbor."
   E. "I don't believe in idol threats."

26. **Why were Aaron and the Israelites afraid to approach Moses after his second marathon visit with God?**
A. They feared he would be extremely angry.
B. An unusual radiance shown from his face.
C. His rod had a fire "like lightning."
D. The first person who touched him fell dead.
E. They figured after forty days and nights without food, he might try to take a bite out of the first thing he saw.

27. **What animal's hide served as the outside covering for the tabernacle tent?**
A. Badger
B. Dolphin
C. Camel
D. Ram
E. Ox

28. **The altar of burnt offering was overlaid with this material, and its accompanying utensils were made of it as well:**

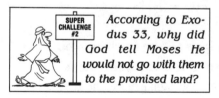

SUPER CHALLENGE #2 *According to Exodus 33, why did God tell Moses He would not go with them to the promised land?*

A. Bronze
B. Gold
C. Silver
D. Teflon
E. Onyx
F. Acacia wood

29. **Which one of the following precious stones was NOT among those used in the breastpiece the Lord commanded Moses to have assembled?**
A. Ruby
B. Sapphire
C. Emerald

D. Diamond

E. Amethyst

30. **What was the tabernacle called?**
    A. The Holy Tabernacle
    B. Tabernacle of the Tent of Meeting
    C. First Independent Church of the Wilderness
    D. The Altar of The Most High God
    E. The Sanctuary of Jehovah

31. **Who were brought to the finished tabernacle to be anointed as priests?**
    A. Moses and his two sons
    B. Joshua and his sons
    C. Aaron and his sons
    D. Bezalel and Oholiab

32. **At the end of Exodus, we are told that Moses could not enter the newly finished tabernacle. Why not?**
    A. Moses had locked it and forgotten where he put the key.
    B. A cloud with God's glory rested upon it and filled it.
    C. An angel stood at the entrance to hail God's coming.
    D. The light coming from the structure was blinding.
    E. God was angry with him for disobedience.

The Israelites' Song

*(Sung to the tune of
"I'd Like to Teach the World to Sing")*

(Strangely enough, you can also use the tune from the "Gilligan's Island" theme song. I have no idea why this happened, but I have a feeling YOU may know.)

We'd like to teach our kids to pray,
And follow all God's laws,
But we are Jews—"stiff-necked" Hebrews
With lots of human flaws.

We hated Egypt, we were slaves—
They really made us work,
We washed their walls, and swept their halls
And Pharaoh was a jerk.

And so when Moses led us out
We knew our God would reign,
Then cried big tears—for forty years
All WE did was complain.

And now we stand at Canaan's door
The place we're meant to be—
With sunny days we'll catch some rays
And live in luxury.

No doubt we'll pat each other's backs
We've done it on our own,
We'll buck the odds, make phony gods
And set them on a throne.

Then when God drives us from the land
To scatter us abroad
As we're chased out, we'll scream and shout
That Moses was a fraud.

ANSWERS TO EXODUS QUESTIONS

#	ANS	REF		#	ANS	REF
1.	C	1:5		25.	D	32:2
2.	B	1:9–10		26.	B	34:30
3.	D	1:16, 22		27.	A,D	36:19
4.	B	2:2–3		28.	A	38:2, 3
5.	C	2:11		29.	A	39:10–13
6.	A	3:1		30.	B	39:32
7.	D	3:18		31.	C	40:12–15
8.	A,C,E	4:2–3, 6–7		32.	B	40:35
9.	A,E,F, G	8:6, 17; 9:6, 10				
10.	E	13:19		Super Challenges:		
11.	B	14:25		#1:	leaven or yeast	
12.	E	15:25			(12:15)	
13.	D	16:31		#2:	". . . lest I consume	
14.	A	17:11			you on the way, for	
15.	C	18:21–22			you are a stiff-	
16.	B,E	19:10, 15			necked people."	
17.	B	20:13			(33:1–3)	
18.	E	21:12, 17, 29; 22:18				
19.	D	24:9				
20.	A	24:18				
21.	A	25:23, 31; 26:1				
22.	C	28:2				
23.	C	30:12–13				
24.	B	31:15				

~LEVITICUS~

(c. 1500–1400 B.C.)

1. **What requirements did God mandate for an animal sacrificed from the herd?**
   A. If the animal is female, it must have never given birth, and must be washed prior to being killed.
   B. The animal must be male and without blemish.
   C. The animal must be at least as tall as Aaron's chest and must be without split hoof.
   D. The animal may be male or female but must be washed prior to killing, and if it has horns, they must be severed before it is burned.

2. **Moses closed the instructions regarding burnt offerings of all three types with what information?**
   A. Blood is the only atonement for sin.
   B. Moses prefers all his steaks medium-well.
   C. Man lives only by the breath of God.
   D. The aroma of the sacrifice pleases God.
   E. God always sees the sacrifice of the giver.

3. **If someone brought a grain offering of flour, part of it was mixed with oils and incense, then burned. What happened to the remainder?**
   A. It went to Aaron and his sons.
   B. Joshua used it to make chocolate chip cookies.
   C. It was to be "scattered across the courtyard."
   D. It was to be sold, and the money given to the priests.
   E. It was to be distributed to the widows.

4. **What two things were the Israelites forbidden to eat "throughout your generations," in Leviticus 3:17?**

A. Insects and pork
B. Big Macs and fries
C. Female goats and two-day-old manna
D. The kidneys and the fat near the loins
E. Fat and blood

5. **If a priest or the general community was guilty of unintentional sin, the sacrifice required was:**

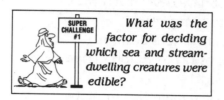

SUPER CHALLENGE #1

What was the factor for deciding which sea and stream-dwelling creatures were edible?

   A. A large quantity of flour and a dove
   B. A female sheep that had not given birth
   C. A young bull, without blemish
   D. The biggest, greenest watermelon in their garden
   E. A male goat, without defect

6. **According to Leviticus 5, certain sins require the sacrifice of a female lamb or goat. What would constitute acceptance of the offender substituting doves or pigeons?**
   A. If he had previously contracted to sell all of his female lambs and goats
   B. If his only female lambs and goats were somehow defective
   C. If the doves were actually Dove Bars
   D. If the amount of doves and pigeons were equal in value to the price of a female lamb
   E. If he could not bring a female lamb or goat

7. **Along with an animal sacrifice to God, a person who stole goods or somehow obtained them dishonestly from his neighbor, was required to make restitution. What was the requirement?**

A. He must repay the owner in full plus one fifth.
B. He must repay the owner twice the amount that was due him.
C. He must repay the owner and agree to work for him for seven weeks, resting only on the Sabbath.
D. The owner was allowed to choose from the person's livestock and goods an amount equal to what had been stolen from him plus ten per cent.
E. The thief had to say, "I'm sorry," and be given a thirty minute "time-out."

8. **Regulations for the burnt offering included:**
   A. The burnt offering was to remain on the altar hearth until morning.
   B. The priest must put on linen clothes before removing the ashes from the altar.
   C. An additional change of clothes was required before carrying the ashes away.
   D. The fire was to be kept burning continuously and was not allowed to go out.
   E. All of the above were requirements.

9. **Which of the following was NOT true concerning fellowship offerings?**

A. Waving the breast of an animal before the Lord was considered a "wave offering."

B. The priest was to burn the fat, but the breast belonged to Aaron and his sons.

C. The right thigh of the sacrifice was to be a contribution to the priest.

D. The fellowship offering was the only sacrifice that Aaron and his sons did not administer.

10. **During the ordination of Aaron and his sons, how long were they to remain at the entrance to the tabernacle of meeting according to Moses' commandment?**

A. Until the Lord spoke

B. Until they had shaken everyone's hand after the service

C. Until seven animal sacrifices were completed

D. Seven days

E. Forty days

EPIC OF GILGAMESH, now available!
(c. 1200 B.C.)

11. **Why did God destroy Aaron's sons Nadab and Abihu with fire?**

A. Because they approached the altar without the "anointed robes" they were commanded to wear

B. Because they offered "profane fire" to the Lord

C. Because their "hearts had hardened toward God"

D. Because Aaron had sinned before God and had not made an atoning sacrifice

12. **What three things did Moses tell Aaron and his two remaining sons NOT to do, so that the Lord would spare their lives?**

A. Blame God; abandon their duties as priests; forget the holy ordinances.

B. Leave the tabernacle; become unclean; eat forbidden meat.

C. Threaten to call their attorneys; give God two weeks' notice that they were finished as priests; send out resumés to pagan gods.

D. Cry out to the Lord; tear their clothes; offer an unacceptable sacrifice.

E. Uncover their heads; tear their clothes; leave the tabernacle.

13. **Leviticus 11 offered several examples of land animals, birds, and fish that were to be considered unclean, and not to be eaten or touched by the Israelites. Which of the following were part of that list?**

The Top Ten Comments Overheard During the Wandering in the Wilderness

10. "Gershom just hit me!"

9. "Your compass IS busted! We're going in circles!"

8. "If your goat nuzzles me one more time, I'm gonna SACRIFICE him!"

7. "I think that 'Red Sea' thing was just an optical illusion."

6. "Mom, are we having manna again!"

5. "It is sooooooo written in stone!"

4. "And I thought the flood was a bummer!"

3. "Check out this sand angel I just made!"

2. "C'mon Moses, aren't they more like guidelines?"

1. "Are we there yet?"

A. Camel
B. Rabbit
C. Panther
D. Sea Gull
E. Pheasant
F. Chameleon
G. The Loch Ness Monster

14. **How long was a woman "customarily unclean" after giving birth?**
    A. Twenty-one days, regardless of the baby's sex
    B. Seven days for a boy baby, fourteen for a girl
    C. Until the baby grew up, graduated from high school and moved out of the house
    D. There was no customary uncleanness regarding giving birth
    E. Seven days, regardless of the baby's gender

15. **Chapter 13 of Leviticus discussed various skin diseases. It also gave instructions for:**
    A. Exorcising evil spirits
    B. Embalming
    C. Disposing of dead unclean animals
    D. Treating blindness
    E. Dealing with garments that have "leprous plague"

16. **What was the significance of the "scapegoat"?**
    A. It meant that the Hebrews were continually "getting God's goat."
    B. The goat symbolized the Israelites continual running away from God's righteousness.
    C. It meant that eventually mankind would need a messiah to blame all their sins on.
    D. Once released, it symbolized the Israelites wandering in the wilderness.

E. The goat symbolically carried away all of the sins of the Israelites.

17. **Two offenses were mentioned in Leviticus 17 as punishable by "being cut off from [one's] people." Can you name them?**

    A. Eating dead animals that have been torn apart by other animals; not observing sacrifice rules for uncleanness

    > The book of Leviticus, in chapters 18 and 20, mentioned the name of a pagan (Ammonite) god, and God warns the Israelites about sacrificing their children to it. Can you name the pagan god?
    >
    > SUPER CHALLENGE #2

    B. Bringing lesser sacrifices to the tabernacle of meeting than the giver is capable of; working on the Sabbath

    C. Tailgating; singing the "Barney" theme song

    D. Sacrificing at places other than the Tent of Meeting; eating blood

    E. Eating blood; working on the Sabbath

18. **What reason did God give in Leviticus 18 for driving nations out of the land?**

    A. Because they had made gods of metal

    B. As a sign to the twelve tribes of Israel

    C. Because they had defiled themselves through sexual perversion

    D. To open the land He had promised to the children of Israel

19. **Which of the following was NOT one of God's decrees of Leviticus chapter 19:**

    A. "Do not mate different kinds of animals."

    B. "Do not plant your field with two kinds of seed."

    C. "Do not wear clothing woven of two kinds of material."

D. "Do not plant a vineyard within view of the tabernacle of meeting."

20. **What did Leviticus 21 state as the penalty for a man who married his brother's wife?**
   A. The woman would be put to death; the man sent away.
   B. They would have no children.
   C. They would be "cut off" from the people.
   D. They had to make an additional sacrifice every Sabbath while both of them remain alive and married.
   E. Some truly interesting family reunions would follow.

21. **Which of the following were priests forbidden to do? (three answers)**

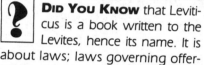

DID YOU KNOW that Leviticus is a book written to the Levites, hence its name. It is about laws; laws governing offerings, spiritual leadership, individual righteousness, sanctification, the feasts and Sabbath, and various vows, etc.

   A. Marry
   B. Shave their heads
   C. Cut their bodies
   D. Any work other than keeping the tabernacle
   E. Uncover their heads
   F. Accept gifts from any non-Hebrew

22. **Animals brought for sacrifice to God were to be free from "defects." However, one of the following was allowable as a freewill offering:**
   A. Animals which were deformed or had stunted growth
   B. Blind animals
   C. Animals that walked with a cane
   D. Animals with festering sores
   E. Animals with warts

23. **This feast was commanded by God to take place on the first day of the seventh month and was to be**

commemorated with trumpet blasts. What was it called?

A. The Feast of Tabernacles
B. The Feast of My Worries
C. Memorial of Trumpets
D. Feast of Weeks
E. Feast of Firstfruits
F. Passover
G. Beauty and the Feast

24. **Why was Shelomith's son stoned to death, according to Leviticus 24:11?**
A. For blasphemy
B. He committed adultery
C. He was found lying with a beast
D. For murdering one of Aaron's remaining sons

25. **The fiftieth year in the new land was called the "Year of Jubilee," with special rules governing it. Which of the following were to be observed during that celebration?**
(three answers)
A. Each person was to return to their family/clan.
B. A "festival sacrifice" was to be made on the altar daily.
C. For the entire year there was to be free parking.
D. Each person was to return to their own property.
E. Countrymen who sold themselves as slaves were to be released.
F. Fifty new judges of the people were to be appointed.

26. **What did God say the Israelites could will to their children as inherited property?**
A. Flocks and herds
B. Their portions of "this land I have given you"
C. Mutual funds, insurance policies, and CDs

D. Their slaves
E. All of the above
F. Their silver and gold

27. **Which of the following was NOT one of the conditional promises God offered to the Israelites, as a reward for keeping His decrees and commands?**
   A. Increasing their numbers
   B. Giving their priests and fathers long life
   C. Removing savage beasts from the land
   D. Providing excellent weather for raising crops

28. **On the flip side, if the people chose to disobey God, which of the following were problems they could expect?**
   (three answers)

   A. The death of their firstborn male child
   B. Diseases causing blindness
   C. Wild animal attacks
   D. Sour tasting (contaminated) water
   E. Violent weather
   F. Destruction of their livestock

Who Am I?

Her willingness to draw water from the well for a young man's camel influenced him to ask her to be his wife. She married him and became the mother of some quite influential children.

REBEKAH

29. **How did the book of Leviticus end?**
   A. With the Israelites finally entering the promised land
   B. With a return to God's prior discussion regarding punishment for sexual perversion
   C. With rules on tithing from the land, herd, and flock
   D. With the death and burial of Moses
   E. With: ". . . and they all wandered happily ever after."

ANSWERS TO LEVITICUS QUESTIONS

#	ANS	REF	#	ANS	REF
1.	B	1:3	19.	D	19:19
2.	D	1:9, 13, 17	20.	B	20:21
3.	A	2:3	21.	B,C,E	21:5, 10
4.	E	3:17	22.	A	22:23
5.	C	4:3, 14	23.	C	23:23
6.	E	5:7	24.	A	24:11
7.	A	6:2–5	25.	A,D,E	25:10, 13, 40–
8.	E	6:8–13			41
9.	D	7:28–34	26.	D	25:45–46
10.	D	8:33	27.	B	26:4–5, 6, 9
11.	B	10:1–2	28.	B,C,F	26:16, 22
12.	E	10:6–7	29.	C	27:30–33
13.	A,B, D,F	11:4, 6, 16, 30			
14.	B	12:2, 5	Super Challenges:		
15.	E	13:47–58	#1: Fins and scales		
16.	E	16:22	(11:9–10)		
17.	D	17:8–10	#2: Molech (18:21)		
18.	C	18:24			

Q. Why should you read the book of Leviticus?

A. Because it's the Law.

∼NUMBERS∼
(c. 1445–1405 B.C.)

1. **Numbers derived its name from which of the following:**
   A. The Israelite nation, although still not at their "promised land" destination, had grown substantially in number.
   B. God instructed Moses to "number" the people by taking a census.
   C. Moses attempted to teach quantum theory equations to the twelve tribes of Israel.
   D. God instructed Moses to divide the nation into specific amounts of people to organize living arrangements in Canaan.
   E. The Israelites were in the process of establishing their own numerical system.

2. **In case of war, who would serve as Israel's soldiers?**
   A. Healthy males over twenty-five years, and unmarried females who had no children
   B. All able-bodied persons over the age of sixteen
   C. All men over the age of twenty
   D. A specially trained group of about 10,000 men

3. **Why were no members of the tribe of Levi included in the army?**
   A. Because they were appointed to be in charge of the tabernacle and its furnishings
   B. Because they were all conscientious objectors
   C. Because the House of Levi had so few young males

D. Because they had abandoned Moses over a disagreement about sacrifices

E. Because they had previously been sent north to Kadesh to establish an encampment site

4. **This tribe numbered 186,400 and was designated to "set out first." Who were they?**
   A. The tribe of Benjamin
   B. The tribe of Judah
   C. The tribe of Reuben
   D. The tribe of Sitting Bull
   E. The tribe of Dan

5. **Which of the following statements was true concerning the official census of the Levites?**
   A. All were counted, including women and children; they numbered 22,000.
   B. Only males over the age of twelve were counted; they numbered 8,500.
   C. Only males at least a month old were counted; they numbered 22,000.
   D. They counted both males and females over the age of seven years; the total was 144,000.
   E. The census was never finished; the man who was counting kept forgetting the count.

6. **When the priest "tested" a woman to see if she had been unfaithful to her husband, the ceremony included all of the following EXCEPT:**
   A. Loosening the woman's hair
   B. Burning the husband's grain offering on the altar
   C. Putting the woman under oath
   D. Making the woman drink bitter holy water
   E. Having the woman provide a "truth" sacrifice

7. Which of the following were part of the require-
ments of taking the Nazirite vow (a vow of separa-
tion to the Lord)?
(three answers)
A. Must abstain from fermented drink
B. Must refrain from sexual relations
C. Must have no contact with alien tribes
D. May not cut hair
E. May not allow nakedness to be seen
F. Must not go near a corpse

8. All of the following were part of God's rules for the
ceremonial cleansing of the Levites EXCEPT:
A. Sprinkling water on them
B. Having them shave their bodies
C. Washing their clothes

Top Ten Reasons Adam & Eve Never Ate at McDonald's

10. Sign outside said "None Sold"
9. Meat was from a yet unnamed animal
8. Sign on the door said: "No clothes, no service."
7. Serpent told them it was a "drive-through only"
6. Adam figured if apples were forbidden, a Big Mac
   would REALLY get him in trouble
5. Angel with a flaming sword stood at the entrance to
   playland
4. Feared Cain might kill his brother for French fries
3. No styrofoam containers for burgers
2. Pepto Bismol not yet invented
1. Eve was holding out for ribs

D. Having them abstain from sexual activity for the seventy-day "purification" period

9. **What instructions did God give to Moses regarding the celebration of Passover by those who were considered unclean, due to contact with a corpse?**
   A. They should wait one month, then celebrate Passover.
   B. They must not observe it until the next year.
   C. They may celebrate it one day after ceremonial washing.
   D. Any person who was ceremonially unclean at the time of any Passover was prohibited from ever taking part in the observance for the rest of their lives.

10. **What determined whether the Israelites traveled or camped while they wandered in the desert?**

BALAAM'S ASS

... OH, AND ON A PERSONAL NOTE, YOU'RE MAKING MY STIRRUPS TOO TIGHT.

A. God's speaking through the ark of testimony (covenant) and directing them

B. The movement of a cloud

C. Reports from the scouts they had sent out to ensure safe passage

D. Moses' mood, and if there was anything decent on TV (which is why they traveled a lot)

E. The weather and seasons

11. **What was the PRIMARY purpose of the two silver trumpets the Lord told Moses to make?**

A. Calling the community together and having the camps sent out

B. To signal to God while they were engaged in battle

C. To announce the beginning of feasts and celebrations

D. To see if Joshua and Caleb could do some old Tiajuana Brass tunes

E. God's preparation to destroy the walls of Jericho

F. As a memorial to be sounded over burnt offerings

12. **Why did Moses encourage Hobab, his brother-in-law, not to leave them and return to his homeland?**

A. Because Moses knew that Zipporah, Moses' wife, would be heartbroken if Hobab left

B. Because he owed Moses money, and Moses knew that if Hobab left, he'd never see a dime of it

C. Because Hobab could be a valuable advisor regarding encampment sites in the desert

D. Because Hobab was a well-known warrior, and Moses knew he could help them greatly in battle

E. Because Hobab was extremely knowledgeable with the herds

13. **Why did God consume part of the outskirts of the Israelites' camp with fire?**

A. So He would prevent their enemies from attacking them.

B. He was angry because they were complaining.

C. He wanted to mark their encampment as a sacrifice to Him.

D. So He could destroy the tribe of Gad, who were conspiring against the people.

14. **Moses told God that if He wouldn't lift his burden, he would prefer God do what?**
    A. "Let the people return to Egypt."
    B. "Let Aaron become their new leader."
    C. "Let each tribe go their own way."
    D. "Put me to death."
    E. "At least give me a couple of weeks on the beach."

15. **What did God provide for the Israelites when they complained about the manna diet?**
    A. Meat from fifty thousand sheep and goats
    B. Flocks of doves
    C. Gift certificates to Bob Evans Restaurants
    D. Flocks of quail
    E. Thousands of cattle from an enemy nation

16. **This person spoke against Moses and was stricken by God with leprosy and confined outside the camp for seven days:**
    A. Miriam
    B. Aaron
    C. Joshua
    D. Benjamin

17. **When Moses sent the team of explorers out to scout Canaan, which of the following was NOT one of the things he asked them to report on?**
    A. Did the inhabitants worship Baal or foreign gods?
    B. How many people were in the land?

C. Were the towns walled or unwalled?

D. Were there trees?

E. Was the soil fertile?

18. **Apparently due to fear of being defeated, some of the men who scouted Canaan reported seeing people there of great physical stature. What did the scouts say they seemed like in comparison to these people?**

    A. Young children

    B. Dwarfs

    C. Ants

    D. Grasshoppers

    E. Beanie Babies

A modest and meek man, but a poor communicator, even stuttering at times. Sometimes he blows his stack and acts rashly. Some say that he has once committed murder—but you wouldn't think it to know him.

Who Am I?

MOSES

19. **What was their response to the scout's report?**

    A. They believed that God would ultimately give them victory.

    B. They were afraid, and asked Moses to request God's instruction.

    C. They discussed finding a new leader and returning to Egypt.

    D. They told Moses to send a new group of scouts to verify the report.

20. **What happened to the men who had filed false reports concerning the land of Canaan?**

    A. They were stoned to death.

    B. They died from a plague.

    C. They were arrested for fraud.

    D. They were struck blind.

    E. They were "cut off" from the people.

21. **In Numbers Chapter 15, a man was stoned to death for breaking the Sabbath. What specifically was he doing?**

A. Gathering manna
B. Picking grapes
C. Gathering wood
D. Mowing his lawn
E. Carrying his son

22. **A rebellion against Moses, led by a Levite named Korah and about 250 men, ended in what way?**

SUPER CHALLENGE #1 *When the Israelite camp was moving, the Kohathites were to Cover, with a cloth, the ark of the covenant, the table of the Presence, the lampstand, the gold altar, and the articles used in the sanctuary. What color was the cloth to be?*

A. God called the dissenters away from the camp, then rained fire and brimstone from heaven, and consumed them all.
B. Moses contacted the U.N., and they sent a peacekeeping force.
C. A violent wind struck the camp of Korah and his followers, and they and their families were never seen again.
D. The earth opened and swallowed Korah and the leaders of the rebellion, and the 250 men were destroyed by fire.
E. The men of the rebellion left for Canaan, where they were violently slaughtered in the Valley of Eshcol.

23. **How many more people did the Lord cause to die (from a plague), because they complained that Moses and Aaron were allowing the Lord's people to die?**
A. 250
B. 14,700
C. 144,000
D. Several hundred men from each of the twelve tribes

24. **What method did God use to show Aaron's authority as a priest?**

A. Selected his staff (from among the staffs of the tribal leaders) to sprout blossoms

B. Struck all the other tribal leaders mute when Aaron spoke

C. Wrote Aaron's name in fire on the side of the Tent of Meeting

D. Had Aaron hit a rock with his staff, and water streamed from it

E. God gave him the first MasterCard

25. **Which of the following was NOT true concerning purification ordinances?**

A. Only the priest could touch or move a corpse without being required to fulfill the rites of purification.

B. Anyone who entered a tent where a corpse resided would be considered unclean for seven days.

C. Every open container within the tent where a corpse resided was considered unclean.

D. Anyone touching a human bone or grave was considered unclean for seven days.

26. **Miriam, the sister of Aaron and Moses, died at Kadesh. What caused her death?**

A. The leprosy God had stricken her with earlier

B. A fever

C. Starvation

D. A motorcycle accident

E. The Bible doesn't say

27. **The king of Edom refused the Israelites passage through his land, even though they promised THREE of the six things on this list.**

A. To give the king a tenth of all their possessions

B. To not trespass through any field or vineyard

C. To spend no more than 40 days crossing their country

D. To leave 70 of their alien slaves for the king

E. To stay only on the main road

F. To pay for any water the people or livestock consumed

28. **Where did Aaron die?**
    A. In battle at the border of Edom
    B. Kadesh
    C. In the emergency room at Jerusalem General
    D. Canaan
    E. Mt. Hor

29. **After God gave the Israelites victory over the Canaanites, they soon began to complain again. How did God respond?**
    A. By miraculously providing them with fresh unleavened bread and fruit
    B. By causing many more to die of leprosy
    C. By sending large locusts to attack the people
    D. By sending poisonous snakes to attack the people
    E. By abandoning them and running the following ad in the national newspaper: "Wanted immediately: A nation to become My chosen people. Must be willing to make some sacrifices, and work well with staff. Leadership abilities desirable, but have been known to work with those who are less than perfect. Please, no whiners. If interested, chisel resumé and leave at top of Mt. Sinai. Be direct, no beating around the bush."

30. **When King Sihon would not let Moses and the Israelites pass through his land, he called up his army. The Israelites were victorious and took all their cities. What nation did the Israelites defeat?**
    A. Ammonites
    B. Amorites
    C. Navajo

D. Philistines

E. Zuphites

31. **Balaam's donkey spoke to him while they were traveling to meet Balak, the Moabite king. What was the basis for the donkey's words?**

    A. The donkey was questioning Balaam's judgment in meeting with an enemy of Israel.

    B. He was asking Balaam what it might take to get God to turn him into a gazelle.

    C. The donkey was telling Balaam that if he refused to curse Israel, Balak would surely kill him.

    D. He was complaining about being beaten by Balaam.

    E. The donkey was exhausted and wanted to rest.

Silk fabrics exported from China!

(*c.* 1300 B.C.)

32. **Why did Balaam ultimately bless the Israelites rather than curse them as Balak had requested?**

    A. Because Balak only offered half the reward he expected

    B. Because he could not go beyond the word of the Lord

    C. Because he feared reprisal if the Israelites were victorious over Balak

    D. Because Aaron had once saved his life

33. **When an Israelite man brought a Midianite woman into his family, they were both slain. How?**

    A. They were beheaded by one of the priests.

    B. They were bound together and burned alive.

    C. They were run through with a spear.

D. They were sentenced to the electric chair.

E. They were stoned publicly by the judges.

34. **Only two men who were counted by Moses and Aaron in the first census remained alive for the second. Who were they?**
   A. Caleb and Joshua
   B. Balaam and Zimri
   C. Ithamar and Eleazar
   D. Joshua and Reuben
   E. Laurel and Hardy

35. **Why did Moses ask God to commission a new leader over the Israelites in Numbers 27?**
   A. Because God told Moses he would be dying soon
   B. Because Moses believed the people no longer trusted him as their leader
   C. Because Moses needed to take his wife to Midian to see her dying father
   D. Because Moses had fallen into idol worship
   E. Because Moses had been offered a large church in Los Angeles

36. **Which was true concerning nullification of women's vows to the Lord?**
   A. Only the woman herself could nullify her vow, if she made a sacrifice and publicly recanted.
   B. Vows to the Lord, whether made by male or female, could not be broken without penalty of death.
   C. A married woman's husband could nullify her vow, as could an unmarried young woman's father.
   D. A young unmarried woman's vow could be nullified by her mother; a married woman's could be nullified by her father.

37. **After the Israelite army defeated the Midianites, Moses gave specific instructions to the officers and com-**

manders of the army regarding the plunder they had acquired. Which of the following were part of Moses' directions?
(three answers)

A. "Leave all of the gold, silver, and bronze items beside the Tent of Meeting."
B. "Kill all the boys you have brought back."
C. "Kill every woman who has slept with a man, but save the virgins for yourselves."
D. "All women who have slept with a man, and all boys over the age of twelve shall become our slaves."
E. "Every garment must be purified."
F. "You and all of your men shall do no work for one month as the Lord sees your efforts."

38. **Why did the officers of the Israelite army make a special offering to the Lord upon their return?**

A. To honor their fellow soldiers who had died in battle
B. Because they had been spending their tithes on video games for several months

What was the name given to the place where God caused water to run from a rock?

C. Because Caleb had died while they were away in battle
D. Because they had not lost a single man
E. Because so many of their men had returned with injuries

39. **What compromise did Moses make with the two tribes who didn't want to enter Canaan, but rather settle east of the Jordan, in Gilead?**

A. They must stay with the Israelites until Canaan was settled, then they were free to return to Gilead.

B. They could build houses for the women and children, but the men must help fight to secure Canaan before they could return.

C. Moses would trade them the land east of the Jordan, but they had to give him Boardwalk and Park Place, with the hotels.

D. The two tribes could stay there and build cities, but they must continue to supply the Israelites with food, and be ready to fight if needed.

E. They would cast lots to see which tribe would stay, but the other must accompany the rest into Canaan.

40. **What did God tell Moses would happen if he did not drive out all the inhabitants of Canaan?**
  A. They would eventually lead the Israelites to false gods.
  B. They would become a thorn in the side and bring God's judgment on Israel.
  C. Those few may grow to do what Israel did to the Egyptians.

41. **Which of the following were part of the defining boundaries of the promised land (Canaan)? (three answers)**
  A. The Wilderness of Zin
  B. Mt. Hor
  C. Paran
  D. Scorpion Pass
  E. Lebanon
  F. The Salt Sea
  G. The Rio Grande

42. **In the new land, six Levite towns were to be set aside as "cities of refuge." What was their purpose?**
  A. A place where the poor or widowed could live when they could no longer sustain themselves

B. A place for those who wished to take special holiness vows

C. A place where those who had killed someone could stay until their trial

D. A place for orphaned children, especially those whose fathers died protecting the nation

E. A place where teenagers could come, when their parents were hassling them too much

43. **The book of Numbers ended with the Lord's commandment to Moses about what controversy?**
    A. The changing of land rights through inheritance
    B. Rights of the two (and a half) tribes east of the Jordan
    C. Whether the Fox Network should be allowed to do its planned TV special: "When Moses Attacks"
    D. The tribe of Manasseh's request to retain some captured Canaanite people as slaves
    E. The proper location for the Tent of Meeting

Q. Who played tennis in the Bible?

A. Jospeh; he served in Pharaoh's court.

ANSWERS TO NUMBERS QUESTIONS

#	ANS	REF	#	ANS	REF
1.	B	1:2	25.	A	19:14–16
2.	D	1:3	26.	E	20:1
3.	A	1:50	27.	B,E,F	20:17–19
4.	B	2:9	28.	E	20:27–28
5.	E	3:39	29.	D	21:6
6.	E	5:18–26	30.	B	21:23–25
7.	A,D,F	6:3, 5, 6	31.	D	22:28–30
8.	D	8:7	32.	B	24:13
9.	A	9:11	33.	C	25:8
10.	B	9:17	34.	A	26:65
11.	A	10:2	35.	A	27:12–18
12.	C	10:31	36.	C	30:3–14
13.	B	11:1	37.	B,C,E	31:17–20
14.	D	11:15	38.	D	31:49–50
15.	D	11:31	39.	B	32:20–27
16.	A	12:1, 10, 14	40.	B	33:55, 56
17.	A	13:18–20	41.	A,B,F	34:3–10
18.	D	13:33	42.	C	35:10–12
19.	C	14:4	43.	A	36:7–9
20.	B	14:37			
21.	C	15:32			
22.	D	16:31–35	Super Challenges:		
23.	B	16:49	#1: blue (4:6–12)		
24.	A	17:8	#2: Meribah (20:13)		

~DEUTERONOMY~

(c. 1500–1400 B.C.)

1. **What analogy did Moses use to describe the current population of Israel?**
   A. Like the grains of sand of the deserts we have crossed
   B. Like the stars of heaven
   C. Like the fish of the Great Sea
   D. Like the snowflakes of winter

2. **Moses' recollection of God's advice about passing through the hill country of Esau was:**
   A. If they refuse to give you passage, I will give them over to you, and you will destroy every man.
   B. Travel around the outskirts of this land, and if anyone would hinder you, tell them that the Most High God is with you.
   C. Offer a tithe to the descendants of Esau, and with their leaders present, offer a sacrifice to me, and they will let you pass.
   D. Do not upset them, and pay for any food and water you consume.
   E. Only you can prevent forest fires!

3. **According to Moses, who died in the thirty-eight years from the time they left Kadesh Barnea until they crossed the Zered Valley?**
   A. All the generation of Israelite soldiers
   B. All of those faithless ones who mistrusted the Lord
   C. Many of the strongest leaders of our enemies
   D. Those evil ones that the Lord cursed
   E. No one

4. **What possession that belonged to Og, king of Bashan, did Moses find worthy of mention?**
   A. A palace with fourteen terraces
   B. A bronze statue of Baal, twenty feet tall
   C. A "really awesome" foosball table
   D. An iron bed thirteen feet long
   E. A chariot with wheels overlaid in gold

5. **Moses said that because God was angry with the people, He would not allow Moses to do what?**

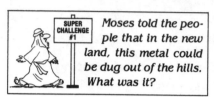
Moses told the people that in the new land, this metal could be dug out of the hills. What was it?

   A. Relinquish all of his authority to Joshua
   B. Place his blessing on all the twelve tribes
   C. Cross the Jordan and see the land
   D. Be buried with his ancestors
   E. Wear his NASCAR hat

6. **Moses' first interval in discussing the history of the Israelites' journey was to warn them of the potential danger of:**
   A. Intermarriage with aliens and unholy tribes
   B. Idolatry
   C. Failure to make proper sacrifices and honor the holy days
   D. Adultery
   E. Lacking true faith in the Lord

7. **Moses reminded Israel that on the day the Lord gave the commandments, the people showed great fear. What were they afraid of?**
   A. That they would be unable to keep all of God's laws, and He would destroy them
   B. That Moses would return with super powers, and only be vulnerable to Kryptonite

C. That Moses would die from being in the presence of a powerful God, and they would have no leader

D. That their flocks and herds would die if they could not tend them on the Sabbath

E. That they would be consumed by the fire from which God was speaking

8. **Which of the following were Moses' suggestions for reinforcing the laws upon one's children? (three answers)**

A. "Do not spare the rod on children who disobey God's laws."

B. "Talk about God's laws when you're sitting at your house and when you're walking down the road."

C. "Write the laws on the doorposts of your houses."

D. "Save them on your hard drives."

E. "Discuss them in the marketplace and in the fields."

F. "Bind the laws on your foreheads."

9. **There were seven nations in the promised land that God assured the Israelites He would defeat. Four of those seven tribes' names are listed below. Good luck!**

A. Hittites

B. Ammonites

C. Outasites

D. Jebusites

E. Canaanites

F. Moabites

G. Perizzites

H. Midianites

I. Pinktights

10. **Moses told the people that God would drive the inhabitants of Canaan out "little by little." What did**

he say the result would be if they were eliminated all at once?

A. The Israelites would not be able to bury the dead and a plague would follow.

B. God's plan regarding the land inheritance of the tribes would not come to fruition.

C. Wild animals would multiply around them.

D. Much of the land would go barren before they could till the ground.

11. **What TWO miracles took place during the forty years of wandering, according to Moses?**

A. No children died, and no mothers died giving birth.

B. People stepped on scorpions and were not harmed, and God protected the judges from disease.

C. The tabernacle and its utensils remained intact, and all of the Levites survived.

D. Their clothes did not wear out, and no one had swollen feet.

12. **One of the tribes that Israel faced in the new land was the Anakim. They were described as:**

A. Great and tall, and difficult to stand up to

B. The fiercest of warriors; men who fight to the death

C. A tribe, which, without God's help, could not be defeated

D. Skilled with bows and highly trained for battle

E. Having neat weapons, but not very bright

13. **Why did Moses say that the Levites were not to receive an inheritance among their brothers?**

A. Because they had turned away from God's laws

B. Because the Lord was their inheritance

C. Because they had failed to use their turn signals one too many times

D. Because God had cursed them

E. Because they were to receive a special gift from the Lord in the generation to come

14. **According to Deuteronomy 11, how was the new land to differ from Egypt?**
(two answers)
A. It required no irrigation.
B. It would sustain far more herds of cattle.
C. It had mountains and valleys.
D. The trees were more plentiful.
E. The pharaoh who lived there was much nicer.

15. **After the place for the Lord's dwelling was established, the people were to bring all of the following there EXCEPT:**
A. Burnt offerings
B. Tithes
C. Bronze utensils

Top Ten Old Testament Witticisms

10. Give him an inch and he'll take a cubit!
9. You can lead a Hebrew to water, but he'll only cross if God parts it.
8. Don't have an Egyptian conniption!
7. Life is like a box of pomegranates.
6. I'll bet you a shekel to a bagel.
5. Sodom? Don't go there!
4. Make like Moses and go plague somebody else!
3. Grab your yarmulke and run.
2. Wouldn't that just sink your ark!
1. You bet your sweet birthright!

D. Firstborn of their herds and flocks

E. Special gifts

16. **Which of the following are true concerning eating in the new land?**
    (three answers)

Bronze now available from Scandinavia!
(*c.* 1300 B.C.)

A. Since the Lord would now be in their land, no food would be considered unclean.

B. Animals could be slaughtered in any of the towns.

C. The tithe of grain could be eaten anywhere, as long as the Lord's blessing had been invoked.

D. The prohibition regarding eating blood was lifted.

E. Both the ceremonially clean and unclean could eat the meat from slaughtered animals.

F. The people could eat as much meat as they desired.

G. God told them to banish anyone who mentioned "fast food."

17. **Moses told the people that if one of the towns in the new land turned to false gods, they should respond with what actions?**
    (three answers)

A. They must investigate thoroughly first, to determine if it was true.

B. Charge the idolaters a "sin tax."

C. The Levites should be God's hands in dealing with the idolatry.

D. All the people were to be killed with swords.

E. The town and all its plunder were to be burned.

F. They must send one appointed member from each of the tribes to talk with the leaders of the town.

18. **The list of unclean birds (not for eating) appeared in Chapter 14. All of these were on the list EXCEPT ONE. Find it!**
   A. Any kind of falcon
   B. Bats
   C. The white owl
   D. Doves
   E. The stork
   F. Any kind of raven

19. **If a person lived too far from the potential tabernacle site to carry his tithe there, how was he to resolve the situation?**
   A. He should sell his tithe for money, go to the tabernacle site, purchase a new tithe, then eat it at the site with his household.
   B. Invite one of the Levites to his house. The Levite was to consecrate the tithe, and then stay to eat with the man and his household until all were filled.
   C. He was to craft a model of the tabernacle, have it consecrated by the priest, and set it above his doorway. The family could then eat their tithe with God's blessing.
   D. He should ship his tithe to the tabernacle via UPS, then travel there on Amtrak with his family. Travel expenses would be deductible under the new covenant.

20. **Which of the following were true concerning "seven year" obligations?**
   (two answers)
   A. Creditors must cancel debts from brothers and foreigners.

B. Hebrew slaves who desired freedom must be set free.

C. You should still loan freely to a poor man, even in the sixth year, knowing his debt must be forgiven the following year.

D. Hebrew slaves who were released, were not to request or receive anything other than their freedom from their owners.

E. Israelite men who had the "seven-year itch" may take an extra wife or two to help them through it.

21. **Which were true concerning the Feast of Tabernacles? (three answers)**

A. It was celebrated for seven days after gathering the produce from the threshing floor and winepress.

B. Only the men and their sons were to take part in the observance.

C. Pizza served could have any topping except anchovies.

D. It was one of three times per year that all men must appear before the Lord at His appointed place.

E. It was an exclusively Hebrew event, and aliens were forbidden from participating.

F. No one was to show up empty-handed.

22. **In Deuteronomy 17, Moses told the people they would need to elect a king. All of the following were criteria for the new king except one:**

A. He must be a brother, not a foreigner.

B. He must be of stature and physically strong.

C. He must not take many wives.

D. He must not acquire a great number of horses.

23. **In the following list, find the three practices that Moses said were detestable to the Lord, according to Leviticus 18.**

A. Marrying foreign women
B. Abusing Hebrew slaves
C. Interpreting omens
D. Consulting the dead
E. Allowing a brother to go hungry
F. Sacrificing sons or daughters in the fire
G. Going through the "Express Lane" with more than ten items

24. **What criteria did Moses tell the people they should use to discern if a prophet's message was from the Lord?**
    A. They should send God a fax, and He would get back to them as soon as He could "free up" some time.

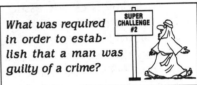

What was required in order to establish that a man was guilty of a crime?

    B. God would always provide a sign, beyond what was spoken.
    C. The prophet's words must come true.
    D. God would immediately judge a false prophet, and the people would know an evil had befallen him.
    E. The council of judges must be in complete agreement.

25. **What example did Moses give of an unintentional murder, which might cause the perpetrator to flee to a city of refuge?**
    A. Two men are in a boat, and one falls out and drowns due to the other's mistake.
    B. A man is slaughtering a bull with a helper; the blade accidentally severs the leg of the helper, causing him to bleed to death.
    C. Two men are training for battle, and one accidentally kills the other.

D. Two men are cutting wood, and the first man is swinging an axe. The head flies off, striking and killing the other man.

E. Someone is playing old "Sonny and Cher" records, not realizing that it's killing their neighbors.

26. Which of the following were NOT acceptable reasons for a man to be excused from battle? (two answers)

A. Having a new home which was not yet dedicated

B. A bad hangnail

C. Being engaged, but not yet married

D. Having a seriously ill wife or child

E. Fear

DID YOU KNOW that the structure of the book of Deuteronomy is closely associated with that of a Near Eastern vassal treaty of the Mosaic age? A vassal treaty declared that, though a nation had been captured, they were free but must pay homage to the capturing King. Moses was relating this concept to the Hebrew's relationship with God.

27. Which of the following were true concerning the scenario of a man found slain and no knowledge of who killed him? (two answers)

A. The town closest to the body was responsible for making an atonement for it.

B. The sacrifice involved was a heifer.

C. The priest should make inquiry of the neighbors in an attempt to find the murderer.

D. If the murderer was an alien, he may be convicted on the testimony of one Israelite.

E. Anyone arrested for the murder should try to blame it on a one-armed man.

28. If an Israelite soldier brought back a female captive of war, all of the following were true EXCEPT:

A. He must forbid her to cut her hair.
B. He may take her into his home.
C. She must trim her nails.
D. He may be her husband after she has mourned her parents for one month.
E. If, after marriage, he decided he didn't like her, he could set her free.

29. **According to Deuteronomy 22, which TWO of the following were true?**
    A. In a dispute involving the virginity of a bride, there was no penalty to a husband for false accusation.
    B. Men and women were not to wear each other's clothing.
    C. Only the two fastest donkeys in the land were allowed to have racing stripes.
    D. If a man raped an unpledged virgin, he was to be stoned to death.
    E. If an engaged virgin slept with another man, they were both to be stoned to death.

30. **Only one of the following groups were allowed to enter the assembly of the Lord. Which one?**
    A. Those born of a forbidden marriage
    B. The third generation of Egyptian children
    C. Ammonites and Moabites
    D. Males who had been emasculated

31. **What money must never be brought to the house of the Lord to pay a vow?**
    A. Interest earned on money loaned to a fellow Israelite
    B. Money earned from selling grapes or grain that was harvested from another's inheritance
    C. The earnings of prostitutes
    D. Money made through casting lots (gambling)
    E. Any of those weird looking twenty dollar bills

32. **THREE of the following statements were true concerning various laws.**

    A. A man who divorces a wife could not remarry her if she since had another husband.

    B. A "newlywed" man may serve in battle if he had been married at least six months.

    C. A pair of millstones was the acceptable collateral for a loan between Hebrew brothers.

    D. Israelites caught kidnapping were to be put to death.

    E. If a man's son or daughter was to be put to death, the father may give his own life as a ransom for their transgression.

    F. When harvesting, leave a little behind for the stranger, the fatherless, and the widows.

    G. Make certain you came to a complete stop before turning right on red.

33. **If two brothers lived together, and one of them died, it was the obligation of the other to marry his widow and continue the family line. If he refused, certain steps were to follow. Which three of the following were part of the procedure?**

    A. She was to move from his household.

    B. She was to report his hesitance to the elders.

    C. The elders were to talk with the man.

    D. He was to make a pledge to provide for her.

    E. He was to move from the household and allow her to live there.

    F. She would spit in his face.

34. **Moses told the people that once they were settled in the new land, the Levites would recite curses against certain transgressions. Which one of the following was NOT one of the violations mentioned?**

A. Accepting a bribe

B. Withholding justice from an alien

C. Moving the neighbor's boundary stone

D. Allowing evil on the property of one's inheritance

E. Leading the blind astray on the road

35. **Leviticus 28 suggests that some very nice things will happen to the Israelites if they follow God's laws. Find the THREE *blessings* that the text lists.**

    A. "God will bless you whether you are in the city or the country."

    B. "You will be blessed with many slaves to help in your fields and in your households."

C. "You will be blessed with many sons."

D. "Your baskets and kneading troughs will be blessed."

E. "Your wealth will multiply tenfold in this generation."

F. "The Lord will send a blessing on your barn."

36. **Here is a list of ten curses that Moses proclaimed would befall the Hebrews if they failed to serve their God. Unfortunately, seven of them are accurate and THREE of them I personally fabricated to confuse you.**

    A. "The calves of your herds will be cursed."

    B. "You will choke in the desert and drown in the sea."

    C. "Your children will rise up and kill you."

    D. "Your carcasses will feed the birds of the air."

    E. "You will end up in an unknown nation, where you will worship gods of stone."

    F. "The seed you sow will be eaten by locusts."

    G. "The Lord will strike you with blindness."

    H. "Your fiancee' will be ravished by another."

    I. "Your livestock will be swallowed up by the earth."

    J. "The Lord will afflict your legs with boils."

37. **What TWO things did Moses mention that the aliens living in the camps did?**

    A. Cared for the herds and guarded the lands

    B. Chopped wood and carried water

    C. Washed the cars and thatched the lawns

    D. Were allies in battle and worked with the Israelites in the fields

    E. Gathered grain and worked in the vineyards

38. **Moses told the people that the words of his commandments were not abstract or far away, but very close to them. How did he describe them?**

A. As being burned into their minds by the fire of the Lord
B. As written for Hebrews, not rocket scientists
C. As being in their mouths and in their hearts
D. As being in their presence always, on two stone tablets, written with the Lord's hand
E. As being written within their very souls

39. **Moses told the people he would not be crossing the Jordan to lead them into Canaan. Who did he say would cross ahead of the people?**
   A. The Lord Himself, and Joshua
   B. Joshua, and the army of the Israelites
   C. Joshua, and the sons of Aaron
   D. The Lord Himself, the Levites with the ark, and the army
   E. Those who had committed crimes would be sent up the river first

Her willingness to draw water from the well for a young man's camel influenced him to ask her to be his wife. She married him and became the mother of some quite influential children.

REBEKAH

40. **What did God tell Moses to write down in Deuteronomy 31?**
   A. A song
   B. The name of a good restaurant that served something besides manna
   C. A blessing on the people, prior to crossing the Jordan
   D. A new law concerning sacrifices in the new land
   E. The names of the leaders of each tribe

41. **The Book of Deuteronomy was the last book of Moses, and ends with his death. While that tends to make us sad, we have to realize that if Moses hadn't died, he would be about 3400 years old today. I have no idea how someone (even someone able to do**

great wonders) could afford that many years in a nursing home. So, which of the following were true concerning Moses' death?
(three answers)

A. Moses died without seeing the "Holy Land."
B. Moses died on Mt. Nebo.
C. Moses' grave became a shrine where the Israelites feasted once a year to celebrate his life.
D. Moses was very weak and nearly blind when he died.
E. The Lord buried Moses.
F. Moses was 120 years old when he died.

Q. What did God tell Moses when He spoke with him in the wilderness?

A. "I'm bushed."

ANSWERS TO DEUTERONOMY QUESTIONS

#	ANS	REF	#	ANS	REF
1.	B	1:10	26.	B,D	20:5–8
2.	D	2:5, 6	27.	A,B	21:1–6
3.	A	2:14	28.	A	21:10–14
4.	D	3:11	29.	B,E	22:5, 23–24
5.	C	3:25–29	30.	B	23:8
6.	B	4:15–19	31.	C	23:18
7.	E	5:25	32.	A,D,F	24:1–4, 7, 19–
8.	B,C,F	6:7–9			21
9.	A,D,	7:1	33.	B,C,F	25:5–10
	E,G		34.	D	27:17, 18, 19,
10.	C	7:22			25
11.	D	8:4	35.	A,D,F	28:3, 5, 8
12.	A	9:2	36.	A,D,	28:16–52
13.	B	10:9		E,F,G,	
14.	A,C	11:10–12		H,J	
15.	C	12:5–6	37.	B	29:11
16.	B,E,F	12:15–17	38.	C	30:14
17.	A,D,E	13:12–16	39.	A	31:3
18.	D	14:12–18	40.	A	31:19
19.	A	14:23–26	41.	B,E,F	34:1, 6, 7
20.	B,C	15:7–9, 12			
21.	A,C,F	16:13–17			
22.	B	17:14–20	Super Challenges:		
23.	C,D,F	18:10–11	#1: Copper (8:9)		
24.	C	18:22	#2: two or three wit-		
25.	D	19:5	nesses (19:15)		

~JOSHUA~
(c. 1405–1390 B.C.)

1. **The VERY FIRST thing God told Joshua was which of the following?**
   A. "Be strong and courageous, for I am with you."
   B. "Moses is dead."
   C. "I'm thinking of looking for a different job."
   D. "Be careful to obey all of My laws."
   E. "You will lead these people into the promised land."

2. **What instructions did Joshua give to the Reubenites, Gadites and half-tribe of Manasseh, (the tribes who had decided to stay east of the Jordan, and not live in the new land)?**
   A. Their armies would lead the Israelites into the new land.
   B. They would be expected to assist the effort with horses and supply additional food to the people.
   C. Serve the Lord always, and remember His laws.
   D. Be ready to come to their aid if needed.

3. **Joshua sent out two spies to investigate Jericho, and they stayed with a woman named Rahab. What was her occupation?**
   A. A seller of purple cloth
   B. A prostitute
   C. A seamstress/maker of garments
   D. A laborer in the vineyards
   E. All of the above

4. **What was the sign to the Israelite army that Rahab's household was to be spared in the siege on Jericho?**

A. Blood would be splattered above the doorway of her house.

B. Rahab was to appear in the doorway with a red letter "A" sewn on her garment.

C. A cloud was to cover the house.

D. A scarlet cord would hang from the window.

E. She would set a large basket of apples on her porch with a large sign which read: "Spies—help yourself."

5. **When the instructions were given for setting out for the new land, how far away were the people supposed to stay from the ark of the covenant?**

A. Fifty paces

B. A thousand yards

C. They were to stay as far away as possible without losing view of it.

D. There was no distance requirement, but they were not to touch it, or they would die.

6. **Which is correct regarding the parting of the Jordan River, which allowed the Israelites to cross?**

A. Aaron raised the staff of Moses, and God stopped the flow of water from the north.

B. The priests knelt at the river's edge, and Joshua raised his arms and cried out to the Lord.

C. The priests carried the ark of the covenant to the water's edge and the upstream water stopped flowing.

D. Joshua cried loudly, and God sent ten thousand beavers from a nearby woods, and within an hour they had constructed the largest dam known to man. The Israelites then crossed over, shouting "Leave it to beavers! Leave it to beavers!"

E. A cloud appeared ahead of the Israelite army, and a great wind blew back the water.

7. **How did God tell the Israelites to commemorate the miraculous crossing of the Jordan?**
   A. By initiating "The Festival of Crossing," to take place at that site each year
   B. By having Joshua read the Ten Commandments and the law to the people
   C. By having a member of each tribe carry a rock from the river to set up at their camp
   D. By building a small tabernacle at the western edge of the river, and dedicating it to the Lord

8. **Why did God tell Joshua to circumcise the Israelites again?**
   A. Because all of those born in the desert remained uncircumcised
   B. As a sign to the tribes that were to be conquered that the Lord's mark was on the Hebrews

What city was considered the "head" of the northern kingdoms that allied against Joshua?

SUPER CHALLENGE #1

   C. To humble them before the final conquest of Canaan
   D. To identify them with the covenant of their father and ancestor, Abraham

9. **Which of the following was true concerning manna?**
   A. The people continued to eat manna until just after the fall of Jericho.
   B. The people had not had manna since the death of Moses. They had been living off the flocks and herds of the tribes who stayed east of the Jordan.
   C. Manna's little baby loves shortnin' bread.
   D. Manna stopped two days after Passover.
   E. Manna stopped on the day of Passover, when the people ate some of the produce of the land.

10. **What did the "man with a drawn sword," who claimed to be commander of "the army of the Lord" say to Joshua?**
   A. "Take your sandal off your foot."
   B. "Get off my foot!"
   C. "Take a cup of water from the Jordan River, and drink it."
   D. "Be not afraid, be of good courage."
   E. "Personally bless each of your troops before they go into battle, kissing the forehead of each."

11. **Which of the following were NOT true concerning the fall of Jericho?**
   A. All of the armed men marched around the city once each day for the first six days.

Joshua's Top Ten Alternative Plans for Conquering Jericho

10. Having everyone form a circle around the walls and sing "Here we go 'Round the Mulberry Bush"
9. Having his army build a large wooden horse . . .
8. Putting on some sneakers and sneak in
7. "If everyone pushes really hard . . ."
6. Setting up loudspeakers and playing country and western music until Jericho surrendered
5. Breaking down and purchasing *The Idiots Guide to Conquering Jericho*
4. Threatening to spread lies about them on the Internet
3. Hiring the Big, Bad Wolf to blow it down
2. Luring Godzilla to the area
1. Just waiting for them to die of old age

B. On the seventh day everyone marched around the city twice.

C. The city walls collapsed after the Israelite people shouted.

D. Jericho cried out: "Help, I've fallen, and I can't get up!"

E. Rahab and her family were spared.

12. **What reason did God give to Joshua about his men being defeated in their first attempt to take the region called Ai?**

    A. Because the army had not sent the ark of the covenant before them

    B. Because the men had not had sufficient rest since the fall of Jericho

    C. Because some of the men of the army had slept with the women at Ai

    D. Because some of the men kept back part of the plundered goods from Jericho, that were supposed to be the Lord's

13. **Which of the following were true concerning the second attempt to take Ai?**
    (three answers)

    A. Joshua's army set up an "ambush" on Ai.

    B. God told Joshua to kill the people, but leave the buildings intact.

    C. All of the plunder was to be taken outside the city and burned.

    D. Joshua took a vote on whether to attack, saying, "All in favor, say Ai."

    E. All 12,000 people of Ai, including men and women, were killed in one day.

    F. The king was taken alive, then hanged later.

14. In order to save their people, the Gibeonite spokesmen pretended to be from far away and managed to trick the leaders of Israel into a peace treaty. All of the following were part of their scheme except:
    A. Their donkeys carried worn-out sacks.
    B. The men wore shabby, patched sandals.
    C. They told Joshua they had buried three members of their party along the way.
    D. All their bread was moldy.

15. Five kings and their armies formed an alliance against Gibeon and attacked them, after hearing of the treaty with Israel. I've added two extra ones. Which are they?

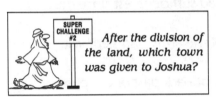

SUPER CHALLENGE #2 *After the division of the land, which town was given to Joshua?*

    A. Adoni-Zedek, king of Jerusalem
    B. Hoham, king of Hebron
    C. Piram, king of Jarmuth
    D. Sihon, king of Heshbon
    E. Elvis, king of Rocknroll
    F. Debir, king of Eglon
    G. Japhia, king of Lachish

16. When Israel went to Gibeon's aid, they soundly defeated the five armies. During the course of the action, which TWO miracles did God perform to help Israel?
    A. Struck the kings of the enemy armies blind
    B. Provided full medical insurance coverage for the Israelites without preexisting conditions limitations
    C. Caused the sun to stand still
    D. Struck many of the enemy with fierce fire from the sky
    E. Confused the enemy troops so that they turned on each other
    F. Rained large hailstones down on the enemy

17. **After Joshua defeated these armies, what did he do next?**
    A. Went back to the Gibeonites and dissolved their treaty with Israel
    B. Went to each of the cities of the five kings and destroyed them, leaving no survivors
    C. Took his armies back to their camp near Ai, where they made sacrifices to God, and Joshua read the law to them
    D. Went to Disney World
    E. Moved the entire camp close to Jerusalem to prepare to conquer it, and establish it as the city of the Lord

18. **When the northern alliance came against Israel, they too, were soundly defeated. Which of the following best describes the aftermath of the battle?**
    A. The Israelite army spent seven days burying the dead.
    B. They had only burned one city, but left the others standing.
    C. They carried away plunder, but killed all of the livestock along with the people.
    D. Israel began its accumulation of slaves by bringing hundreds of them from each of the northern kingdoms it destroyed.
    E. Joshua stood in the center of the battlefield, and, backed up by a quartet of his best soldiers, sang a powerful rendition of "My Way."

19. **At the beginning of Joshua 13, God tells Joshua that he is getting old, but there still remained a problem. What was it?**
    A. There were still tribes to be driven out of the land.
    B. They had not yet built a temple for God.
    C. They had yet to establish Jerusalem as the Holy City.

D. The two and a half tribes east of the Jordan were being threatened by Ammonites.

E. Joshua had no son to succeed him.

20. **What request did Caleb and the men of Judah make to Joshua?**
    A. To begin construction of God's temple
    B. To give them the northern territories near the Sea of Chinnereth (Galilee)
    C. To be called "eradication engineers" rather than "soldiers"
    D. To allow them to go to the southern borders of Canaan and drive out any remaining tribes who may be there, according to God's orders
    E. To give them the hill country, Hebron, which the Lord had promised them

21. **What did Caleb offer as a reward to the man who attacked and captured Kirdath Sepher?**
    A. The right to succeed him as the leader in the land
    B. Whatever part of the land he chose for his inheritance
    C. His daughter
    D. One half the plunder of the city, after removing the items that must be presented to the Lord's treasury
    E. His "Spiderman" issue #1 comic book, in primo condition

22. **Manasseh and Ephraim received an inheritance of land beginning at the Jordan and heading west. The Bible tells us that they were the descendants of:**
    A. Benjamin
    B. Reuben
    C. Levi
    D. Joseph
    E. Adam

23. **Manasseh's people encountered Canaanites in the towns on their inherited land. What was the outcome of this?**
   A. They settled outside the towns and left the Canaanites alone.
   B. They subjected the Canaanites to slavery, but could never totally eliminate them.
   C. Manasseh's tribe slaughtered all of them.
   D. The Canaanites negotiated an agreement of reciprocity, and the tribe of Manasseh established the area as an "Enterprise Zone."
   E. God destroyed all of the Canaanite towns with fire, and Manasseh's tribe killed all of the males.

24. **"The children of Joseph" were concerned about something they felt was an advantage to the Canaanites. What was it?**
   A. The Canaanites knew the territory so well that the tribes feared an ambush.
   B. The Canaanites had trained everyone, including women and older children, to fight.
   C. The Canaanites had weapons made of bronze and iron headed spears.
   D. The Canaanites had iron chariots.
   E. The Canaanites had light sabers, and the Israelites feared "the force" may be with the Canaanites.

King Tut dies!
(c. 1352 B.C.)

25. **At this time, there were still seven tribes who had not received their inheritance of land. How did Joshua resolve this?**
   A. He drew a map, dividing the land into seven districts. Then he let the elders of each tribe choose their land,

beginning with the largest tribe and ending with the smallest.

B. He sent three men from each tribe out to survey the land and create descriptions. Then he cast lots to decide which tribe got what land.

C. He drew a map, then cast lots to decide where each tribe would go.

D. Joshua and the elders of the tribes met before the ark of the covenant. The Lord spoke to them through the ark, and gave them instructions as to which tribe would occupy the various areas.

> **DID YOU KNOW** that Joshua's birth name was actually *Hoshea*, which means "salvation." Moses changed it to *Joshua*, which means, "the Lord saves"? *Jesus* is the Greek form of *Joshua*.

E. The leaders of each tribe were given a nickel. After several rounds of "odd man" the land was divided.

26. **If someone accidentally killed another, they could flee to one of the "cities of refuge," to avoid being punished unfairly. What TWO things must take place before they could return to their home?**
    A. The accused must stand trial before the assembly.
    B. The priest must invoke "the truth of God."
    C. The high priest who is serving at that time must die.
    D. If the accused is found to have partial guilt, he must make a sacrifice to God, and pay the family of the deceased, according to the law.
    E. They must pay their attorney fees in full.

27. **Which was the last group of Israelites to receive their inheritance in the new land?**
    A. The Levites
    B. Benjamin's tribe
    C. Simeon's tribe
    D. Dan's tribe

E. The Gadites (They never wanted to settle down, just gad.)

28. **How many towns were given to the priests from the lands of the Israelite tribes?**
    A. 12
    B. 3
    C. 48
    D. 144

29. **After all of the land had been apportioned and all the tribes had settled in their lands, the Bible says the Lord kept His promises, and all were fulfilled. What did Joshua do next?**
    A. Went to his inheritance in the hill country of Ephraim, and rested for seven months
    B. Passed his leadership role on to Caleb
    C. An interview with Barbara Walters
    D. Talked with Caleb about a full conquest of Jerusalem
    E. Sent the Reubenites, Gadites and half-tribe of Manasseh to their homes east of the Jordan

30. **What controversy nearly caused a civil war between the Israelites shortly after the land had been apportioned?**
    A. The location for the Tent of Meeting
    B. The construction of a large altar near the Jordan
    C. The decision of Joshua regarding who should lead the people
    D. When Joshua decided to ban phenphen
    E. Intermarriage with some of the remaining Canaanites

She bore the child of her master at his wife's bidding. This later caused conflict in their relationship and in the relationship between their children.

HAGAR

31. **What did Joshua say to illustrate the favor God had shown toward the Israelite soldiers?**
    A. "God has carried your swords in His hand."
    B. "One of you chases a thousand."
    C. "Your enemies tremble at the sound of your approaching footsteps."
    D. "Your weapons have carried out the justice of the Lord."

32. **Joshua died and was buried on his inherited land. How old was he at his death?**
    A. 110 years old
    B. 89 years old
    C. 145 years old
    D. The Bible doesn't say.
    E. He was 175, but he didn't look a day over 150.

33. **Following the death of Joshua, the book ends with two more events. Select the TWO correct answers.**
    A. The birth of Samson
    B. The appointing of a new leader
    C. Caleb and some of his buddies sitting around a campfire singing "Achy Breaky Heart"
    D. The death of Aaron's son
    E. An attack on one of the tribes by the remnant of Canaanites
    F. The burial of Joseph's bones

Q. Who had a motorbike in the Bible?

A. Joshua; his Triumph was heard throughout the land.

ANSWERS TO JOSHUA QUESTIONS

#	ANS	REF	#	ANS	REF
1.	B	1:2	25.	B	18:4–6
2.	A	1:14	26.	A,C	20:6
3.	B	2:1	27.	A	21:3
4.	D	2:18	28.	C	21:41
5.	B	3:4	29.	E	22:1–4
6.	C	3:15–17	30.	B	22:10–34
7.	C	4:2–3	31.	B	23:10
8.	A	5:4–8	32.	A	24:29
9.	D	5:11–12	33.	D,F	24:32–33
10.	A	5:15			
11.	B,E	6:11–14, 20, 25			
12.	D	7:11–12		**Super Challenges:**	
13.	A,E,F	8:9, 23, 25, 29		#1: Hazor (11:10)	
14.	C	9:4–5		#2: Timnath Serah, in	
15.	D,E	10:3		the hill country of	
16.	C,F	10:11–13		Ephraim (19:50)	
17.	B	10:29–40			
18.	B	11:10–13			
19.	A	13:1			
20.	E	14:12–13			
21.	C	15:16			
22.	D	16:4			
23.	B	17:12–13			
24.	D	17:16			

∼JUDGES∼
(c. 1050–1000 B.C.)

1. Which tribe did God tell the Israelites was to lead them against the Canaanites?
A. The tribe of Simeon
B. The tribe of Asher
C. The tribe of Dan
D. The tribe of Judah

2. After the victory over the Canaanites and Perizzites, the Israelite tribes captured the enemy's leader, Adoni-Bezek. What did they do to him?
A. Beheaded him
B. Cut off his thumbs and big toes
C. Shaved his head and hanged him from an oak tree
D. Gouged out his eyes

3. Which of the following was true concerning the fall of Bethel to the Hebrew army?
A. Israelite spies coerced a man who lived there to give them information about access to the city, and, in return, spared his life.
B. An angel of the Lord opened the gates of Bethel so that the Hebrew army could take the city.
C. The only casualty of the battle was a homely Chihuahua who ran up to Caleb and said, "Yo quiero Taco Bell."
D. The uncle of Rahab (the harlot who had assisted them in Jericho) was utilized in gaining access to the city of Bethel.

E. The leaders of Bethel had hoped to defeat Israel through a plan which included pretending to form an alliance with them.

4. Which of the following statements best summarizes the Israelites' status in the new land, according to Judges 1?
  A. They were well-established there, but there were still Canaanites and others that were successfully resisting.
  B. Once they donned their "Old Navy" garments, they were considered the ultimate avant-garde nation.
  C. The Israelite nation was severely weakened by the alliances of their enemies and in danger of collapse.
  D. They were extremely strong in the middle and northern territories, but the southern territories were constantly under siege.
  E. God had given over all the lands, and the Israelites ruled fully and completely.

5. Who came to Bokim and told the people that they would suffer for turning away from the Lord?

A. The ghost of Joshua
B. Caleb and his son-in-law, Othniel
C. Micah
D. An angel of the Lord
E. A Western Union clerk to whom God had sent a telegram

6. **After Joshua's generation died, another rose up that ignored God's laws, worshiping Baal and his female companion, Ashtoreth (the supreme goddess). As a result, all of the following things happened to Israel except one. Which was it?**
A. They were given to rebels, who plundered them.
B. They were sold to their enemies.
C. They suffered great plagues, and thousands died.
D. God was not with them in battle, and they were defeated.

7. **What was the only temporary "salvation" the Israelites enjoyed throughout their years of disobedience and punishment?**
A. On Wednesday nights, their captives would sometimes allow them to watch old "I Love Lucy" reruns on "Nick at Night."
B. When God saw that a few of His people repented, He protected them in battle.
C. Occasionally, God would raise up a judge who would save the people from their enemies.
D. An angel of the Lord would come down during the time of Passover, and the peoples' burdens were lightened for seven days.
E. Some of them were able to find some favor with their captives, and become overseers of their fellow slaves.

8. **The Bible says that God gave the Israelites a deliverer named Ehud. What fact does it mention about him?**
   A. He was a very hairy man.
   B. He was left-handed.
   C. He looked just like a member of ZZ Top.
   D. He was small in stature.
   E. He had only one leg.

9. **Which of the following were correct regarding the slaying of the Moabite king, Eglon, by Ehud? (three answers)**
   A. Ehud tricked Eglon into sending away his attendants.
   B. Ehud was wounded by Eglon, but survived.
   C. Ehud shoved an eighteen-inch sword into Eglon's belly.
   D. Ehud gained access to the king by delivering tax money to him.
   E. Ehud looked at King Eglon and said, "Well punk, do ya feel lucky?"
   F. Ehud killed two of Eglon's attendants with the same sword in order to escape.

10. **In Judges 4, we found the first mention of a woman leading Israel. Can you name her?**
    A. Ruth
    B. Esther
    C. Shirley "We Need to Build a" Temple
    D. Deborah, a prophetess
    E. Acsah, daughter of Caleb

11. **When the Israelites, led by Barak, defeated the Canaanites under Sisera, Sisera fled on foot. What was his fate?**
    A. A woman he trusted drove a stake through his head.
    B. Barak and his men tied his body between two horses, and they pulled him apart.

C. He was dragged to death behind his own iron chariot.

D. He escaped, but drowned trying to swim across the Jordan River.

E. He was imprisoned and died of thirst.

12. **When God called Gideon to save Israel from the Midianites, one of the first things He told Gideon to do nearly got him killed. What was it?**

A. To slay his own father and three other men from his village

B. To remove an altar to Baal and replace it with an altar to Him

C. To sneak into the camp of the Midianites and cut off the head of their leader

D. To walk through a tough part of town at night, with twenty-dollar bills hanging out of his pockets

E. To enter a cave where a family of lions lived

13. **The concept of "putting out a fleece" came from Gideon. What did it involve?**

A. Gideon asked God to make the fleece wet with dew and keep the surrounding ground dry; then do the opposite.

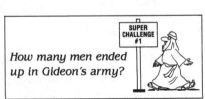

SUPER CHALLENGE #1

How many men ended up in Gideon's army?

B. Gideon asked God to change the fleece from white to red (with blood), then change it back to white.

C. Gideon had been to the movies, where he paid eight dollars for a ticket, five dollars for popcorn, two-fifty for a Coke, and two bucks for some M&M's. He told God he finally realized what it meant to be "fleeced."

D. Gideon asked God to turn the fleece pale with age, then restore it the next night.

E. Gideon asked God to remove the fleece from his threshing floor, then return it the next night.

14. **What criteria did God tell Gideon to use in choosing the men who would be in his army?**
    A. He was to use only the left-handed men.
    B. He was to take only those who were uncircumcised.
    C. It depended on how they drank water from a stream.
    D. They must be able to answer a riddle from the Lord.
    E. They must all be over forty years old, and have fought in twelve previous battles.

Troy destroyed in Trojan War!
(c. 1183 B.C.)

15. **Who actually killed the Midianite army?**
    A. God, with fire and hailstones from heaven
    B. Gideon's men, with the element of surprise
    C. An army of Ammonites, who, unbeknownst to Gideon, were waiting in the hills where the Midianites fled
    D. Themselves
    E. Troops whom Gideon had sent back to camp

16. **How did Abimelech (Gideon's son by a concubine), come into power?**
    A. God appointed him upon the death of Gideon, in accordance with Gideon's wishes.
    B. He unwittingly ate some Imperial margarine, and a crown miraculously appeared on his head.
    C. When all of Gideon's other sons were slaughtered by a surprise attack at Ophrah by a small group of Perizzites, Abimelech was the only remaining son of Gideon left to lead.
    D. There was a rebellion against the coalition of Gideon's sons, lead mainly by worshipers of Baal. They installed Abimelech as their leader.

E. He hired some ruthless mercenaries and killed all but one of Gideon's sons.

17. **How did Abimelech die?**
    A. He accidentally fell on his own sword while running toward the tower at Thebez.
    B. One of his own men hit him over the head with a rock.
    C. He ordered one of his own men to kill him with a sword after being injured by a woman.
    D. Two women of Thebez managed to strangle him with rope.
    E. An iron chariot wheel ran over his head.

18. **Why was Jephthah, the son of Gilead, reluctant to lead Israel against the Ammonites when he was asked to do so?**
    A. Because his family had disinherited him earlier, saying that he was not the son of their mother
    B. Because his mother was an Ammonite, and he loved her dearly
    C. Because he felt that the Ammonites so greatly outnumbered the Israelites there, that there would be no chance of victory
    D. Because he was essentially a farmer and had never fought in battle

19. **What did Jephthah's vow to the Lord end up costing him?**
    A. His only child, a son
    B. His wife
    C. His own life
    D. His only child, a daughter
    E. None of the above

20. **After the victory over the Ammonites, Jephthah's men had a skirmish with the Ephraimites. Then his**

army defeated them, and they killed thousands more based on what?

A. Their unwillingness to worship the Israelite's God

B. How the Ephraimites pronounced the word *Shibboleth*

C. Whether or not they were found to be circumcised

D. Their knowledge of the law and the commandments

E. The type of mood they were in

21. **Which of the following was NOT true concerning the birth of Samson?**

SUPER CHALLENGE #2

What happened to Samson's first wife?

A. His mother had been previously barren (sterile).

B. His mother was made pregnant by an angel of the Lord.

C. His mother was to drink no wine or fermented drink.

D. They were not to cut the baby's hair.

E. When Samson's father, Manoah, offered a burnt offering to the Lord, the angel that was with them ascended in the flame and disappeared.

22. **What was the first evidence of God's enhancement of Samson's strength?**

A. He killed thirty Philistines.

B. He bench-pressed Goliath fifteen times.

C. He killed a young lion without any kind of weapon.

D. He knocked over part of a city wall at the outskirts of Philistia.

E. He uprooted a large tree with his bare hands.

23. **What was the name of Samson's first wife?**

A. Delilah

B. Leah

C. Annah

D. The Bible doesn't say.

24. How did Samson destroy the fields of the Philistines, along with their vineyards and olive groves?
A. He dragged two large trees through the fields, for two entire days without ceasing.
B. He stampeded five thousand cattle through the fields and vineyards until everything was destroyed.
C. He filled fifteen hollow tree logs with locusts, and plugged each end of the logs with the carcasses of thirty lions he had killed. Then he dragged the trees to the Philistine fields and released the locusts.
D. He collected three hundred foxes and tied their tails together in pairs. Then he set their tails on fire and released them in the fields.
E. He attacked them with "Greek fire."

25. What weapon did Samson use to slay one thousand Philistines, according to Judges 15?
A. A donkey's jawbone
B. The femur (legbone) of a lion
C. A large tree branch
D. A scourge (a whip with metal fragments attached to it)

26. What was to be Delilah's reward for "selling out" Samson to the Philistine leaders?
A. She would receive eleven hundred pieces of silver.
B. She would become one of the king of Philistia's favored wives.
C. She would receive gold and become a concubine of the king.
D. She would receive no reward, but they would spare her life.

This prostitute trusted Israel's God and aided Israel's spies. After Jericho fell, she married an Israelite and entered the family line from which both David and Jesus would come. RAHAB

E. She would receive a Carnival cruise on the Dead Sea.

27. What was the FIRST lie Samson told Delilah, regarding what would cause him to lose his great strength?
A. Binding him securely with new ropes
B. Binding him with seven fresh bowstrings
C. Weaving his seven locks of hair into a loom
D. Giving him intoxicating drink

28. How many people were on the roof of the temple when Samson demolished it?
A. Five hundred men
B. Six thousand men and women
C. One thousand men, including the leaders of the city
D. Three thousand men and women

29. When we were introduced to Micah in Judges 17, what TWO sins was he involved in?

 DID YOU KNOW that the judges were military leaders in Israel? God raised them up to deliver Israel from oppression. They were divinely appointed and empowered; they did not rule by heredity.

A. Adultery and false witness (lying)
B. Theft and idolatry
C. Breaking the Sabbath and theft
D. Murder and lying

30. When the army of Dan came to Micah's house, what did they take from him?
A. His mother, his livestock, and some silver
B. His daughter, a visiting priest, and two slaves
C. His only copy of the 45 rpm record of Peter, Paul & Mary singing "Micah Row the Boat Ashore"

D. His livestock, his daughter, and a Levite priest

E. A Levite priest and some idols

31. What event led to a war between Israel and the tribe of Benjamin?

A. Benjamin's attempt to convince all of Israel to worship the idol, Asherah

B. An argument over which is superior: peanut butter or jelly

C. The sexual assault on a Levite's concubine, leading to her death

D. The tribe of Benjamin was trespassing on lands of two of the other tribes, and ignoring the rulings of the tribal council

E. The violent murder of a Levite priest

32. Which statement most accurately describes the war that was between the tribes of Benjamin and Israel?

A. Israel won in the end, but suffered great losses.

B. The Israelites quickly defeated the Benjamites, with few casualties of their own.

C. The Benjamites defeated Israel in four successive battles and the Israelites abandoned the effort when they realized God would not help them.

D. There was only one battle, in which both sides sustained serious losses. After that, the matter was resolved by the execution of ten men who had been the cause of the hostility.

E. The Israelites won by a whisker, when they cried out "G-2!" and sunk the Benjamite's battleship.

33. Judges came to a close with what occurrence?

A. The Israelites turning again to idolatry

B. A mass kidnaping of women

C. The execution, by stoning, of a Levite priest

D. The Israelites lamenting their defeat to Benjamin

E. A scandal regarding the location of the next Hebrew Olympic games

Q. Why did Abraham bargain with God?

A. He was hoping to save a Lot.

ANSWERS TO JUDGES QUESTIONS

#	ANS	REF	#	ANS	REF
1.	D	1:2	25.	D	15:4, 5
2.	B	1:6	26.	A	15:15
3.	A	1:24–25	27.	A	16:5
4.	A	1:27–36	28.	B	16:7
5.	D	2:1–2	29.	D	16:27
6.	C	2:13–15	30.	B	17:2–4
7.	C	2:16, 18	31.	E	18:18–20
8.	B	3:15	32.	C	20:4–5
9.	A,C,D	3:15–26	33.	A	20:20–48
10.	D	4:4	34.	B	21:19–24
11.	A	4:21			
12.	B	6:25–27, 30			
13.	A	6:36–40	Super Challenges:		
14.	C	7:5, 7	#1: 300 (7:7)		
15.	D	7:22	#2: She was given to		
16.	D	8:16–17	his best man.		
17.	E	9:5	(14:20)		
18.	C	9:53–54			
19.	A	11:1–7			
20.	D	11:30–40			
21.	B	12:5–6			
22.	B	13:2, 4, 5, 20			
23.	C	14:6			
24.	D	14:1–20			

~RUTH~
(c. 1010–970 B.C.)

1. **What was the name of Ruth's FIRST husband?**
   A. Elimelech
   B. Boaz
   C. Mahlon
   D. Chilion

2. **What did Naomi tell her two daughters-in-law after the death of her husband and sons (their husbands)?**
   A. "Stay with me, for I am old and cannot support myself."
   B. "Return to your mothers' houses."
   C. "This is a total bummer."
   D. "I desire to live no more."
   E. "We will surely die in this famine."

3. **Ruth stayed with her mother-in-law, Naomi, and returned with her to Naomi's homeland. Which was:**
   A. A nice suburb just outside Nashville
   B. Damascus
   C. Megiddo
   D. Bethlehem
   E. Egypt

4. **How did Ruth and Boaz meet?**
   A. While Ruth was working in one of Boaz's fields
   B. At a wedding celebration
   C. Boaz rescued Ruth from being robbed by sojourners
   D. In the marketplace
   E. At a Hebrew hoedown

5. Which of the following was NOT one of the ways that Boaz showed favor toward Ruth?

    A. Had his servants bring her new garments

    B. Commanded the young men not to touch her

    C. Gave her bread and parched grain to eat

    D. Told the reapers to purposely let grain fall so that she could get it

Classic paganism dominates Greece!
(*c.* 1000 B.C.)

6. Which of the following were part of Naomi's instructions to Ruth, regarding going to see Boaz?
(three answers)

    A. "Go to him first thing in the morning."

    B. "Wash and anoint yourself."

    C. "Sing to him."

    D. "Put on your best garment."

    E. "Uncover his feet."

    F. "Tell him you will be his wife."

    G. "Let's synchronize our watches."

 DID YOU KNOW that the Moabite lands, in which the story of Ruth begins, were lands that belonged to the children of the incestuous relationship between Lot and his daughters? The Moabites were pagan enemies of the Israelites; they received many pronouncements of judgement from the prophets.

7. What did Boaz give Ruth to take back to Naomi?

    A. A ring of gold

    B. Twenty pieces of silver

    C. Barley

    D. A purple cloth

    E. A ferret

8. Before Boaz married Ruth, what did he do?

    A. Sent his three concubines away

    B. Sold his fields and bought a dwelling in the town

    C. Asked for Naomi's blessing

D. Redeemed some property that was in Naomi's family

E. Prepared a pre-nuptial agreement

9. **When Ruth gave birth to her son, Obed, Naomi was then reminded by her friends that God had not forgotten her. They also told her that Ruth was:**

A. Chosen by God to be a mother of kings

B. Better than having seven sons

C. The most honorable woman in Bethlehem

D. Working for the Moabite Secret Service

E. Truly a light among women

This "hairdresser's" name means small *or* dainty. *This is interesting since she is paired in history with the strongest man to ever live.*

DELILAH

ANSWERS TO RUTH QUESTIONS

#	ANS	REF	#	ANS	REF
1.	C	4:10	6.	B,D,E	3:3–4
2.	B	1:8	7.	C	3:15–17
3.	D	1:1, 22	8.	D	4:8–9
4.	A	2:3	9.	B	4:15
5.	A	2:9, 14, 16			

~FIRST SAMUEL~
(c. 1050–750 B.C.)

1. Which of the following statements was true concerning the birth of Samuel?
A. Samuel's father had four wives.
B. Samuel was a "preemie," and was in an incubator for three weeks before being released from the hospital.
C. Samuel's mother died giving birth to him.
D. Samuel's mother had been previously barren.
E. Samuel was the third son of Elkanah and Peninnah.

2. How were Samuel's early childhood years spent?
A. Helping to tend his father's flocks in Ephraim
B. Serving Eli, the priest of Israel
C. Traveling across Judah with his family, who were merchants
D. Being very ill until he became a young man
E. Just hangin' in the 'hood

3. The Bible mentioned TWO things that were happening at Shiloh that angered the Lord. What were they?
A. There was no reverence for sacrifices.
B. The priest's sons were having sexual relations with women who came to the tabernacle.
C. Some of the men had built an altar to Baal at the entrance to the city.
D. Incest occurred among the tribe of Benjamin.
E. Vendors who sold animals and birds to be sacrificed were cheating the people.

4. **When God first spoke to Samuel, what did His message concern?**
   A. The death of Samuel's father
   B. Samuel updating his wardrobe
   C. A potential attack on Israel by the revived tribe of Benjamin
   D. The coming judgment on the house of Eli
   E. His call to Samuel to become the leader of Israel

5. **In Chapter 4 of First Samuel, the Israelite army suffered a great defeat at the hands of the Philistines. THREE of the following were results of that battle.**
   A. Samuel's brother was killed.
   B. Both of Eli's sons died.
   C. Eli's daughter-in-law went into labor and died.
   D. The tabernacle of the tent of meeting was destroyed.
   E. Samuel's wife was molested and killed.
   F. Eli fell off a bench, broke his neck, and died.

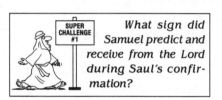

SUPER CHALLENGE #1

What sign did Samuel predict and receive from the Lord during Saul's confirmation?

6. **Which TWO of the following were true concerning the capture of the ark of the covenant by the Philistines?**
   A. When the Philistines placed the ark next to their idol, Dagon, he kept falling over.
   B. The Philistines who touched the ark were struck dead instantly.
   C. When the ark was set on the altar of Dagon at Ashdod, fire like lightning came from it, striking one hundred men blind.
   D. The people of Ashdod were forced to listen to Egyptian rap music until they went insane.
   E. The people of Ashdod were struck with tumors.

F. Once the Philistines realized they couldn't touch the ark, they transported it using poles, without further incident.

7. **After seven months, the Israelites got the ark of the covenant back. How?**

   A. A group made up of twelve Levite priests and twelve foot soldiers went into the Philistine temple very early in the morning, and were able to retake the ark and escape.

   B. Two words: Indiana Jones.

   C. After discussing the problems they were having, the Philistines returned the ark based on the advice of their priests and diviners.

   D. They agreed to serve the Philistines as slaves for seven years, in return for the ark.

   E. When the Philistines were defeated by the Gathites, they allowed the Israelites to come and get the ark.

8. **After Samuel convinced the people to rid themselves of their idols, God helped them defeat the Philistines and recover their towns. What specific thing did He do?**

   A. Created a thunder that disoriented the Philistines

   B. Divided the enemy with a "wall of fire" so that the Israelites could conquer them in smaller groups

   C. Opened the earth beneath the Philistine leaders, swallowing them up

   D. Made the Philistines so sleepy that they could not fight

9. **When Samuel was getting old, what did the people ask him to do?**

   A. A commercial for Geritol

   B. Allow the councils to serve as judges over their cities

   C. Appoint a king for the nation

D. Let the leaders of each of the twelve tribes rule their own people

E. Appoint his sons to rule over them

10. **How did Saul meet Samuel?**

A. Saul had gone into the city of Zuph to take part in the celebration of sacrifice.

B. Saul and two of his servants had taken some of Saul's father's livestock to the city, to sell it for others to use as sacrifices.

C. Samuel came to Saul's house in Ephraim, as God had told him, seeking out a king for Israel.

D. Saul and a servant were seeking some lost donkeys, and they coincidentqally met Samuel.

11. **Before Saul departed from Samuel, Samuel told him to expect several things on his return trip. THREE of the following were part of that list.**

A. He would see two men by Rachel's tomb, who would mention his father's concern for him.

B. His plane would be overbooked, and he would be "bumped" to a later flight.

C. Three men would greet him and give him two loaves of bread.

D. He would meet a group of men playing instruments and prophesying.

E. He would find two virgins in a woods. He was to take the taller one as his wife, and the other as a concubine.

F. He would encounter a wild beast. When he raised his right hand, the beast would fall dead.

12. **Saul proved himself a worthy king to the Israelites early on, by helping them defeat the Ammonites. All of the following facts concerning this were true except one.**

A. The Ammonites were the aggressors.
B. Saul had two fingers of his left hand severed in the battle.
C. The Ammonites offered to take the Israelites as slaves if they could poke out all of their right eyes.
D. Saul threatened to destroy any of the Hebrew tribes who refused to aid in the battle.
E. Saul spared the lives of a handful of Israelites who opposed his being king.

13. **Which of the following statements most accurately reflects Samuel's sentiments at this time?**
    A. Samuel was pleased that Israel now had a strong leader.

Top Ten Old Testament Manuals

10. "Ten Easy Trumpet Tunes to Bring Down the Walls" by Joshua
9. "Eat Right or Die: the Levitican Nutritional Handbook"
8. "Jonah's Pre-*Moby Dick* Guide to Marine Life"
7. "The Sodom and Gomorrah Primer: First Aid for Fire and Brimstone Related Injuries."
6. "It All Boils Down to Patience" authored by Job, with his friends Larry, Darrell and Darrell
5. "Choosing Your Staff" by Moses
4. "Bone Up on Prophecy" by Ezekiel.
3. "Treading Water: Your Guide to Flood Survival" (author unknown, presumed drowned.)
2. "When Workouts Get Hairy: Samson's Guide to Muscle Building"
1. "Arks for Dummies"

B. Samuel was impressed with Saul, but was disappointed that Israel had wanted a king, and feared for their future.

C. Now that Saul had defeated the Ammonites, Samuel knew that God was with him. Thus, Samuel could die with an assurance of peace for Israel's future.

D. Although Samuel outwardly supported Saul, he was inwardly disappointed that his own sons were not to be rulers of the Hebrews.

14. **When Israel was in battle with the Philistines, only Saul and his son Jonathan had swords or spears. Why?**

   A. Because God had told Saul that his army should not take weapons; He would deliver their victory

   B. Because the Philistines had taken the Hebrews by surprise, and the soldiers had not had time to get their weapons

   C. Because Israel had no blacksmiths

   D. Because the Israelites had fallen into idol worship, and had melted down their swords to make an iron god

   E. Because they had all ordered new weapons from "Swords 'R Us," and they hadn't been shipped yet

15. **Who went to the Philistine garrison prior to battle on a whim to see if the Lord might help them?**

   A. Saul and two of his advisors

   B. Saul and Jonathan

   C. Ichabod and Ahijah

   D. Jonathan and his armor carrier

   E. Jonathan and David

16. **What curse had Saul uttered during the day of battle?**

A. A curse on any of his men who ate before Saul had gotten vengeance on his enemies

B. A curse on any man who turned from battle out of fear

C. A curse on the enemies of the Lord, who were "the uncircumcised worshipers of Dagon"

D. A curse on Samuel for appointing him as king

17. **What did Saul want to do with his son Jonathan, who had (unknowingly) violated his order?**
A. Kill him
B. Banish him from the Israelites forever
C. Cut off his hand
D. Forgive him

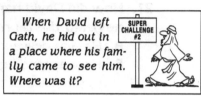

When David left Gath, he hid out in a place where his family came to see him. Where was it?

SUPER CHALLENGE #2

18. **Why were God and Samuel displeased after the victory over the Amalekites?**
A. Because the Israelites slaughtered the young children
B. Because Saul had allowed certain soldiers to sexually assault the Amalekite women
C. Because many Israelite soldiers were killed due to disobeying God's specific instructions for attack
D. Because the Israelites had brought back animals for sacrificing to God

19. **How did Agag, the king of the Amalekites who was defeated, die?**
A. Saul personally killed him using his bare hands.
B. He was dragged behind a horse by the leaders of the Israelite army.
C. He was milking a cow and accidentally kicked the bucket.
D. He killed himself, when he realized defeat was imminent.

E. He was thrown in a pit full of poisonous snakes.

F. He was cut into pieces by Samuel.

20. Why did Saul originally send for David?

A. He had heard that Samuel had anointed David, and planned to kill him.

B. He wanted David to play the harp for him.

C. He wanted to see David's skill in slinging stones.

D. Saul wanted him for a friend to his son Jonathan.

E. He wanted to train David to be his successor as king.

21. How did David happen to be in the army camp when he heard the taunting of Goliath?

A. He was delivering food to the soldiers.

B. He was tending sheep when God called him to go to the place of battle.

C. He was accompanying Saul as part of his training to be king.

D. He was reporting on the battle for CNN.

E. He was appointed to sound the trumpet signals for the Israelite army.

22. **David told Saul that he (David) was a worthy opponent for Goliath. What were his reasons?**
    A. God had promised David he would live to be old; David was one of the better fighters in Saul's army.
    B. His ability to sling stones would allow him to keep Goliath at a safe distance; his spear throwing arm was very strong.
    C. Although he was much smaller, he was also younger and able to move more quickly; Goliath had poor eyesight and would not be able to see David's quick movements.
    D. While protecting sheep, he had killed both lions and bears; the Lord would protect him.
    E. He used to be in *Roller Derby*; he was a superstar whom they would never dare to injure.

23. **What did Jonathan give to David, as a token of his friendship?**
    (three answers)
    A. A gold earring
    B. A robe
    C. Armor
    D. A sword
    E. A red Lamborghini
    F. A javelin
    G. A lamb

24. **Why did Saul turn against David?**
    A. Because Jonathan told Saul that David hoped to be king
    B. Because David refused to marry Saul's daughter

C. Because some women had praised David's battle victories as greater than Saul's

D. Because David had confronted Saul about his lack of obedience to God

25. **Saul's jealousy increased, and the Bible says the Lord departed from him (18:12). Then he tried to kill David in several ways. Which of these is NOT one of the methods?**
    A. Throwing a spear at him
    B. By sending him to collect Philistine foreskins
    C. By attempting to poison him
    D. By telling his servants to kill David
    E. By threatening his own son Jonathan to bring David to him

26. **When David fled from Saul, he went to a place called Gath. The Bible says David was very much afraid of the king there. What did he do to avoid trouble?**
    A. Promised an alliance with Achish (the king) when Saul was deposed
    B. Pretended to be insane
    C. Assumed the identity of Jonathan
    D. Pretended to be very ill
    E. Wore a T-shirt reading "Support Your Local King"

27. **What was Saul's response when he learned that a priest named Ahimelech had helped David by giving him bread and the sword of Goliath?**
    A. He ordered all the priests of the kingdom sent out of the land.
    B. He had 85 priests put to death.
    C. He personally killed Ahimelech, and ordered his household cut off from the people.
    D. He vowed to destroy David and his entire family.
    E. He blessed the priest for his kindness.

28. **When Saul and his men had nearly caught David, they abruptly abandoned their quest. Why?**

A. A messenger came and told them the Philistines were attacking again.

B. Saul learned of the death of his father, Kish, and returned to bury him.

C. God appeared to Saul in a dream and told him to spare David's life.

D. They realized it was bingo night.

E. The men who were with Saul rebelled, and threatened to kill Saul if he proceeded against David.

29. **David was able to prove to Saul that he would not hurt him, even though Saul was seeking his life. He did this by obtaining a piece of Saul's robe, then showing it to Saul later, saying that he could have killed Saul if he wished. Now that I've said all that, how did David get the fragment?**

A. He sneaked into Saul's camp when everyone was asleep and cut off the piece of cloth.

B. He found it in some briars and recognized it as being from Saul's robe.

C. Saul's son, Jonathan, got it secretly and took it to David.

D. David cut it off Saul's robe when Saul was in a cave "powdering his nose."

E. He bought it at a charity auction.

The most promising leader around, despite the fact that he had an affair with his neighbor's wife.

DAVID

30. **When David sent his men to a man named Nabal to ask for provisions, he refused them, even though David's men had protected his shepherds. What was the outcome of this?**

A. Nothing. David and his men left and went back to the mountains of Maon.

B. David and his men routed the place, killing Nabal. David took Nabal's wife Abigail as his concubine.

C. David withheld action. Shortly thereafter, Nabal died, and David married Abigail.

First Olympic Games!
(*c.* 776 B.C.)

D. One of David's men was attacked by Nabal, and killed him to save his own life. Nabal's wife and servants then came with David and his men.

E. David looked at his messengers and said "Same stuff—different day!"

31. A second time, David spared Saul's life. What happened?

A. Saul was captured by David's men. They brought him to David, who made them set him free.

B. David's men were camped in the mountains when Saul and a small army rode beneath them. David's men trapped them, then released them without harm.

C. David and Abishai went down into Saul's camp where he was sleeping and took his spear and water jug to prove that he would not kill Saul.

D. The Philistine army had attacked Saul's band of men and was routing them, when David and his army of about six hundred men arrived to fend off the attackers, saving Saul's life in the process.

32. What did David do during the sixteen months that he spent living among the Philistines at Gath?

A. Defended the house of Achish, the king of Gath

B. Raided Philistine settlements, then lied about it to the king

C. Practiced his guitar, wrote some music, and hung out

D. Lived with his two wives and hid from Saul

E. Raided the Israelite encampments in the southern areas of Judah, bringing back the plunder to Achish

33. **In chapter 28, Saul visited a medium to call Samuel back from the dead. This was unusual because:**
   A. Saul had previously expelled all of the mediums and spiritists from the land.
   B. God specifically prohibited sorcery in the law.
   C. Samuel was actually still alive, and living in a village in the western part of Judah's territory.
   D. Saul's own daughter was a prophetess.
   E. Saul would never even read his own fortune at the bottom of Bazooka comics.

34. **How was David able to avoid going to battle against Saul and Israel?**
   A. The other Philistine leaders didn't trust David, and made Achish (king of Gath), send him back.
   B. David started a false rumor that the Israelites planned to ambush Gath, so Achish told David and his 600 men to stay there in case that happened.
   C. He told Achish that he had requested his vacation for that week way back in January, and he was sick and tired of getting the small end of the stick, while everyone else in the place got away with murder.
   D. Jonathan showed up in disguise, and told David of Saul's plan to kill him in battle. He and David then left and spent the next few days hiding in a cave.
   E. Saul's encounter with the medium, combined with his fear of the huge Philistine army, made him decide to surrender before the battle was fought.

35. **When David and his men returned to their home in Philistine territory, what did they find?**
   A. An army of Israelites waiting to kill them
   B. A great celebration honoring the victory over Israel

C. An angel of the Lord standing at the city's gate instructing them to go to Shiloh

D. The city burned and all the people taken

E. A new billboard at the entrance to the city which read: Welcome to Ziklag, Home of the National Champion Stoning Team

36. First Samuel closed with an important battle between Israel, under Saul, and the Philistine armies. THREE of the following were true.

A. The Israelites soundly crushed the Philistines, thanks to God's intervention.

B. Many Israelites were slain on Mt. Gilboa.

C. Saul's three sons, including Jonathan, were killed in battle.

D. David was standing on a hill above Saul and watched as he was slain.

E. The Israelites fought valiantly down to the last man.

F. Saul had been wounded by archers but died by his own hand.

Q. Who wrote the sequel to Numbers?

A. Paul; all his books are letters.

ANSWERS TO FIRST SAMUEL QUESTIONS

#	ANS	REF	#	ANS	REF
1.	D	1:5	23.	B,C,D	18:4
2.	B	2:11	24.	C	18:7–9
3.	A,B	2:17, 22	25.	C	Ch 18—20
4.	D	3:10–14	26.	B	21:13
5.	B,C,F	4:11, 18–20	27.	B	22:16–18
6.	A,E	5:3–4, 6	28.	A	23:27–28
7.	C	6:2	29.	D	24:3–4
8.	A	7:10	30.	C	25:38–42
9.	C	8:5	31.	C	26:6–25
10.	D	9:3–17	32.	E	27:8–12
11.	A,C,D	10:2, 4–5	33.	A	28:3
12.	B	11:1–13	34.	A	29:4
13.	B	12:19–20, 25	35.	D	30:3
14.	C	13:19, 22	36.	B,C,F	31:1–4
15.	D	14:1			
16.	A	14:24			
17.	A	14:44	Super Challenges:		
18.	D	15:19–21	#1: thunder and rain		
19.	F	15:33	(12:17–18)		
20.	B	16:17–19	#2: cave of Adullam		
21.	A	17:17–18	(22:1)		
22.	D	17:34–37			

~SECOND~ SAMUEL

(c. 1010–970 B.C.)

1. **When the Amalekite man came and told David about Saul and Jonathan's death, what proof did he show David?**
   - **A.** The bow that David had given Jonathan
   - **B.** Saul's spear
   - **C.** A newspaper showing their names in the obituary section
   - **D.** Saul's crown and a bracelet
   - **E.** An ephod with Saul's crest on it

2. **After they had mourned Saul and Jonathan's deaths, David and his household went up to Hebron, where he was anointed king of Judah. Who was installed as king of Israel?**
   - **A.** David
   - **B.** Ishbosheth, Saul's son
   - **C.** Abner, commander of the army
   - **D.** Joab, son of Zeruiah
   - **E.** No one

3. **Which were true concerning Abner's visit to David's house?**
   (three answers)
   - **A.** He insulted David and was sent away.
   - **B.** He came to work out a covenant with David regarding the leadership of Israel.
   - **C.** David accused him of being a traitor.

D. David provided a feast for Abner and his men, and they left in peace.

E. Shortly after Abner left, he was killed by an ally of David's.

F. Abner returned to Gilead, where he stabbed Saul's son.

G. Abner had come down to make an offer to purchase David's house, but changed his mind when he found out it was zoned "battle."

4. **Which of the following is NOT true, regarding the death of Ishbosheth?**

A. He was killed by two of his own troop captains.

B. He was slain while in his own bed.

C. His head was taken to David.

D. Two Philistines attacked him, and he killed one, but the other slew him with a sword.

E. David had those responsible killed and dismembered.

5. **After Ishbosheth's death, David was anointed king. How old does the Bible say he was at this time?**

   A. 30 years

   B. 6 years (but that was measured in Hebrew "dog years")

   C. 50 years

   D. 35 years

   E. 42 years

6. **The first thing the Bible recorded after David became king of Israel was:**

   A. David's plan for the Hebrew Air Force

   B. David's reading of the law to the people

   C. The conquest of Jerusalem

   D. David's plan to build a temple to the Lord

   E. A problem with the Philistines

7. **Why was Michal, David's wife, angry at him?**

   A. He continued to take wives and concubines, ignoring her and her children.

   B. She believed he had dishonored Saul, her father, by making a treaty with the Philistines.

   C. She felt he had disgraced himself while celebrating the return of the ark of the covenant.

   D. Every time it was his turn to do dishes, he always had to go fight the Philistines.

   E. She believed he was not taking proper precautions regarding his personal safety.

8. **What message did God give to David through Nathan the prophet?**
   A. That He would no longer speak through the ark of the covenant, but through the king and the prophets
   B. That David's seed (son) would build Him a house
   C. That David was to take no more wives
   D. That the twelve tribes of Israel would soon be scattered like "dust in the wind"

9. **Which tribes/nations from this list were specifically mentioned as being defeated during David's conquest of Israel, according to chapter 8? (three answers)**

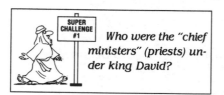

   SUPER CHALLENGE #1 *Who were the "chief ministers" (priests) under king David?*

   A. The Moabites
   B. Asher
   C. Phoenicia
   D. The Eskimos (David's army set fire to their igloos)
   E. The Philistines
   F. The Syrians
   G. Zobah

10. **David extended grace toward Jonathan's son, Ishbosheth, as a memorial to his friend, and the house of Saul. What was Ishbosheth's handicap?**
    A. He was "lame in his feet."
    B. He was "crooked in stature" (probably a spinal defect).
    C. He had lost his left arm in battle.
    D. He had a "leprous skin."
    E. He was "soft in the head."

11. **When the king of Ammon died, David sent some servants to extend sympathy to Hanun, the king's son. How were they received by the Ammonites?**

A. They tortured them brutally, in retaliation for David's past dealings with Ammon, then released them.

B. They received them warmly, and signed a treaty strengthening their loyalty to David.

C. Hanun had them put up at the Hyatt, and put everything on his tab.

D. They thought the servants were spies, and intimidated them by shaving off half of their beards and mutilating their garments. Then they sent them away.

E. The Ammonites believed the servants of David planned to kill Hanun. They cut off the feet of the servants, then publicly hung them.

12. **After David committed adultery with Bathsheba, he received word from her that she was pregnant. What was his first plan to solve the "problem"?**
    A. To have her husband, Uriah, killed in battle
    B. To bring her husband from battle to sleep with her
    C. To beg Uriah's forgiveness, and offer to make him commander of all his armies
    D. To conspire with Bathsheba, and fabricate a story that she was sexually assaulted by a stranger

13. **Who came to David and rebuked him for his sin with Bathsheba?**
    A. Nathan
    B. Joab, his military commander
    C. His wife Michal (Saul's daughter)
    D. An angel of the Lord
    E. His twelve mothers-in-law

14. **What was the name of David and Bathsheba's second son?**
    A. Absalom
    B. Amnon

C. Fox

D. Solomon

E. Gilead

15. **As part of David's punishment for his sin, there was trouble in his house. Which of the following best describes what happened next?**

Celts invade England!
(c. 850 B.C.)

A. Absalom, David's son, raped his sister, Tamar, and was murdered one week later by Amnon.

B. Jonadab, David's nephew, began a conspiracy to overthrow David, leading to the death of Amnon.

C. David's son Amnon, raped his half-sister Tamar, and was killed two years later on orders from Absalom.

D. Tamar seduced her cousin Jonadab, and both of them were murdered by David's servants.

E. None of the TV remotes in David's house worked. Light bulbs blew out every other day, and his lap top was stolen. His chariot was carjacked, and his job performance polls dropped below thirty per cent. (The Gallup polls didn't horse around, and the Ropers could get you strung up.)

16. **Why did Joab (David's nephew and army commander) enlist the help of a "wise woman" of Tekoa, to pose as a mourner before King David?**

A. To warn David of an uprising among the Edomites

B. As a decoy to help disguise Joab's plan to overthrow David

C. To convince David to bring Absalom back to Jerusalem

D. Because David's grief was not being adequately shared by his people

17. **The Bible indicates that David's son Absalom was an extremely good-looking man. Which of the following was true concerning the account?**
    A. His eyes were the bluest of any man.
    B. His hair was extremely thick and heavy.
    C. He wore a bone through his nose.
    D. His jaw was strong and square.
    E. His face was ruddy (rosy-cheeked).

Top Ten Tribes NOT Mentioned in the Old Testament

10. Fishbites (Their favorite saying was "ya shoulda been here LAST week!")
9. Troglodytes (They had seniority.)
8. Flyakites (this name worked well with their clan chant: "Goooo Flyakites!")
7. Uptights (very nervous group)
6. I'mallrights (forever cool, ain't nobody worried 'bout them)
5. Sticktites (always around when you didn't need 'em)
4. Electrolytes (had lots of energy; hyper)
3. Amalgamites (industrious group)
2. Samsonites (traveled a lot)
1. Stalactites (just hung around; did nothing)

18. **What did David do when he heard that Absalom had captured the "hearts of the men of Israel"?**
   A. Instructed Joab to organize an army against them
   B. Sent for Absalom to request a treaty
   C. Went into a rage and killed the messenger
   D. Fled to the wilderness
   E. Answered, "He can have their hearts. I hold all their mortgages."

19. **Why did David send his friend Hushai to serve Absalom?**
   A. He wanted to show Absalom that David was willing to hand over the kingdom.
   B. David knew that Hushai's loyalty for him was gone.
   C. He believed that if Absalom killed Hushai the people would turn on him.
   D. David could only afford to pay him minimum wage.
   E. He sent Hushai to spy on Absalom.

20. **What advice did Ahithophel, who was a counselor to Absalom, give him in order to make "the hands of all who are with you strong"?**
   A. "You must attack and kill your father."
   B. "Go and have sexual relations with your father's concubines."
   C. "Make them all squeeze tennis balls for an hour every day."
   D. "Put to death your remaining two brothers who are still loyal to David."
   E. "Appoint your own priests to bring the ark of the covenant out to the people."

21. **When Absalom decided to take the advice of Hushai regarding battle plans, what did Ahithophel do?**

A. Put his affairs in order, then hung himself
B. Took a job with Morton in the Valley of Salt
C. Defected to King David
D. Left Jerusalem and was never seen again
E. Killed Hushai

22. **Which one of the following was NOT true concerning the death of Absalom?**
    A. He had three spears thrust through his heart by Joab.
    B. He was struck and killed by ten young men.
    C. He was decapitated.
    D. His head got caught in a tree, and he was suspended in air.
    E. David had given an order to "deal gently" with Absalom.

23. **Why did Joab rebuke David after they had won the battle over Absalom?**
    A. Because David danced naked in celebration of the victory
    B. Because David had said the Lord was on Absalom's side
    C. Because David's soldiers believed David would rather they had died than Absalom
    D. Because David had killed the messenger who told him of Absalom's death

This evil temptress of a royal woman attempted to remove the worship of Israel's God and replace it with the worship of Baal. She came to a bitter end though, when she was thrown to her death and eaten by dogs. JEZEBEL

24. **When David and his followers were at Mahanaim, a wealthy man named Barzillai provided supplies for them. What was his main reason for refusing David's offer to come to Jerusalem?**
    A. His wives and family were all satisfied to stay at Mahanaim, and he wouldn't leave them.

B. He was an old man and wished to be buried with his parents.

C. He needed to remain in Mahanaim to keep watch over all of his enterprises there.

D. Property taxes in Jerusalem were just too high.

E. He had enemies in Jerusalem and feared they would find him and kill him.

25. **All of the following except one were true regarding Joab's regaining of his position as commander of the armies. Which one?**

> **DID YOU KNOW** that Second Samuel was intended to give the Hebrew people the facts and implications about David's reign? It focused on the spiritual aspects of his kingship.

A. The leader who had replaced him, Amasa, delayed in carrying out King David's orders.

B. David knew that if he was going to regain the people's trust he must reappoint Joab to the position.

C. Joab killed Amasa, using trickery.

D. Joab spared a city in return for the head of one of David's enemies.

26. **When a famine came upon Israel, David asked God why it was happening. God responded that it was because the Gibeonites had not been protected by the house of Saul. What was the outcome of this?**

A. David went to the Gibeonites with a large offering of silver, gold, and grain. The famine lasted two more years.

B. David argued with God and refused His commandment concerning restitution. As David's punishment, the famine lasted seven more years, and thousands died.

C. The Gibeonites requested permanent territory for themselves and an end to their servitude as slaves. King David granted them release as slaves but refused to give them land. As a result, the famine lasted three more years.

D. The Gibeonites requested seven of Saul's descendants, whom they executed. After this, the famine ended.

E. David agreed to establish "National Gibeonite Week" during which there would be lots of festivities dedicated to recognizing the uniqueness of the Gibeonites. They were all pleased with this, and the famine literally ended overnight.

27. **Second Samuel 23 discusses some of David's "mighty men" and their remarkable deeds. Three of these are mentioned in the text.**

A. Alihud the Berite single-handedly defeated one hundred Philistines after having gone three days without food.

B. Burr, the Sticktite, the enemy just couldn't eliminate him from their presence.

Who became David's chief priest after his conquest of Absalom?

SUPER CHALLENGE #2

C. Benaiah killed two lion-like heroes of Moab and a REAL lion in a pit.

D. Elaim, the Ephraimite, fighting against the troops of Absalom, killed forty men AFTER having his right armed severed by an enemy sword.

E. Eleazar, son of Dodo, fought so hard against the Philistines that "his hand stuck to the sword."

F. Adino the Eznite killed eight hundred men at one time.

28. **Second Samuel ends with what TWO things?**

A. A census and a plague

B. Civil war in Israel, and a second famine

C. Peace in the land, and David and three friends composing "barber-shop" quartet arrangements of his psalms

D. Solomon's rise to power, and the beginning of the temple construction

E. A major battle with the Philistines, and the death of David

Q. Who was known as a great mathematician in Bible Times?

A. Moses; he wrote the book of Numbers.

ANSWERS TO SECOND SAMUEL QUESTIONS

#	ANS	REF	#	ANS	REF
1.	D	1:10	26.	D	21:3–9
2.	B	2:8, 9	27.	C,E,F	23:8–10, 20
3.	B,D,E	3:20–27	28.	A	24:2, 15
4.	D	4:2–12			
5.	A	5:4			
6.	C	5:6–7	Super Challenges:		
7.	C	6:16–23	#1: David's sons (8:18)		
8.	B	7:12–13	#2: Ira the Jairite (20:26)		
9.	A,F,G	8:1–6			
10.	A	9:3			
11.	D	10:4			
12.	B	11:6–13			
13.	A	12:1–12			
14.	D	12:24			
15.	C	13:1–14, 28–29			
16.	C	14:1–3			
17.	B	14:25–26			
18.	D	15:13–23			
19.	E	15:34–37			
20.	B	16:21			
21.	A	17:23			
22.	C	18:5–15			
23.	C	19:5–7			
24.	B	19:35, 37			
25.	B	20:5			

~FIRST KINGS~
(c. 600–500 B.C.)

1. **Why did David's servants send for a young virgin named Abishag?**
   A. To be the bride of Solomon
   B. To restock the pop machines in the palace
   C. To care for the aging David, and keep him warm
   D. To become wife to Adonijah
   E. She was a prophetess, and David wished to ask her how much longer he would live.

2. **Just before David told his confidants to install Solomon as king, another man was attempting to set himself up as king. Who was it?**
   A. Adonijah
   B. Joab, the army commander
   C. Benaiah
   D. Eleazar, one of the "mighty men"
   E. Some guy who claimed he could make the trains run on time

3. **Before David died, he instructed Solomon to seek some level of revenge against TWO of the people from this list. Who were they?**
   A. Joab, the army commander
   B. Shimei, son of Gera
   C. The oldest son of Barzillai the Gileadite
   D. Adonijah

4. **Why did Solomon order the death of his half-brother Adonijah?**

A. Because news reached Solomon that Adonijah was planning a revolt against him
B. Because he was tired of Adonijah always coming over to borrow money
C. Because Adonijah had killed one of Solomon's priests
D. Because Adonijah had sent Bathsheba to request that Solomon give him Abishag
E. Because Solomon's mother, Bathsheba, told him that Adonijah had cursed her

5. **Which of the following were true concerning Solomon's purging of his new kingdom? (three answers)**

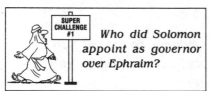

SUPER CHALLENGE #1 Who did Solomon appoint as governor over Ephraim?

A. To be completely safe, Solomon ordered everyone in Israel to kill everyone else. Then he ruled no one, quite successfully, for his entire life.
B. Solomon had Joab put to death, and he died in the tabernacle.
C. Abiathar the priest was stoned by the people on orders from Solomon.
D. Shimei was sent away with specific orders. He was later executed for violating those instructions.
E. Abiathar was spared because he had served David.
F. Solomon spared Joab but removed him as commander.

6. **In Solomon's dream, God asked him what he wanted. What was Solomon's response?**
A. All of the knowledge of the heavens
B. An understanding heart
C. To complete the Lord's temple
D. Great and vast riches
E. A pink Cadillac

7. **Solomon's first test regarding his ability to judge fairly involved what?**
   A. A land dispute between the Gadites and the Benjamites
   B. Bathsheba's request to return to Ephraim
   C. Two harlots and an infant
   D. A clarification of the rites of sacrifice
   E. Movie ratings

8. **How was Solomon's house supplied?**
   A. Each year, a different tribe was responsible for bringing supplies.
   B. Twice each year, each tribe was to bring a tithe (tenth) of their animals, grain, silver, and gold.
   C. One of Solomon's first investments was a national grocery chain.
   D. The twelve tribes alternated on a monthly basis.
   E. Solomon sent an army of one hundred men to various tribes, as he had need, to obtain sustenance.

9. **When Solomon began preparations for construction of the temple, he was first contacted by Hiram, king of the Sidonians. Why?**
   A. The Sidonians had cedars and timber cutting skills.
   B. Hiram was well known in the land for his ability to construct great buildings.
   C. The Sidonians were renowned artisans, especially with gold.
   D. Solomon had granted special favors to Hiram and wanted the favors returned in the form of manual labor from the Sidonians.
   E. Hiram was in charge of issuing building permits.

10. **Concerning the temple, all but one of the following were true. Find the incorrect statement!**

A. The temple took twelve years to complete.

B. It featured a vestibule and beveled windows.

C. The temple was paneled with cedar beams and boards.

D. The inner sanctuary and its altar were overlaid in gold.

E. Two of the doors featured carvings of angels, palm trees, and open flowers.

11. **After the temple was finished, Solomon had other structures created, including a house for himself. The last thing(s) brought into the temple was/were what?**

A. Ten beautifully ornate bronze carts (stands)

B. An altar overlaid in gold

C. The bulletins for the first Sunday service

D. The ark of the covenant

E. The tent of meeting and sacrificial articles which had been used in the desert

12. **What miracle took place after the temple was furnished, and the priests came out?**

A. Solomon's face shown radiantly, and the people feared God.

B. A cloud, full of the glory of the Lord, filled the temple.

C. The priests were struck and fell as if they were dead.

D. A dove descended from the heavens, landing on Solomon's shoulder.

E. Everyone liked the wallpaper.

13. **All of the following were true concerning the dedication of the temple except one.**

A. There was an altercation, and two priests were accidentally killed.

B. Solomon personally offered up the prayer of consecration and thanks.

C. Solomon had over one hundred thousand sheep slaughtered for sacrifice.

D. Everyone went away happy.

E. The feast lasted fourteen days.

14. **What did Solomon give to Hiram, king of Tyre, in return for his help with the construction of the temple and house?**

    A. 120 talents of gold

    B. Ten virgins, rolls of expensive cloth, and twenty thousand bulls

    C. Twenty cities

    D. An extended kingdom, into the territory of the Danites, leading to a war

    E. A really nice thank-you card

    Prone to depression. Collapses under pressure. Had unusual experience with wildlife while spending time alone in the wilderness.

    ᴡʜᴏ Aₘ I?

    ELIJAH

15. **What does the Bible say Solomon also built at Ezion Geber, near the shore of the Red Sea?**

    A. An altar to God (The Altar of Sunset)

    B. A smaller temple

    C. A walled city (probably a fort)

    D. A fleet of ships

    E. A marina and beach house

16. **When the queen of Sheba came to visit Solomon, she brought gifts. In fact, the Bible says there never again was such an abundance of what given to the king.**

    A. Rubies of the purest red

    B. Spices

    C. Gold

    D. Fine silk

    E. Reese's Peanut Butter Cups

17. **First Kings 10:22 tells us that Solomon had a shipping arrangement with Hiram. Every three years, ships would come in bringing which FOUR things from the following list?**
    A. Sapphires
    B. Ivory
    C. Spices
    D. Apes
    E. Slaves
    F. Gold
    G. Flowers (bulbs)
    H. Monkeys

18. **Solomon, at his peak, had how many wives and concubines?**
    A. Thirty wives and twenty concubines
    B. Seven hundred wives and three hundred concubines
    C. One hundred fifty wives and eighty concubines
    D. Nine hundred wives and six hundred concubines
    E. None of the above. Solomon was a confirmed bachelor.

19. **What did the Bible say was Solomon's downfall?**
    A. His many foreign wives led him into idolatry.
    B. He became obsessed with his wealth and forgot the Lord.
    C. He found nothing to please him as he aged and became evil and defiled.
    D. He grew restless and was intoxicated with much wine and strong drink until his death.

20. **When Solomon died, his son Rehoboam became king. What early mistake did he make?**
    A. Telling the people he would be their servant
    B. Canceling the appointed feasting days

C. Ignoring the advice of the elders regarding his policy toward the people

D. Allowing Solomon's former servant, Jeroboam, to control the northern kingdoms

E. Believing that wisdom was in his genes

21. **What happened when Rehoboam sent out Adoram, his first revenue officer?**

A. He was stoned to death by the people.

B. He was threatened and injured but escaped with his life.

C. He was captured, and his abductors sent word to Rehoboam that they would send him Adoram's head unless Rehoboam agreed to renounce his kingship.

D. The people grumbled among themselves about who should succeed Rehoboam.

E. The people didn't Adoram.

Top Ten Things David Did After Becoming King

10. The "Tarzan yell"
9. Established a center for nuclear arms research
8. Had "The Boss" painted on the side of his chariot
7. Took down all the Philistine signs that read "Eat more pork"
6. Went shopping for wives
5. Got his own key to the executive washroom
4. Canceled the investigation into Saul's political action committee
3. E-mailed all of his friends
2. Interviewed with Barbara Walters
1. Went to Disney World

22. **When all of the tribes except Judah made Jeroboam their king, he started off on the wrong foot. What did he do?**
    A. Told the Israelites that Solomon had been an evil ruler
    B. Ordered Solomon's temple torn down
    C. Built two golden calves for the Israelites to sacrifice to
    D. Attacked Rehoboam at Jerusalem and was soundly defeated

23. **What TWO miracles did God use against Jeroboam, through a prophet that had come from Judah?**
    A. Caused Jeroboam's men to become deaf so that they couldn't hear his orders
    B. Made Jeroboam's spear hover in the air just above his reach
    C. Made Jeroboam's feet sink into the earth so that he could not move
    D. Withered the hand of Jeroboam
    E. Made an altar split apart

24. **What happened to the prophet before he made it home?**
    (three answers)
    A. Another old prophet deceived him into accepting a dinner invitation.
    B. God allowed him to kill two men sent by Jeroboam in order to save his life.
    C. Someone stole the CD player out of his mule.
    D. He was attacked and killed by a lion.
    E. He refused an invitation to dine with King Jeroboam.
    F. He fell sick, and Jeroboam assisted in his recovery.

25. **Why did Jeroboam send his wife, in disguise, to the prophet Ahijah?**

A. He heard the prophet was dying and sent his wife to pay their respects.

B. He was concerned about losing the kingdom and wanted to know Ahijah's prophecy.

C. He wanted to see if Ahijah would come back with her to help Jeroboam try to regain God's favor.

D. Their son was ill, and Jeroboam wanted to know what would happen to him.

E. He wanted to see if Ahijah would become a downline in their Amway group.

26. **According to First Kings 14:25–26, who came against Jerusalem in the fifth year of King Rehoboam and took all the "treasures of the house of the Lord and . . . the king's house"?**

    A. The House of Judah

    B. Shishak, king of Egypt

    C. The Philistines under Mephistopheles

    D. The tribes of Arabia

    E. Genghis Khan

27. **Why did Asa (king of Judah) remove his grandmother from the position of queen mother?**

    A. She had attempted to kill him.

    B. She was going insane.

    C. She made an obscene image.

    D. She had stolen holy items from the house of the Lord.

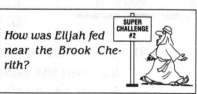

SUPER CHALLENGE #2

How was Elijah fed near the Brook Cherith?

28. **Elah, the son of Baasha, was king of Israel for about two years. What happened to him?**

    A. His poor decision-making led to a famine; he starved to death.

B. He became a deadhead and left Jerusalem in a flowered VW van. He returned after the death of Jerry Garcia.

C. He was captured by the army of Asa and burned alive.

D. He died of the plague at the age of forty.

E. His commander conspired against him, killing Elah, who was in a drunken stupor.

29. What city was built by Omri, when he was king of Israel?

Papyrus introduced in Greece!
(c. 650 B.C.)

A. Samaria
B. Gaza
C. Tel Aviv
D. Cleveland
E. Damascus

30. According to the author of First Kings, this Israelite king "did more to provoke the Lord . . . to anger than all . . . before him."

A. Jeroboam
B. Omri
C. Elah
D. Ahab

31. What TWO miracles took place while Elijah was staying with the widow?

A. The neighbor's dog stopped barking at night.
B. The woman's dead son was revived.
C. The woman's silver was increased tenfold.
D. The woman's crippled leg was healed.
E. God increased her oil and flour.

32. How did God help Elijah convince the Israelites that Baal was a false god?

A. By striking all 450 of Baal's prophets dead

B. By sending rain on the land and ending a drought

C. By causing the ground to "swallow up" the idols of Baal

D. By consuming a sacrificial bull with fire

E. Through a mature, scientific, dialectical debate

33. **Why did Elijah flee to Beersheba after the victory over Baal?**

    A. Because civil war had broken out between the tribes there

    B. Because Ahab's wife, Jezebel, threatened to kill him

    C. Because God warned him in a dream that harm would come to him if he remained where he was

    D. Because God threatened to destroy the land and people around Mt. Carmel, due to their idol worship

34. **Which of the following were true concerning the victory of Israel over Ben-Hadad and the Syrians? (three answers)**

    A. Ahab and the Israelites had attacked Syria twice already without success.

    B. Ahab had originally agreed to make significant concessions to Syria.

    C. The prophets were silent regarding the war, even though Ahab inquired of them.

    D. When the Israelite army came out, Ben-Hadad was in the command post getting drunk.

    E. Israel was losing until Elijah showed up in a tank.

    F. Ben-Hadad survived and agreed to a treaty.

    G. Ben-Hadad was brutally slaughtered early in the second battle.

35. **Why did Ahab's wife, Jezebel, create a conspiracy to kill Naboth?**

A. Because she had been involved in an affair with Naboth, and couldn't risk having Ahab find out about it

B. Because Ahab wanted Naboth's vineyard, and he wouldn't sell it

C. Because she wanted to attack Judah, and Naboth was a hindrance to her plan

D. Because it was part of her larger plan to destroy her husband, Ahab, and become ruling queen of Israel

36. How did Ahab die?

A. He was killed by a bow in battle.

B. He drowned in the Jordan River while retreating.

C. He died laughing at a comedy club in Jericho.

D. He died of old age.

E. He was killed in his sleep by Jezebel.

Solomon's version of that old Springsteen tune was "Pink Battle Axe" and the chorus went something like:

A pink battle axe, swing it left and right,
Slaughter everybody on a Saturday night—
My pink battle axe, ya know what it means
A great way to irritate those nasty Philistines.
I'm tellin' all you people, they really get the facts
With my pink battle axe
Yeah my pink battle axe
Oh my pink battle axe

(Repeat and fade)

ANSWERS TO FIRST KINGS QUESTIONS

#	ANS	REF	#	ANS	REF
1.	C	1:1–4	22.	C	12:28–33
2.	A	1:5–9	23.	D,E	13:4–5
3.	A,B	2:5–9	24.	A,D,E	13:7–8, 18, 24
4.	D	2:13–25	25.	D	14:1–3
5.	B,D,E	2:26–46	26.	B	14:25–26
6.	B	3:9	27.	C	15:13
7.	C	3:16–27	28.	E	16:8–14
8.	E	4:7	29.	A	16:24
9.	A	5:6	30.	D	16:33
10.	A	6:38	31.	B,E	17:15–16, 22
11.	D	8:6–8	32.	D	18:22–40
12.	B	8:10–11	33.	B	19:1–3
13.	A	8:22–53, 63, 65–66	34.	B,D,F	20:4, 16, 34
			35.	B	21:7
14.	C	9:10–13	36.	A	22:34–35
15.	D	9:26			
16.	B	10:10			
17.	B,D, F,H	10:22	Super Challenges:		
18.	B	11:3	#1: Ben-Hur (4:8)		
19.	A	11:4–13	#2: by ravens (17:4–6)		
20.	C	12:6–15			
21.	A	12:18			

~SECOND KINGS~

(c. 600–500 B.C.)

1. **What accident did Israel's King Ahaziah (Ahab's son) suffer at the beginning of Second Kings?**
   A. He was thrown from a horse on the way to visit the king of Moab.
   B. He fell through the lattice of an upper room.
   C. He was pierced through the wrist with his own arrow while shooting a bow.
   D. He was severely burned with fire from a sacrifice.

2. **What happened to the troops Ahaziah sent to inquire of Baal-Zebub, regarding the outcome of his injury?**
   A. They were captured by Moabites on the way, and all were beheaded.
   B. They were surrounded by lions, and thirty men were killed.
   C. Elijah called down to them from a tree, and told them Ahaziah would die unless they turned from idolatry.
   D. 102 men were consumed by fire, and Elijah predicted Ahaziah's death.
   E. They defected to Judah, and were ultimately responsible for Ahaziah's death.

3. **Which of the following were true concerning the parting of Elijah and his protege, Elisha?**
   (three answers)
   A. Elisha wanted to leave before Elijah was "taken," but Elijah forbade him to do so.

B. Elijah parted the Jordan by striking it with a rolled up cloak.

C. Elisha requested double the spirit of Elijah.

D. Elijah climbed a golden ladder into the heavens, until Elisha could no longer see him.

E. Elisha agreed to allow men to go and search for Elijah.

F. Two angels carried Elijah up and set him in a chariot of fire.

4. When Elisha was on his way to Bethel, he pronounced a curse on some youths from the city; many of them were mauled by bears as a result. Why did he curse them?

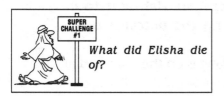

SUPER CHALLENGE #1

What did Elisha die of?

A. They attempted to sexually assault him.

B. They beat and robbed him.

C. They called him a "prophet of Baal."

D. They profaned the Lord.

E. They made fun of him for being bald.

5. All of the following were true concerning the battle of Israel and Judah versus Moab, except one.

A. The king of Moab rebelled.

B. Jehoshaphat (Judah's king), although joined with Israel in appearance, was actually conspiring with the Moabite king.

C. God provided water for the Israelite/Judaean armies in the wilderness.

D. Elisha advised the troops to attack all of the choice cities, cut down every good tree, and stop up their springs.

E. The king of Moab offered his son as a burnt offering.

6. God performed several miracles through Elisha, which were recorded in Chapters 4 through 6. Of the following list, FIVE are correct, and the rest are more of my fabrications. Can you identify the right miracles?

A. He made the sun stand still for three hours.

B. He felled a tree with his mantle (cloak).

C. He raised a young boy from the dead.

D. He made poisoned stew safe.

E. He restored a woman's foot.

F. He healed a leper.

G. He made an ax head float, not to be confused with a root-beer float.

H. He turned water into wine.

I. He struck an entire army blind.

J. He beat Michael Jordan in a game of "horse."

7. Why did the king of Israel tear his clothes during a famine?

A. He watched his own son starve to death.

B. He got hung up on a barbed wire fence while trying to steal chickens.

C. He heard a report of cannibalism.

D. His people were reverting back to Baal worship in hopes of receiving food.

E. The Syrians who were attacking at the time carried off his wife and servants.

8. Who discovered that the Syrian camps had been deserted, leaving all kinds of animals and supplies for the taking?

A. Four lepers

B. A widow, who had left the city in order to die by her husband's tomb

C. A small army of Israelites

D. Elisha

9. **What happened to the city gatekeeper when the people rushed to raid the deserted Syrian camp?**
   A. The ladder he was on was knocked over by the crowd, and he fell to his death.
   B. He was caught behind the great door and crushed to death.
   C. He was trampled to death.
   D. He stayed to protect the city and was killed by Syrian spies.
   E. He dove into a ditch to escape the stampede, muttering to himself, "I gotta get outta this job."

10. **When the king of Syria, Ben-Hadad, was ill, he sent an officer named Hazael to inquire of Elisha as to his prognosis. THREE of the following were accurate regarding Elisha's response.**
    A. "Tell him he is going to recover."
    B. "Tell him he is going to die."
    C. "He will reign for seven more years."
    D. "The Lord has shown me that he will die."
    E. "You [Hazael] will become king and do much evil to the children of Israel."
    F. "You will not live to see your king again."

11. **Who was killed in Chapter 9?**
    A. King Joram of Israel
    B. King Ahaziah of Judah
    C. Jezebel, former queen and widow of Ahab
    D. Both A & B
    E. All of the above

12. **What did Jehu, new king of Israel, mandate and receive from the Samarians?**
    A. The sons of their king
    B. Deluxe time-shares on the Great Sea

C. The heads of Ahab's sons

D. An annual *gift* (tax) of gold, silver, and sheep

E. The destruction of all their idols

13. **How did Jehu eliminate Baal worship in Israel?**

   A. He decreed it an illegal practice, punishable by death.

   B. He allowed all the worshipers of Baal one month to leave the land; after that, they would be killed.

   C. God provided miracles through Jehu, so that the people returned to the Lord and destroyed their idols.

   D. He lured all the Baal worshipers into their temple, then slaughtered them.

   E. He disallowed income tax deductions for donations to Baal's religion.

14. **When Ahaziah (Judah's king) died, what did his mother (Athaliah) do, when the news reached her?**

   A. Called FTD and sent a nice flower arrangement to each of his wives

   B. Committed suicide by falling on her husband's sword

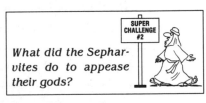

What did the Sephar-vites do to appease their gods?

   C. Ordered an attack on Jehu, offering leadership of the kingdom to his killer

   D. Fled to Joppa and made a pact with the Philistines

   E. Killed all of the heirs she could find

15. **Which were true concerning the new king of Judah, Joash (Jehoash)?**
   (three answers)

   A. His coronation led to Athaliah's death.

   B. He had been rescued from death by a woman named Jehosheba.

   C. Elisha sent his servant to kill Joash.

   D. He was only seven when he became king.

E. God cursed him through Elijah for ignoring the temple.

16. **What did Joash send to Hazael, king of Syria?**
    A. The head of Hazael's messenger, in a wooden box
    B. All of the gold and sacred items from the treasuries
    C. His only daughter, to marry Hazael as part of an alliance
    D. A subscription to *Judah Today*
    E. A bronze statue of Baal

17. **What was the common thread of the kings Jehoahaz and Jehoash (his son) mentioned in Chapter 13?**
    A. Both kings were instrumental in rebuilding the army.
    B. Both did evil in the sight of the Lord.
    C. Both fought the worship of Baal.
    D. Both reigned for less than five years.
    E. Both were renowned warriors.

Top Ten Old Testament Night Clubs

10. Hard Ark Cafe, Ararat
9. Burning Bush Golf and Country Club
8. Planet "Everything's Made of" Wood
7. The Joppa Cabana
6. Meggido Re Me
5. Sidon n' Stay Awhile
4. 77 Gaza Strip
3. The Sands
2. The Pink Behemoth
1. Cave 54

18. **What miracle took place at Elisha's tomb?**
   A. An angel of the Lord saved a small army of Israelites from certain slaughter by Syrians.
   B. A chariot of fire hovered above it as a sign to Joash regarding victory over Syria.
   C. Elisha's bones reassembled as a skeleton and walked in the wilderness near his tomb.
   D. A dead man placed in Elisha's tomb came back to life.

19. **Which of the following were true concerning the war between Amaziah, king of Judah, and Jehoash, king of Israel?**
   (three answers)
   A. Jehoash and Israel provoked the battle.
   B. Amaziah tried three times to avert a war.
   C. The battle took place on Judah's territory.
   D. Jehoash pretended to retreat, as a ploy.
   E. Israel soundly defeated Judah.
   F. Jehoash and his men destroyed the wall of Jerusalem and looted the treasuries there.

20. **What was unique about Azariah, king of Judah?**
   A. He had twelve fingers and twelve toes.
   B. He claimed to be God and was stoned by his own people.
   C. He was struck with leprosy and lived in isolation.
   D. He was only three and a half cubits (4½ ft.) tall.
   E. He could say the Hebrew alphabet backwards.

21. **What did King Ahaz of Judah have built for the king of Assyria (Tiglath-Pileser)?**
   A. An altar
   B. A palace
   C. A jeweled chest

D. An iron chariot

E. A golf cart with the Assyrian logo on it

22. **According to Second Kings 17, God finally rejected "all the descendants of Israel." What does the author say happened to the nation?**
    A. They were carried off to Assyria.
    B. They were brought under the captivity of Babylon.
    C. They were scattered across the land.
    D. They fell into utter depravity and wickedness.

23. **When the king of Assyria brought foreigners into the Samarian cities, they each worshiped their own pagan gods. What does the Bible say the Lord did about this?**
    A. Smote them with plagues
    B. Burned many with fire
    C. Caused their women to be barren
    D. Sent lions among them, killing some
    E. He turned his face from them

24. **The Bible says that Hezekiah began to reign over Judah and that he did "what was right in the sight of the Lord. In fact, he did all of these things except ONE:**
    A. Removed the high places (altars to false gods)
    B. Put to death the worshipers of Asherah
    C. Cut down the wooden images
    D. Broke the bronze serpent of Moses

25. **The king of Assyria sent his messengers, along with a great army, to give a message to the people of Judah. Which best sums it up?**
    A. Enemies are all around you, and you need our help. Form an alliance with us, and your king, Hezekiah, will become an advisor to our king, Sennacherib.

B. You are a dying nation. You have few resources and are unable to withstand our armies. Take a lesson from your neighbors and see the future. Be our slaves, and we will let you live.

C. If you are counting on Egypt for help, remember, Pharaoh is not trustworthy. If you are relying on your gods, ask yourself what help the gods of our enemies have been to them. Pay a tribute to our king, and you will live.

D. We have come in peace. Our leaders have supported each other for three generations. We can both benefit greatly by allying against the Edomites and Moabites. However, if you refuse now, we will not be sorry if you are destroyed by their armies in the future.

E. We'd like to challenge you all to a few rounds of ping-pong. It's probably the best thing that's happened to Assyria since we discovered the hot mineral springs!

Aesop's FABLES, now available!
(*c.* 650 B.C.)

26. **Which prophet did Hezekiah's assistants approach, regarding the dilemma with Assyria?**
    A. Ezekiel
    B. Hosea
    C. Isaiah
    D. Obadiah
    E. Micah

27. **All of the following except ONE were true concerning Sennacherib, king of Assyria.**
    A. The prophet sent word to Hezekiah that God would protect Judah.

B. An angel of the Lord killed nearly 200,000 Assyrian soldiers while they slept.

C. Sennacherib was slain by his sons.

D. The army of Judah slew over one hundred thousand Assyrians in the first and only battle, and the remaining soldiers retreated.

28. **What miracle did God perform as a sign to Hezekiah that he would live fifteen more years?**

   A. Multiplied figs in a basket

   B. Made the sundial shadow go backward

   C. Gave Hezekiah a credit card that expired in fourteen years and eleven months

   D. Piled huge stones at the entrance to Hezekiah's family tomb

   E. Made rain travel from the earth to the clouds

29. When King Hezekiah died, his son Manasseh became king. The Bible says he did all of the following except one. Which?
    A. Built altars for Baal
    B. Made his son pass through the fire
    C. Used witchcraft
    D. Shed much innocent blood
    E. Murdered Hephzibah, his mother

30. Josiah became king of Judah at eight years of age. THREE of the following were true regarding him:
    A. He initiated repairs on the house of the Lord.
    B. He was saddened when he heard the law, because he realized his ancestors had sinned greatly.
    C. A prophetess told him that Judah would suffer for its sins, but Josiah himself would die in peace.
    D. He kept a poster of Helen Hunt on his bedroom wall.
    E. Although he purged the idols from the temple, he allowed the altars in the high places.
    F. Josiah had no sons, and when he died his nephew became king.
    G. Josiah died in his sleep at the age of eighty-four.

31. Nebuchadnezzar's armies came from Babylon, and did all of the following except one:
    A. Wrote Nebuchadnezzar's name above the door of the temple
    B. Took over much of the king of Egypt's territory
    C. Took Judah's king as prisoner
    D. Destroyed the golden articles that Solomon had created for the temple
    E. Installed the king's uncle as the new king

32. The book of Second Kings ended with the final plundering and desolation of Judah. Which THREE of the following were correct?

A. Nebuchadnezzar returned three more times to over-see the total destruction of Jerusalem.

B. The king of Judah was caught fleeing, and had his eyes put out by the enemy.

C. After the second assault on Judah, every remaining person was either killed or carried off.

D. Nebuchadnezzar appointed a governor over the handful of people who would remain in Judah.

E. Jehoiachin, the former king of Judah, was eventually released from the Babylonian prison, and given a prominent seat there.

F. An angel of the Lord closed the door of the looted temple and erased the name of Nebuchadnezzar from above it.

Q. Why was Moses arrested?

A. He had broken the Law.

ANSWERS TO SECOND KINGS QUESTIONS

#	ANS	REF		#	ANS	REF
1.	B	1:2		20.	C	15:5
2.	D	1:9–17		21.	A	16:10–12
3.	B,C,E	2:8, 9, 17		22.	A	17:20–23
4.	E	2:23		23.	D	17:25
5.	B	3:5, 19–20, 27		24.	B	18:4
6.	C,D,F,	4:34, 35, 40–		25.	C	18:17–37
	G,I	41; 5:1–14;		26.	C	19:2
		6:5–6, 18		27.	D	19:32–37
7.	C	6:28–30		28.	B	20:11
8.	A	7:3–5		29.	E	21:3, 6, 16
9.	E	7:20		30.	A,B,C	22:5, 11–13,
10.	A,D,E	8:10, 12–13				20
11.	E	9:23–24, 27,		31.	A	24:7, 12–13,
		30–33				17
12.	C	10:6–7		32.	B,D,E	25:7, 22, 27–
13.	D	10:18–25				28
14.	E	11:1–3				
15.	A,B,D	11:2, 13–16,				
		21		Super Challenges:		
16.	B	12:18		#1: "an illness" (13:14)		
17.	B	13:2, 11		#2: burned their chil-		
18.	D	13:21		dren in fire (17:31)		
19.	C,E,F	14:11–14				

~FIRST~ CHRONICLES

(c. 500–400 B.C.)

1. **The first nine chapters of First Chronicles contain what?**
   A. Several psalms written by both David and Solomon
   B. Crossword puzzles
   C. Genealogies of the Hebrews
   D. Harsh judgments on Israel
   E. The prayers of the priests

2. **What does the writer say the Philistines did to Saul after finding his body?**
   A. Took his armor and head, and placed his head in the temple of Dagon
   B. Tied rope to his feet, and hung his body over the side of Mt. Gilboa for the birds to eat
   C. Cut his body into small pieces, and threw them off the mountain in every direction
   D. Took his armor, and returned his body to the Israelites

3. **What reason does the author give for Saul's death? (three answers)**
   A. He had an evil jealousy regarding David.
   B. He went to war against God's orders.
   C. He consulted a medium.
   D. He did not inquire of the Lord.
   E. He studied under General Custer.
   F. He was unfaithful to the Lord.

4. **How did Joab, the son of Zeruiah, become the head captain under David?**
   A. He was David's nephew.
   B. He had served Saul's army extremely well.
   C. He was the first to attack Jerusalem.
   D. He had once saved David's life, when Saul was trying to kill David.

Parthenon built in Athens!
(c. 500–400 B.C.)

5. **When David was holed up in a cave, he told his men that he thirsted for water from the well of Bethlehem. When three of his best men risked their lives to get it for him, what did he do?**
   A. Poured it over the heads of the men, anointing them
   B. Made all of the men drink, taking none for himself
   C. Filled his Water Blaster Squirt Gun, and went after the Philistines
   D. Poured out the water to the Lord, not drinking any of it
   E. Tore his clothes because he was humbled by their deed

6. **When David was a fugitive from Saul, several "mighty men" aided him. According to Chapter 12, all of the following were true except:**
   A. They were armed with bows.
   B. They could shoot arrows and/or sling stones with either hand.
   C. Their faces were like lions.
   D. They feared nothing.

7. **When David was bringing the ark of the covenant back to Israel, there was a celebration. Which of the**

following musical instruments were included in the festivities?
(four answers)
A. Harps
B. Trumpets
C. Lutes
D. Drums
E. Synthesizers
F. Flutes
G. Tambourines
H. Cymbals

8. During the second raid on the valley by the Philistines, David was to attack when God gave what sign?
A. A shaking of the ground
B. A marching sound in the treetops
C. An exit sign from the freeway
D. A cloud covering the enemy
E. Two ravens flying just above the trees

9. When the ark was finally brought back to the city, who carried it?
A. King David and three of his sons
B. The leaders of the four largest tribes of Israel
C. The children of the Levites
D. A cart pulled by two oxen

Who did the Ammonites hire to help them battle Israel?

10. What THREE items did King David distribute to each Israelite to eat, in celebration of the ark's return?
A. A piece of meat
B. A little chocolate doughnut
C. A loaf of bread

D. A cake of raisins

E. A pomegranate

F. A cluster of grapes

11. **Concerning worship, David left people in charge of all of the following EXCEPT:**

   A. Burnt offerings morning and evening

   B. Collecting the money offerings of the people

   C. Keeping the gates

   D. Giving thanks

   E. Playing trumpets

12. **How did David learn that God did not want him to build a temple for Him?**

   A. Through the prophet Nathan

   B. Through an angel of the Lord who appeared to him at Gibeon

   C. Through his wife Michal who heard it at the beauty parlor

   D. Through a dream, in which God appeared as a lion

   E. Through Elijah, the prophet

13. When David defeated Zobah, First Chronicles says he went as far as Hamath, to establish his power by what river?
   A. The Euphrates
   B. The Nile
   C. The Tigris
   D. The Jordan
   E. The Swanee

14. After David's men were humiliated by the Ammonites, he told them they could return when what took place?
   A. The feast of Passover
   B. The end of harvest
   C. The other soldiers' return from Edom
   D. Their circumcision
   E. Their beards grew

> **DID YOU KNOW** that the Hebrew title for the Chronicles is translated, "The Events of the Days" and they were placed at the end of the volume?

15. Whose crown was put on David's head?
   A. The king of Rabbah's (Ammonite king)
   B. Saul's
   C. One they picked up at Burger King
   D. The crown of Israel, created by David's artisans
   E. The Syrian king's

16. Who did David's brother Jonathan slay in a battle with the Philistines?
   A. Goliath's brother
   B. An elderly Philistine midget, who was ill
   C. A large warrior, with twenty-four fingers and toes
   D. Golshek, a seven-foot-tall Philistine king
   E. Sippai, a giant's son

17. Who did the author of First Chronicles say "moved David to number (take a census of) Israel"?

A. The Lord
B. Satan
C. Joab, his army commander
D. Michal, his wife (Saul's daughter)
E. A restless spirit

18. **David was punished for egotism in Chapter 21, and God gave him THREE choices. Find 'em!**

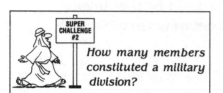

A. Losing three great battles
B. Three years of famine
C. The death of his firstborn son
D. Three weeks of pestilence
E. Three months of defeat by your enemies
F. Three days of devastating plague

19. **According to First Chronicles, David did all of the following EXCEPT:**
    A. Instructed his young son Solomon to build the temple
    B. Made preparation for materials and laborers for the temple
    C. Reassigned all of the religious duties from the Levites to the Benjamites
    D. Commanded all of the leaders to assist Solomon
    E. Charged Solomon to keep the law

20. **How did they decide on the schedule for the priests serving in the temple?**
    A. The king's priest appointed them.
    B. They cast lots.
    C. They were chosen by Solomon.
    D. The oldest men served early; the youngest served through evening.
    E. They did the "scissors, rock, paper" thing until it was all worked out.

21. **Chapter 25 was dedicated to the appointing of men for what function?**
   A. Bringing animals to the temple for sacrifices
   B. Keeping track of Solomon's girlfriends' phone numbers
   C. Overseeing the work of temple construction
   D. Serving as musicians
   E. Care of the widows and orphans

22. **The overseer of the treasuries was a man named Shebuel. What was unique about him?**
   A. He was a half-brother of Solomon.
   B. He was blind.
   C. He had done time for embezzlement.
   D. He was Moses' grandson.
   E. He had once fought against David in battle.

23. **How old did a male have to be to serve in David's armies?**

Top Ten Books NOT Included in the Old Testament

10. *Day by Day Journal,* by Methuselah
 9. *The Goliath Gourmet: A Philistine Cookbook*
 8. *Little Black Book,* by Solomon
 7. *East of Eden*
 6. *Adam's Baby Book*
 5. *Letters from Ham*
 4. *Tuesdays with Moses*
 3. *I'll Be Dagon: The Pagan's Guide to Idols*
 2. *First and Second Megalith*
 1. *Chicken Soup for the Hebrew Soul*

A. 21
B. 30
C. 16
D. 40

24. **David's royal officers included people to oversee which of the following?**
(four answers)

TAMAR

Her rape by her half-brother led to murder and rebellion in Israel under King David.

A. The produce of the vineyards for the wine supply
B. The olive and sycamore trees
C. The video arcade
D. The sundial behind the temple
E. The donkeys
F. The lepers
G. The camels
H. The water from the tiles (irrigation)

25. **When David had assembled his leaders, he told them that God would not allow him to build His temple. What did he say God's reason was?**
A. That David was too full of years to accomplish the task
B. That the temple was to represent the peace of Solomon's Israel
C. That David had been a man of war and bloodshed
D. That David's sin regarding Bathsheba and Uriah had stained the City of the Lord

26. **Where did Solomon get the plans for the temple and its furnishings?**
A. A team of men were appointed to draw the plans.
B. David had prepared them.
C. He, with the artisans, created them over a six-month period.

D. Solomon designed the temple with the help of Joab, and the articles for worship were designed by the artisans under Jehiel.

E. Lenny the Nerdite designed it using a CAD program.

27. **First Chronicles closes with the death of David. Which of the following were true concerning how he was described?**
(three answers)

A. "The most holy king of Israel"

B. "Being in a good old age, full of days"

C. "Being righteous, but for his sin with Bathsheba"

D. "Full of riches"

E. "Full of honor"

F. "Content, and ready to rest with his fathers"

G. "A man you wouldn't want to upset"

Q. What did Samuel tell Saul when he refused to follow God's instruction to give rice to every Israelite?

A. "To obey is better than sacks of rice."

ANSWERS TO FIRST CHRONICLES QUESTIONS

#	ANS	REF	#	ANS	REF
1.	C	1–9	23.	A	27:23
2.	A	10:8–10	24.	A,B, E,G	27:27–31
3.	C,D,F	10:13–14			
4.	C	11:6	25.	C	28:3
5.	D	11:15–19	26.	B	28:11, 19
6.	D	12:2, 8	27.	B,D,E	29:28
7.	A,B, G,H	13:8			
8.	B	14:14–15	Super Challenges:		
9.	C	15:15	#1: the Syrians (19:7–		
10.	A,C,D	16:3	10)		
11.	B	16:37–42	#2: 24,000 (27:1)		
12.	A	17:3–4, 15			
13.	A	18:3			
14.	E	19:5			
15.	A	20:2			
16.	C	20:6–7			
17.	B	21:1			
18.	B,E,F	21:12			
19.	C	22:5, 6, 12, 17			
20.	B	24:5			
21.	D	25:1–31			
22.	D	26:24			

SECOND CHRONICLES

(c. 500–400 B.C.)

1. **Where was Solomon when God asked him what gift he would like to receive?**
   A. In Jerusalem, at the temple
   B. At the high place at Gibeon
   C. In David's house
   D. On the road to Gath

2. **When Solomon was preparing to build the temple, he wrote to Hiram, king of Tyre, for assistance. He told the king that all of the following would be uses for the new temple except:**
   A. Burning incense before God
   B. Submitting burnt offerings morning and evening
   C. The consecration of the priests
   D. The continual showbread

3. **Solomon asked Hiram to provide timber and timbermen, and offered to reward them with which of the following?**
   (four answers)
   A. Sheep
   B. Barley
   C. Wine
   D. A city
   E. A large supply of Ben-Gay
   F. Camels
   G. Ground wheat
   H. Oil

4. **Where did Solomon build the temple?**
   A. Mt. Moriah
   B. Mt. Gilboa
   C. By the Spring of Gihon
   D. At Gethsemane

5. **Who were Jachin and Boaz?**
   A. Two of Solomon's fathers-in-law
   B. Two of the artisans from Tyre
   C. Two prophets who cursed Solomon
   D. The pillars of the temple
   E. A reggae band from Joppa

6. **Solomon had a large washbasin constructed for the temple, which was called the "Sea." What animals were engraved around its base?**
   A. Camels
   B. Oxen

Top Ten Ways the Ark of the Covenant Should Never Be Transported

10. Amtrak
9. Station wagon
8. Dog sled
7. Trunk of taxicab
6. UPS
5. Tied to Orson Welles with bungee cords
4. The *Titanic*
3. Valuejet
2. Sanford & Son pickup truck
1. The *Hindenburg*

D. Sheep

E. Prairie dogs

7. **What was in the ark when it was placed in the temple?**

   A. Just the two tablets which had been placed there by Moses

   B. Twelve scrolls containing the law, and the histories of the Hebrew tribes

   C. Nothing

   D. The Urim and Thummim, and the two tablets of Moses

8. **What happened immediately after Solomon finished his sermon and prayer at the dedication of the new temple?**

   A. The clouds above the temple opened, the sun's rays shone on the temple, and Solomon's robe was "like fire."

   B. Everyone said in unison, "Amen. Can we EAT now?"

   C. Lightning raced across the heavens, the ground shook, and the people feared God.

   D. Fire came down from heaven and consumed the sacrifices.

   E. A voice from the cloud said, "I am the God who brought you out of Egypt. Obey My laws, and be My people."

9. **Solomon built cities in Hamath, at the extreme north boundary of his kingdom. What was their primary purpose?**

   A. To guard against attack from the nomadic tribes just beyond his north border

   B. Mainly for storage

C. To harvest the natural resources, primarily cedar and cypress trees

D. For the production of wine

10. **Solomon made five hundred of these out of gold and put them in the "House of the Forest" of Lebanon.**
    A. Swords
    B. Candle stands
    C. Staffs
    D. Shields
    E. Oscars

11. **Which of the following best describes the reason for the kingdom's division after the death of Solomon?**
    A. The tribe of Judah's ongoing fight against the northern tribes over natural resources
    B. Solomon's failure to establish any of his sons as credible leaders, prior to his death
    C. Rehoboam's decision to tell the people he would increase their burdens
    D. The people's love of Solomon's son Jeroboam, over Solomon's appointed successor, Rehoboam
    E. A disagreement over the designated hitter rule

12. **What prevented a civil war between Israel and Judah?**
    A. The tribes of Judah and Benjamin realized they were greatly outnumbered by the Israelites
    B. An agreement dividing the lands to be ruled by Jeroboam and Rehoboam
    C. The words of Shemaiah to the leaders, saying that the division was God's will
    D. Rehoboam's accidental death, and the tribes of Judah's embracing Jeroboam as their leader
    E. A U.N. negotiating team led by Madeline Albright

13. **What was the outcome of the battle between King Jeroboam of Israel and King Abijah of Judah?**

   A. Abijah and Judah defeated Israel, and Jeroboam's power was gone forever.

   B. It was essentially a draw, as spoken by the prophet Shemaiah.

   C. Israel won a significant victory, but the effect was short-lived.

   D. Israel defeated Abijah, killing him, and effectively re-uniting the kingdom.

14. **After Asa heard the optimistic prophecy of Oded, many of the tribes joined with him to rededicate themselves to seeking God. In fact, they decided that whoever would not seek the God of Israel would be:**

   A. Sent away from Judah

   B. Charged double for harp lessons

   C. Considered evil

   D. Made a slave

   E. Put to death

When Abijah died, his son Asa became king. Asa's first military challenge came from a leader named Zera. Where was Zera from?

SUPER CHALLENGE #1

15. **When Asa engaged the king of Syria to help him deal with a problem he was having with the Israelites, a seer rebuked Asa for not trusting God. What was Asa's response?**

   A. He repented, and God gave him victory over his enemies.

   B. Asa became angry and had the seer imprisoned.

   C. Asa thought the man was insane and had him executed.

   D. Asa considered the man's words but followed through with his plans.

   E. He told the man "Make like Moses and go plague somebody else."

16. **Concerning the life of Judah's King Jehoshaphat, which of the following were true?**
(three answers)
A. He strengthened Judah militarily against Israel.
B. He suffered from palsy.
C. He removed the high places (of pagan sacrifice) and wooden images.
D. He sent leaders out to teach the law.
E. He essentially refurnished the temple.
F. He told the truth but played the lyre.

Hippocrates develops medical oath!
(c. 400 B.C.)

17. **When Judah (under Jehoshaphat) allied with Israel (under Ahab) to do battle with Ramoth Gilead, all of these things happened EXCEPT ONE:**
A. Four hundred of Israel's prophets assured a victory.
B. The king of Israel went into battle disguised.
C. The Lord protected Jehoshaphat from attack.
D. The armies of Ramoth Gilead killed twelve of the commanders of the Judah/Israel armies and several thousand men.
E. Ahab was killed by an arrow.

18. **What happened when the Moabites, Ammonites, and Mount Seirites came to attack Judah?**
A. God led the approaching armies into the Salt Sea (Dead Sea) and they were drowned.
B. The prophet Jahaziel led the children out to meet the approaching armies, as God had instructed him. When the enemies of Judah saw this, they stopped, then went home.

C. Judah's much smaller army managed to divide the enemy into four groups. After they had ambushed two of them, the rest retreated.

D. It was Christmas, and they found the country wrapped in Judah Garland.

E. The three enemy armies destroyed one another.

19. **After Jehoshaphat died, his son Jehoram became king. Which of the following were true about him? (four answers)**

A. He was the youngest of his father's sons.

B. He killed all of his brothers.

C. He attacked the Edomites at night when they revolted.

D. He forbade idolatry and had idolaters executed.

E. The prophet Elijah prophesied against him.

F. He had set up a complete league of women's volleyball teams, using just his own wives and concubines.

G. His possessions and family were carried off by Philistines and Arabians.

H. He lived to be old and was buried in the Tomb of the Kings.

20. **When Ahaziah became king of Judah, he ruled wickedly. Whose counsel encouraged him to do so?**

A. His wife's

B. His chief military advisor's

C. His magic eight ball's (As I see it, "yes.")

D. A prophet of Baal's

E. His mother's

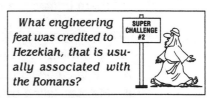

What engineering feat was credited to Hezekiah, that is usually associated with the Romans?

21. **Athaliah was the ruling queen of Judah when her grandson, Joash was anointed as king. Her final recorded words were:**

A. "The gods have made me queen! I am the queen of Judah!"
B. "I order you to kill the child (king) now!
C. "Treason, treason!"
D. "Do wah diddy diddy dum diddy do!"
E. "None shall stand before me! I am your goddess!"

22. **Joash ruled Judah for forty years. What was one of his greatest accomplishments?**
    A. Physical restoration of the temple
    B. Rebuilding Judah's armies as a powerful force
    C. Defeating a much stronger Syrian army
    D. Fortifying Jerusalem
    E. Founding a company called "Juway," a multi-level system for selling swords and shields

23. **What did Amaziah's army do with the ten thousand people they captured from the Valley of Seir?**
    A. Brought them back to Jerusalem as slaves
    B. Took them to the top of a mountain, and threw them off
    C. Allowed them to populate a small village near Jerusalem
    D. Released them, after an angel of the Lord warned Judah of the danger of bringing them back
    E. Brought them back to Jerusalem and slaughtered them before the temple

24. **What happened to Judah's King Uzziah when he burned incense in the temple?**
    A. He became leprous.
    B. He was killed by Azariah and the priests.
    C. The people stoned him when he came out from the temple.
    D. He realized that it wasn't nearly as exciting as sparklers.

E. The vapors from the incense choked him, and he died.

25. **When Israel defeated Judah (under Ahaz), they brought back thousands of captives. What prophet was instrumental in convincing the Israelites to release them?**
   A. Nathan
   B. Elijah
   C. Zechariah
   D. Oded
   E. Nahum

26. **When King Hezekiah restored worship in the temple, the people brought sacrifices. What problem surfaced?**

A. Many of the city's poor brought animals to sacrifice, while the rich did not.

B. Some of the grain sacrifices had previously been offered to the pagan gods.

C. There was not enough room for both people and animals.

D. They had forgotten to put up the signs at various places which read: "From this point it is a three hour wait to sacrifice your animal."

E. Some of the people who didn't know the law had brought diseased animals.

F. There were not enough priests to skin all of the animals.

27. **Which were true concerning King Hezekiah's call to Israel and Judah to come to Jerusalem to celebrate the Passover?**
(three answers)

A. He was coerced into doing it by certain Levites.

> **DID YOU KNOW** that the Septuagint title is translated, "The Things Left Out," and placed the books after the Samuels and Kings because they were thought to be a repetition of these books, with some additional information?

B. He designed it as a trick to lure the Israelite leaders into a trap.

C. The messengers with the invitation were runners, and they were laughed at.

D. He made it a strictly black-tie affair.

E. The people who took part, although ceremonially "unclean," were forgiven.

F. There had not been such joy in Jerusalem since Solomon's time.

G. A small congregation took part in the celebration.

28. **What did the people do when the Passover had ended?**

A. Went home
B. Exchanged phone numbers and e-mail addresses
C. Went out and cut down the altars and wooden images
D. Asked Hezekiah to allow them to stay in Jerusalem
E. Made a covenant to return for the Passover each year at the appointed time

29. **When Hezekiah and Jerusalem were faced with a threat of war from Assyria, which of the following did they do?**
(three answers)
A. Stopped the water from the springs
B. Built an additional wall
C. Sent ambassadors to Sennacherib, king of Assyria, to discuss peace
D. Made weapons and shields
E. Allied themselves with the Moabites
F. Hid their children in the tunnels beneath the city

30. **Which was true concerning the reigns of Manasseh, Amon, and Josiah?**
A. They were all basically evil, with idol worship and little respect for the Lord.
B. Manasseh and his son Amon were both evil rulers, but Josiah was a righteous king.
C. All three men "did what was right in the sight of the Lord."
D. Manasseh was a vile, cruel man, but Amon and Josiah were both upright rulers.

31. **Which of the following were actual events related to the death of King Josiah?**
(three answers)
A. Judah was attacked by Egypt.
B. He was hang gliding off the Mount of Olives.

C. He was wounded at the Valley of Meggido.
D. Judah was suffering from a plague.
E. He died in Jerusalem.
F. He disguised himself to go into battle.

32. **Second Chronicles ends with a proclamation by this king, that God has given him all the kingdoms of the earth:**
A. Cyrus, king of Persia
B. Nebuchadnezzar, king of Babylon
C. Kong, king of the Empire State Building
D. Zedekiah, king of Judah
E. Necho, pharaoh of Egypt

Q. Where is a mention of insurance in the Bible?

A. David gave Goliath a piece of the rock.

ANSWERS TO SECOND CHRONICLES QUESTIONS

#	ANS	REF	#	ANS	REF
1.	B	1:3–7	24.	A	26:16–21
2.	C	2:4	25.	D	28:9
3.	B,C, G,H	2:10	26.	F	29:34
4.	A	3:1	27.	C,E,F	30:10, 17–20, 26
5.	D	3:17	28.	C	31:1
6.	B	4:3	29.	A,B,D	32:3, 5
7.	A	5:10	30.	B	33 & 34
8.	D	7:1	31.	C,E,F	35:22–24
9.	B	8:4	32.	A	36:23
10.	D	9:15–16			
11.	C	10:1–19			
12.	C	11:1–5	Super Challenges:		
13.	A	13:13–20	#1: Ethiopia (14:9)		
14.	E	15:13	#2: Aqueducts (32:30)		
15.	B	16:7–10			
16.	A,C,D	17:1–2, 6–9			
17.	D	18:5, 29, 31, 33–34			
18.	E	20:22–24			
19.	B,C, E,G	21:4, 10, 12–15, 16–17			
20.	E	22:3			
21.	C	23:13			
22.	A	24:4–14			
23.	B	25:12			

~EZRA~
(c. 460–400 B.C.)

1. **Which of the following were true concerning a proclamation made by King Cyrus of Persia?**
   (three answers)
   A. He was making Nebuchadnezzar the ruler over the tribes of Israel.
   B. The Jews were free to return to their homeland.
   C. The Persians were not to intermarry with Jews.
   D. He wanted to restore the temple in Jerusalem.
   E. Jews who remained in Babylon would pay double the amount of tribute (tax) that had been previously collected.
   F. Everyone should support the temple rebuilding efforts in Jerusalem.

2. **Chapter 2 offered a census of the Jews who decided to leave Babylon with Zerubbabel. Not including slaves, how many were there in all?**
   A. 1,500,000
   B. 42,360
   C. 234,350
   D. 510,000
   E. 8 guys who could never get dates in Babylon

3. **What did the Jews (who were returning to Jerusalem) fear regarding making offerings to the Lord?**
   A. They were afraid that if they made regular sacrifices they would eventually starve to death before arriving at Jerusalem.

B. Since they did not have the book of the Law with them, they feared sacrificing improperly and offending God.

C. They didn't have anyone to play the offertory while they were passing the collection plates.

D. They were afraid of running out of the specified offerings for designated feast days.

E. They were afraid of the people whose countries they were passing through.

4. **Why did the work on the temple cease under Artaxerxes?**

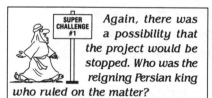

SUPER CHALLENGE #1

Again, there was a possibility that the project would be stopped. Who was the reigning Persian king who ruled on the matter?

A. Because enemies of Judah wrote to Artaxerxes (king of Persia) and protested

B. Because they had forgotten to get a building permit

C. Because the Jews were too busy building homes for themselves

D. Because the shipment of logs from Sidon and Tyre was interrupted, due to war

E. Because the Jews fell back into idolatry

5. **What two prophets were involved in getting the temple project going again?**
   A. Isaiah and Ezra
   B. Haggai and Zechariah
   C. Nehemiah and Jeremiah
   D. Nahum and Micah
   E. Psalm and Proverb

6. **When the king of Persia made his ruling, THREE of the following items were included:**

A. The governor of the lands beyond the river was to to keep himself and his people far away from Jerusalem.

B. Taxes from the lands beyond the river were to be used to assist in the construction of the temple.

C. Animals, grain, or wine were to be given to the Jewish priests as they had need.

D. The governor was to send men to Sidon to assist in the cutting of timber for the temple.

E. The people beyond the river were to receive two million dollars and a first round draft pick.

F. Two men were to be sent from the king to serve as intermediaries between the people.

Soldiers and judges receive regular salaries!
(*c.* 462 B.C.)

7. **Ezra left Babylon to travel to Jerusalem, a distance of about nine hundred miles. The Bible says that "the good hand of God was on him." How long did his journey take?**
A. Four months
B. Seventy days
C. Eight months
D. One year

8. **The king's letter to Ezra gave him the right to do all of the following except:**
A. Avoid taxes to the kingdom for priests and temple workers
B. Take all of the gold with him that he could find
C. Appoint magistrates and judges for the land beyond the river
D. Establish holy altars among the Ammonites

9. **Why did Ezra say he was ashamed to ask the king for an escort of men and horses "to help us against the enemy on the road"?**

? **DID YOU KNOW** that the book of Ezra was written to document the return of a small group of Jewish exiles to Jerusalem? These Jews were responding to the political decree of King Cyrus to rebuild the temple of God.

A. Because the king had already shown extreme generosity toward Ezra

B. Because there was a shortage of horses in the land at that time, and he didn't want the king to forego something he may need

C. Because it would have shown a lack of faith in God

D. Because some of the men going with him had trained in the king's army

E. Because the king had already equipped Ezra's party with bazooka's and M-16s

10. **What frustrated Ezra so much that he tore his garment and plucked hair from his head and beard?**
    A. When some of the Jews who had returned wanted to allow the pagan altars to remain on the hills
    B. The officiating at the Super Bowl
    C. The fact that many of the Jews had intermarried
    D. When he heard that some harlots had been inside the temple
    E. When the Levites began to quarrel over the weighing and division of the silver and gold

11. **This book ends with the Israelites all standing outside waiting to resolve their situation. Why couldn't they remain there until everything was settled?**
    A. It was extremely cold.
    B. It was raining heavily.
    C. There was a minimal food supply.
    D. The Sabbath was approaching.
    E. There was a "No Loitering" sign nearby.

Q. Why were Artaxerxes phone bills always so high?

A. His calls were all Persian to Persian.

ANSWERS TO EZRA QUESTIONS

#	ANS	REF		#	ANS	REF
1.	B,D,F	1:1–4		9.	C	8:22
2.	B	2:64		10.	C	9:1–3
3.	E	3:3		11.	B	10:13
4.	A	4:7–23				
5.	B	5:1				
6.	A,B,C	6:6–9		Super Challenge:		
7.	A	7:9		#1: Darius (6:1–13)		
8.	D	7:15–25				

~NEHEMIAH~

(c. 460–440 B.C.)

1. **What caused Nehemiah's initial distress?**
   A. An order by Artaxerxes that caused great burdens to the Jewish people living in Persia
   B. A report that the Jews back in Jerusalem had been slaughtered by the neighboring tribes
   C. A report that Jerusalem was in distress, and the walls were broken down
   D. Discovering that his king was ill and near death

2. **Nehemiah worked in the Persian palace. What was his job?**
   A. Cupbearer to the king
   B. Baker/cook
   C. Priest
   D. Head of the Persian treasury
   E. Lawnmower maintenance

3. **What request of Nehemiah's was granted by the king?**
   A. To lower the burden of taxes on the Persian Jews
   B. To send financial help to the people in Jerusalem
   C. To allow him to marry Artaxerxes' daughter
   D. To allow him to travel to Judah

4. **When Nehemiah went to view the walls, he passed by and/or viewed FIVE of the following places. Can you find the real Jerusalem landmarks versus the ones I made up?**
   A. The Valley Gate
   B. The Lord's Garden

C. Altar of Zion

D. Serpent Well

E. The King's Pool

F. Fountain of David

G. Solomon's Tower

H. Fountain Gate

I. Refuse Gate

J. The Statue of Liberty

5. **What was Nehemiah's master plan for rebuilding the walls of Jerusalem?**

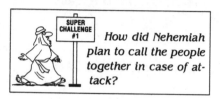

How did Nehemiah plan to call the people together in case of attack?

A. Each person would repair a section nearest to where they lived.

B. The workers from Sidon would make the most difficult repairs, and those less-skilled would make the easier ones.

C. The workers who came with Nehemiah would make the repairs, while the Jews worked to provide food and compensation for them.

D. The gold and silver that Artaxerxes sent with Nehemiah would be more than enough to pay skilled workers, while Nehemiah attended to the spiritual problems of the Jews.

6. **How did Nehemiah counteract threats of possible attack from enemies during the rebuilding effort?**

A. He sent word to Artaxerxes the king and asked for additional protection.

B. He took the Jews who were least able to do construction work and created a small army that patrolled the walls.

C. He instructed everyone to fast and pray for God's protection.

D. He had half of the workers repairing the walls, while the other half stood guard.

E. He planted land mines outside the walls.

7. **When the concern about being attacked had diminished, what internal problem did Nehemiah face?**

A. Some of the Jews had made a large wooden idol and were sacrificing to it.

B. The wealthier Jews were loaning money to the poor and creating hardships for them through interest charges.

C. Since the walls had been repaired, some of the Jews wanted to change the name of Jerusalem to "Wally World."

D. There was an adulterous situation involving one of the rulers.

E. The Jews who had arrived at Jerusalem first were claiming specific rights to food and lands.

Top Ten Television Shows of the Old Testament

10. The Sinai Hillbillies
9. Adam's Family
8. Amorite Bandstand
7. Hebron Five-O
6. I Love Ruthie
5. My Favorite Martyr
4. Gentle Ben-Ammi
3. Little Harem in the Palace
2. The Dukes of Hazor
1. Leave it to Beor

8. **How did Nehemiah set a positive example of unselfishness?**
   A. He loaned money to the people without interest.
   B. He never accepted his full rightful share as governor.
   C. He personally worked longer on the wall repair than anyone else.
   D. He redeemed several of the Jewish people's children from servitude with his own money.
   E. He never entered the game until the fourth inning.

9. **Nehemiah had three main enemies: Sanballat, Tobiah, and Geshem the Arab. They tried to destroy Nehemiah in all of the following ways except:**
   A. Attempting to get Nehemiah to meet them somewhere (probably planning to kill him)
   B. Accusing him of planning to lead the Jews in a rebellion
   C. Trying to entrap Nehemiah using a harlot
   D. Accusing him of wanting to be king
   E. Attempting to convince Nehemiah to hide in the temple, to protect his life

Who Am I?

She was a bit ahead of her time considering her position of leadership. She instructed a soldier to go to battle against Israel's enemy, but he was afraid and asked her to go with him.

DEBORAH

10. **According to Nehemiah 7, what was the status of the city once the doors were hung and the wall finished?**
   A. The city was large and spacious, but there were few people, and the individual houses were not rebuilt.
   B. The city was smaller than it had been originally, but there were many people, and most of the houses had been rebuilt.
   C. The city was large, the houses were nearly all rebuilt, and the population was sizable.

D. The city was about half its original size, and roughly half of the houses had been rebuilt, all of them occupied by those who originally returned with Zerubbabel.

11. **After the project was completed, all the people gathered in front of the Water Gate, to hear the reading of the Law. Who read it to them?**
    A. King Artaxerxes
    B. Nehemiah
    C. Isaiah, the prophet
    D. Ezra
    E. Charlton Heston, dressed as Moses
    F. Moses, dressed as Charlton Heston

12. **Following the blessing of the Levites, the leaders signed a covenant to the Lord which specified all of these things EXCEPT:**

    Aramaic language replaces Hebrew!
    (c. 450 B.C.)

    A. Preventing intermarriage of their sons and daughters with those from foreign tribes
    B. Observing the laws of Moses regarding what was unholy to eat
    C. Not buying on the Sabbath or holy days
    D. Making provision for the service of the temple
    E. Bringing the "firstfruits" to the house of the Lord

13. **How was it decided who would live in Jerusalem?**
    A. Nehemiah ordered everyone to live in Jerusalem until the city was completely restored.
    B. It was strictly on a volunteer basis.
    C. The leaders appointed two people from every ten to stay in Jerusalem. Every five years they would alternate with the others.

D. Nehemiah gave them a choice between living in Jerusalem or living in his 1964 VW van with the flowers painted on the side.

E. The leaders lived in Jerusalem, along with some volunteers. Then they cast lots so that one tenth of the people would remain there also.

14. **Who did Nehemiah say, in Chapter 13, would be excluded from the congregation of God?**
    A. Those who defile the Sabbath
    B. The Danites
    C. The Moabites and Ammonites
    D. Women
    E. Pagans

15. **Nehemiah returned to Persia, then came back to Jerusalem, where he found that the Jews had again**

intermarried with pagan tribes. Which of the following best describes his response:

A. He prayed that God would take revenge on them, then went about the business of the temple.

B. He had some of them stoned to death, others banished from the people, and issued a new decree of punishment for the sin.

C. He cursed them, struck some of them, and pulled out their hair.

D. He realized that his previous efforts were in vain, and returned to the Persian palace, where he died.

Q. Which area of Palestine was especially wealthy?

A. The Jordan River—its banks were always overflowing.

ANSWERS TO NEHEMIAH QUESTIONS

#	ANS	REF	#	ANS	REF
1.	C	1:2–3	11.	D	8:1–3
2.	A	1:11	12.	B	10:28–39
3.	D	2:5–6	13.	E	11:1–2
4.	A,D,E,	2:13–15	14.	C	13:1–2
	H,I		15.	C	13:25
5.	A	3:1–32			
6.	D	4:16			
7.	B	5:1–13	Super Challenge:		
8.	B	5:14	#1: With a trumpet		
9.	C	6:1–14	blast (4:20)		
10.	A	7:4			

~ESTHER~

(c. 470–430 B.C.)

1. **The book of Esther opens with:**
   A. A flip of the pages
   B. A feast
   C. A battle
   D. A sinful marriage
   E. A murder

2. **Why was King Ahasuerus infuriated?**
   A. Because he had been defeated in a battle
   B. Because his son Teresh had been slain
   C. Because he couldn't get the child-proof cap off the aspirin bottle
   D. Because his wife disobeyed him
   E. Because his commanders had disobeyed his orders

3. **Which of the following were true regarding Esther and Mordecai?**
   (three answers)
   A. Esther was a cousin to Mordecai.
   B. Mordecai and Esther were husband and wife.
   C. Mordecai had raised Esther since her parents died.
   D. Mordecai was a descendant of Benjamin.
   E. Esther was one-half Jewish and one-half Persian.
   F. Mordecai was one of the king's eunuchs.

4. **After the king took Esther as his queen, why didn't she reveal her nationality?**
   A. Mordecai had told her not to.
   B. She feared the king might harm her, Mordecai, or both of them.

C. She knew that some of the king's princes despised the Jews.

D. She wanted to wait for the wedding feast.

E. The king had a "don't ask—don't tell" policy.

5. **Who was hanged on a gallows for an alleged plot to murder the king?**

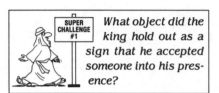

SUPER CHALLENGE #1

What object did the king hold out as a sign that he accepted someone into his presence?

A. Five of the soldiers from the king's army

B. The deposed queen, Vashti, and three others with her

C. Seven nobles from Media

D. Two of the kings eunuchs, who were doorkeepers

6. **Why did Haman convince King Ahasuerus that the Jews should be put to death?**

A. Because Haman had heard that some of the Jews were plotting against the king

B. Because Mordecai had refused to bow to Haman

C. Because Mordecai had offended Haman by asking for separate lands to be inhabited exclusively by Jews

D. Because many Jews were contracting leprosy

E. Because Haman had convinced many of the Jews to put him in their wills.

7. **After the king issued a decree regarding the upcoming destruction of the Jews, correspondence took place between Mordecai and Esther. Which of the following occurred?**
(three answers)

A. Mordecai told Esther that she needed to obtain a copy of the decree and read it for herself.

B. Esther told Mordecai that the king had not called for her in thirty days.

C. Esther told Mordecai, that if an unauthorized person went to the king, he or she would be killed unless the king extended his scepter.

D. Mordecai told Esther that he was old and ready to die, and that she should be safe in the palace.

E. Esther's letters to Mordecai always arrived "postage due."

F. Esther told Mordecai to initiate a three-day fast among all the Jews in the city.

G. Mordecai told Esther that God was going to punish the Jews for remaining in Persia and not returning to their homeland.

8. **Who told Haman that a seventy-five-foot gallows should be built, on which to hang Mordecai?**
   A. Mordecai
   B. King Ahasuerus
   C. Haman's wife and friends
   D. Esther
   E. A eunuch, who was attendant to Esther

Socrates is born!
(c. 470 B.C.)

9. **Why was King Ahasuerus reading through the records when he discovered that Mordecai had uncovered the plot to assassinate him?**
   A. He read the records monthly to attest to their accuracy and seal them.
   B. He was having insomnia.
   C. He was hoping to learn where all of Esther's relatives were.
   D. He was being audited by the IRS.
   E. He believed one of his princes had cheated him out of tribute money.

10. **Who suggested that Mordecai be given royal treatment for potentially saving the king's life?**
   A. Haman
   B. Esther
   C. No one. The king decided this on his own.
   D. Mordecai
   E. The former queen, Vashti

11. **What happened after Esther told King Ahasuerus that Haman was behind the plot to destroy her people?**
   A. The king went into a rage and banished both Haman and Esther from the palace.
   B. The king told them they should try to work it out like mature adults.

C. The king accused her of lying, and ordered her immediately taken away.

D. The king ordered Haman hanged.

E. The king took a dagger and shoved it through Haman's heart.

12. When Esther later requested that the king's decree (regarding the destruction of the Jews) be rescinded, what was his response?

A. He told her that since his seal was on the decree, he could not repeal it.

B. He called for all of the Jews to come to the royal city before the appointed day of destruction, and promised that his army would protect them.

C. He sent out messengers to all the cities to repeal the order.

D. He allowed Mordecai to write a decree which allowed the Jews to defend themselves.

Lived with a single widow while ministering to her. Performed certain unending miracles.

ELISHA

13. After the positive outcome of this situation, Mordecai and Esther decided the two days commemorating it should be celebrated every year by the Jews. What is the name of this event?

A. The Feast of Mordecai

B. The Two Days of Deliverance

C. The Days of Purim (lots)

D. The Fasting Days of Esther

E. The Passover

ANSWERS TO ESTHER QUESTIONS

#	ANS	REF	#	ANS	REF
1.	B	1:3	11.	D	7:10
2.	D	1:12	12.	D	8:3–14
3.	A,C,D	2:5–7	13.	C	9:26
4.	A	2:20			
5.	D	2:21–23			
6.	B	3:5–6	Super Challenge:		
7.	B,C,F	4:6–17	#1: A golden scepter		
8.	C	5:14	(4:11)		
9.	B	6:1			
10.	A	6:6–9			

DENTIST: Oh, no!

MORDECAI: What? What is it?

DENTIST: More decay, Mordecai!

~JOB~

(c. 1200 B.C.)

1. **At the outset of this book, Job had all of the following EXCEPT:**
   A. Seven sons
   B. Seven thousand sheep
   C. Four wives
   D. Three thousand camels
   E. Three daughters

2. **Why did Satan take an interest in Job?**
   A. Because he felt that Job would be easy prey
   B. Because God had pointed out Job's righteousness to him
   C. Because Job was harming Satan by calling the people of the land to God
   D. Because Satan believed that Job was susceptible to sexual immorality
   E. Because he thought Job was cute

3. **Which of the following had Job lost at the end of Satan's first attack?**
   (three answers)
   A. Many servants
   B. One of his wives
   C. His house
   D. His sons and daughters
   E. His gold and silver
   F. Sheep and camels

4. **When Satan came back for assault number two what happened to Job?**

A. He was paralyzed from the neck down.

B. He developed leprosy.

C. He was covered with boils.

D. His ears grew so large that he could flap them and fly.

E. He went blind.

5. **After this happened to Job, his wife advised him to "curse God and die." What was Job's response?**

A. "As for me and my house, we shall serve the Lord."

B. "My life will end soon, and I will endure this evil."

C. He ordered his servants to kill her.

D. He called her foolish and asked her if it was right to only accept good things from the Lord.

E. He told her that if she suffered adversity her soul was in her own hands.

> **?** **DID YOU KNOW** that in the book of Job, Job is never told the reason for his suffering? He never hears the conversations between God and Satan, even after his suffering is over. He was surely a man of faith!

6. **Three of Job's friends showed up to visit him when they heard of his problems. What was the essence of Job's first speech?**

A. I must have sinned to bring this upon myself.

B. Why did I have to be born?

C. I don't want anyone to see me like this.

D. You are my only true friends; no one else has come.

E. Did you guys bring me anything?

7. **The first of Job's friends to speak was a man named Eliphaz. Which of the following best paraphrases his words to Job?**

A. Job's suffering was due to sin, and Job would be foolish to cry out to anyone accept God. He should accept God's judgment, and know that He alone could make things right.

B. Both the righteous and the unrighteous face adversity. Job's predicament had more to do with human problems than with relating to God. Job should face reality and try to make the best of things.

C. Job had gathered up too many worldly goods, believing that they would shelter him from all of life's potential problems. Now, God was showing him that all of man's work could not minimize God's power.

D. He had no answers for Job and could not understand why Job was suffering. He had come in friendship to see if he could lighten Job's burden in some way.

Top Ten "Other Things" Said by Job's Wife

10. "Buy that Honda if you want, Job, but I think the Ford Pinto would be safer."

9. "My husband doesn't just get angry . . . he boils!"

8. "For a guy with a name like yours you sure don't work much!"

7. "Jenga?"

6. "Maybe we should take you to the Wizard of Uz."

5. "The government only wants what's best for us."

4. "I think that whirlwind had something to do with Helen Hunt."

3. "C'mon Job. Everybody knows the world is flat!"

2. "Do you want to be remembered as a guy who complained all the time?"

1. "What would Moses do?"

8. **After Eliphaz finished, Job spoke again. His message was about what THREE things?**
   A. His concern about what will happen when he dies
   B. The extent of his suffering
   C. A cry for sympathy from his friends
   D. Why God is trying him
   E. A request for temporary relief
   F. Reconsidering the words of his wife

9. **Next, Job's second friend, Bildad, addressed him. Essentially, his message was:**
   A. "You were overdue for troubles."
   B. "You are not the first nor the last person to suffer."
   C. "Those who forget God will be destroyed, but the righteous will be remembered."
   D. "Who can know the mind of God?"
   E. "This reminds me of a bad cold I had last winter."

10. In describing God's greatness, Job mentioned THREE constellations that God created. Find them in this list:

A. The Great Ladle (Big Dipper)
B. The Bear
C. The Great Wolf
D. Orion
E. The Pleiades
F. Gemini

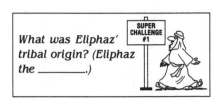

SUPER CHALLENGE #1

What was Eliphaz' tribal origin? (Eliphaz the _____.)

11. When Job's friend Zophar spoke, he basically told Job that if he would cry out honestly to God, he would forget his misery. Job responded by saying (my paraphrase):

A. I have already done so; why hasn't God healed me by now?
B. My pain and suffering is such that I cannot know honesty toward God.
C. With friends like you guys, who needs Chaldean raiders?
D. What makes you think you have a corner on common wisdom; even nature proves the ways of God.
E. God already knows my condition; yet I am blameless and He still makes me suffer.

12. After Job mourned the brevity of life, and Eliphaz speaks again, Job addressed his visitors, referring to them as:

A. Friends who are like brothers
B. Miserable comforters
C. Self-righteous visitors
D. My God-fearing neighbors
E. Larry, Darryl, and Darryl

13. **In Chapter 19, Job lamented his physical condition. THREE of the following are accurate regarding his own description:**

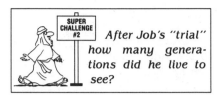

After Job's "trial" how many generations did he live to see?

A. "I am poured out like wax."
B. "My breath is offensive to my wife."
C. "I am repulsive to my children."
D. "My legs and arms barely move."
E. "My bone clings to my skin."
F. "None of my frame has escaped God's wrath."

14. **In Chapter 22, Eliphaz used Job as an example of man's evil and accused him of all of the following except:**
A. Slaughtering the innocent
B. Stripping the naked of their clothing
C. Withholding bread from the hungry
D. Sending widows away empty
E. Taking collateral from others without good reason

15. **Job said that once his testing was over, he would . . .**
A. Be whole again and favored by God
B. Have tried every "boil remedy" known to man
C. Never again question the wisdom of God
D. Know the depths of God's mercy
E. Come forth as gold

16. **Job asked where wisdom could be found and suggested several things which were NOT as valuable as wisdom. Find FOUR of them in the following list:**
A. Onyx
B. Emeralds
C. Sapphire
D. Rubies

E. Ivory

F. Topaz

G. Pet rocks

17. **In Chapters 29–31, Job discussed all of the following except:**
   A. The happiness of his past
   B. How the people who used to respect him now mock him
   C. The people of his household whom God has destroyed
   D. His righteousness concerning sexual immorality

18. **Why did Elihu, a fourth visitor, wait until everyone had spoken before he addressed Job and the others?**
   A. He did not know Job as well as the others.
   B. He liked getting the last word.
   C. He was significantly younger than the others.
   D. He entered late into the debate and wanted to make certain everyone else had spoken their fill.
   E. He, too, was afflicted and wished to hear all of the debate before responding.

Iron Age!
(c. 1200 B.C.)

19. **Elihu was upset with the overall conversation for all of the following reasons EXCEPT:**
   A. He believed that prayer was more effective than discussion.
   B. He felt Job was too self-righteous.
   C. The other three had condemned Job.
   D. He felt that Eliphaz, Bildad, and Zophar had no substantive answers.

20. **Elihu spoke for the next six chapters, addressing Job's ideas. Which of the following were the main points of his arguments?**
    (three answers)
    A. "You have no right to question God."
    B. "Satan is your tempter, and you should be blaming him."
    C. "Your physical malady is related to your humanity; it has nothing to do with good or evil."
    D. "God will not commit iniquity."
    E. "God righteously disciplines all people."

21. **The next person to speak was God. What form did He take?**
    A. An angel
    B. Lightning
    C. A man in a chariot of fire
    D. A voice from a whirlwind
    E. A doctor

22. **God compared the power of Job to that of what animal?**
    A. An ox
    B. A behemoth
    C. A mule
    D. A badger

23. **What THREE things occurred after God had finished speaking to Job?**
    A. Job repented and declared his ignorance.
    B. Job commended Elihu for his wisdom and gave him a gold ring.
    C. God commanded Eliphaz, Bildad, and Zophar to make a sacrifice because He disliked their opinions.
    D. Job witnessed Satan walking away in the distance.

E. God told Eliphaz that Job would pray for him and his friends.

24. **After Job's adversity ended, God blessed him. Which of the following are correct biblical facts concerning Job's "estate"?**
(three answers)
   A. He had forty thousand sheep.
   B. His three daughters were more beautiful than any of the women in the land.
   C. He had six thousand camels.
   D. He had nine sons.
   E. He had one thousand yoke of oxen.
   F. To celebrate his ordeal, he bought a blue '84 Corvette.

Q. Why was everyone in the Old Testament so poor?

A. Because there was only one Job.

ANSWERS TO JOB QUESTIONS

#	ANS	REF	#	ANS	REF
1.	C	1:2–3	18.	C	32:4
2.	B	1:8	19.	B	32:2–3
3.	A,D,F	1:14–19	20.	A,D,E	33:12–13;
4.	C	2:7			34:10, 23–25
5.	D	2:9–10	21.	D	38:1
6.	B	3:3–19	22.	B	40:15–24
7.	A	Ch. 4, 5	23.	A,C,E	42:6–9
8.	B,C,D	6:2–14; 7:1–	24.	B,C,E	42:12, 15
		21			
9.	C	8:1–22			
10.	B,D,E	9:9	Super Challenges:		
11.	D	12:3, 7–10	#1: Temanite (4:1)		
12.	B	16:2	#2: Four (42:16)		
13.	B,C,E	19:17, 20			
14.	A	22:5–11			
15.	E	23:10			
16.	A,C, D,F	28:12–19			
17.	C	29:2–6, 21; 30:1; 31:1–12			

~PSALMS~
(c. 1410–430 B.C.)

1. According to Psalm 1, a man who "walks not in the counsel of the ungodly" was comparable to:
   A. The highest angel
   B. A house on a strong foundation
   C. Microsoft stock
   D. A tree planted by the water
   E. The great men of old

2. Who was David fleeing from when he wrote in Psalm 3: "Lord, how they have increased who trouble me!"?
   A. His son Solomon
   B. His son Absalom
   C. King Saul
   D. Uriah, husband of Bathsheba
   E. The Hebrew FBI

3. Psalm 10 asks God to do what to the wicked man?
   A. Break his arm
   B. Judge him harshly
   C. Slay him in his iniquity
   D. Forgive him

4. From Psalm 14: "The fool has said in his heart" that . . .
   A. "There will be no judgment upon him."
   B. "His sins are hidden by the nightfall."
   C. "There is no God."
   D. "There is no good nor evil."
   E. "The Spice Girls were extremely talented."

5. **What did David say would happen when he called upon the Lord (Psalm 18)?**
   A. "He heard my cry, and lifted my soul toward heaven."
   B. "So shall I be saved from my enemies."
   C. "He forgave my transgressions, and healed me."
   D. "He built a wall around me, and preserved me."

6. **This passage from Psalm 22:14 is often considered prophetic regarding the crucifixion of Christ. Can you complete it? "I am poured out like water, and . . .**
   A. "This corruptible body fails me."
   B. "The pall of death is at my feet."
   C. "All of my friends have abandoned me."
   D. "All my bones are out of joint."
   E. "Life drains from me like sand through an hourglass."

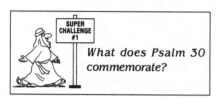

SUPER CHALLENGE #1

What does Psalm 30 commemorate?

7. **According to Psalm 23, David said the Lord does all of the following:**
   (four answers)
   A. Leads his enemies down the paths of destruction
   B. Leads him beside the still waters
   C. Leads him in the paths of righteousness
   D. Fills his soul with the breath of life
   E. Anoints his head with oil
   F. Makes him lie down in green pastures
   G. Covers him with His hand

8. **Psalm 24 says that "what" is the Lord's?**
   A. The earth and all its fullness
   B. The heavens and all their glory
   C. Every living thing
   D. All things seen and unseen

9. **In Psalm 32, David said, "Blessed is he . . ."**
   A. ". . . whose heart cries out to the Lord."
   B. ". . . whose transgression is forgiven."
   C. ". . . who has no car payment."
   D. ". . . who seeks the face of God."
   E. ". . . whose happiness is in honesty."

10. **David stated in Psalm 37 that if you "delight yourself in the Lord"**
    A. "He will bless you in a thousand ways."
    B. "Your life shall be filled with peace."
    C. "He shall protect you from your enemies."
    D. "He shall give you the desires of your heart."

11. **The first psalm of *Book Two* is Psalm 42 and begins as follows:**
    A. "I cried out to the Lord, and He heard me."
    B. "I just got a fax from Job, O Lord, and I guess I'm not so bad off after all."

Top Ten Things Not Commemorated by a Psalm

10. David's hernia surgery
9. Israel's annual chicken barbecue
8. Cain's murder trial
7. Pork Producers Convention
6. Any of Methuselah's 969 birthdays
5. Construction of the pyramids
4. Susan B. Anthony dollar
3. Pharaoh's first rap CD
2. Pharaoh's second rap CD
1. I don't Noah; you tell me.

C. "Remember me, O God, for my enemies surround me."

D. "I shall dwell in the house of the Lord forever."

E. "As the deer pants for the water brooks, so pants my soul for You."

12. **Psalm 47 begins with the words, "Oh clap your hands, all you peoples! Shout to God with the voice of triumph!" This psalm was written by:**

   A. King David

   B. Solomon (for the dedication of the temple)

   C. The sons of Korah (a guild of singers and composers)

   D. An unknown author

   E. Moses (this is his only known psalm)

13. **In Psalm 51, why did David say, "Create in me a clean heart, O God"?**

   A. He had just returned from a battle in which he slew many enemy soldiers.

   B. He had just had his cholesterol checked.

   C. He had just committed adultery with Bathsheba.

   D. His household had just suffered the incident of incest regarding Amnon and Tamar.

   E. He had cursed his son Absalom for attempting to overthrow him.

14. **"Be merciful to me, O God, be merciful to me!" It's Psalm 57, and what was the situation when David wrote it?**

   A. It was the night before David's army was to face a much larger army of Philistines.

   B. David had fled Jerusalem to escape Absalom.

   C. David was on his deathbed and had just instructed his assistants to begin Solomon's coronation as king.

   D. He was in a cave hiding from Saul.

E. He had just finished a large meal in a Mexican restaurant, and his stomach was attempting to kill him.

15. **In Psalm 62, David said that "men of low degree are a vapor." What are men of "high degree"?**
    A. Foolishness
    B. A lie
    C. A shadow
    D. Vain fools
    E. Ph.D.s

16. **What did David number at "twenty-thousand, even thousands of thousands" in Psalm 68?**
    A. The chariots of God
    B. The blessings of the Lord
    C. The righteous judgments of Jehovah
    D. The mercies of the Almighty
    E. The mosquitoes around Jerusalem

17. Only two psalms are attributed to Solomon, and one of them (72) closes out the second book of Psalms. Which of the following are mentioned in this work? (three answers)
A. An asp (poisonous serpent)
B. The gold of Sheba
C. Milk Duds
D. The kings of Tarshish
E. The darkest rubies of the land
F. Lebanon
G. Philistine idols

18. Psalm 74 is credited to Asaph, one of David's chief musicians. In verse fourteen, he mentions a large creature (identity unknown) whose name also appears in Job. Can you name it?
A. Behemoth
B. Hyrax
C. Leviathan
D. Chipmunkus Rex

19. Asaph's Psalm 78 is a history of Israel. It includes all of the following EXCEPT:
A. Moses
B. Jacob
C. The parting of the sea
D. Manna from heaven
E. The plagues on Egypt

20. According to Psalm 84, what would the writer rather do than dwell in the tents of wickedness?
A. Starve in the desert
B. Mourn with the afflicted
C. Sit on a park bench in Damascus and watch the streetlights change

D. Be a doorkeeper in the house of God

E. Be an unknown servant of the Living God

21. **"I will sing of the mercies of the Lord forever," begins Psalm 89. These are the words of:**
    A. Heman the Ezrahite
    B. King David
    C. Ethan the Ezrahite
    D. Asaph, a priest

22. **Psalm 91 says that if you live "under the shadow of the Almighty," He will protect you from which of the following:**
    (three answers)
    A. Arrows
    B. The wrath of kings
    C. Frivolous lawsuits
    D. Plagues
    E. The sword of him who hates you
    F. Cobras

23. **In Psalm 94, the author said the wicked do all of these things EXCEPT:**
    A. Boast in themselves
    B. Steal from the house of God
    C. Murder the fatherless
    D. Break God's people into pieces

24. **Four well-known Bible figures are named in the 99th Psalm. Find the correct four in this list:**
    A. Adam
    B. Samuel
    C. Aaron
    D. Solomon
    E. Esther
    F. Moses

The psalmist cried out in Psalm 102, saying that his "heart is stricken" so badly that he forgot to do what?

SUPER CHALLENGE #2

G. Goliath

H. Jacob

25. **Psalm 104 said, "You have set a boundary that they may not pass over." "They" refers to:**
   A. The wicked
   B. The chosen ones
   C. The wild beasts
   D. The waters
   E. Cattle rustlers

26. **All of the following were part of David's Psalm 108 EXCEPT:**

> **DID YOU KNOW** that the book of Psalms had more than six authors?

   A. Ammon is my footstool.
   B. Ephraim is the helmet for my head.
   C. Judah is my lawgiver.
   D. Moab is my washpot.
   E. Over Edom, I will cast my shoe.

27. **What will be in the house of the man who fears the Lord? (Psalm 112)**
   A. Wealth and riches
   B. Goodness and mercy
   C. A heritage of righteousness
   D. The peace that passes understanding
   E. Lots of good hiding places

28. **Psalm 116 tells us that "precious in the sight of the Lord" is:**
   A. The praise of His people
   B. The little children
   C. The death of His saints
   D. The offerings of His chosen ones

29. **David was glad in Psalm 122. Why?**
   A. Because one of his psalms had just made the top ten on *The Hebrew Hit Parade*

B. Because he was invited to go to the temple

C. Because the altars (to pagan gods) in the high places had been destroyed

D. Because he had just won a victory over the Moabites

E. Because the Israelites had repented from their sin

30. **According to Psalm 133, what is "like precious oil on the head"?**

A. The knowledge of salvation for the righteous man

B. Wisdom

C. Valvoline 10w30

D. The mercy of the Lord

E. When people dwell together in unity

King Nebuchad-nezzar II builds fantastic "Hanging Gardens!"
(c. 600 B.C.)

31. **Where were the Israelites in Psalm 137, when they wept over Zion?**

A. By the rivers of Babylon

B. In the land of the Pharaoh

C. Watching "The Ten Commandments" at a theater in Gaza

D. In Jerusalem, seeing their deteriorated homeland for the first time since returning from captivity

E. Within the walls of Persia

32. **In Psalm 144, David said that if God would rescue and deliver them from foreigners, they would reap all of these benefits EXCEPT:**

A. "Our sons may be as plants grown up in their youth."

B. "Our daughters may be as pillars."

C. "Our barns may be full."

D. "Our wine barrels will overflow."

E. "Our sheep may bring forth thousands (of off-spring)."

33. David said in Psalm 147 that God does lots of things. However, there are many things God does that he DIDN'T include in this Psalm. Therefore, I had to make up, contrive, devise, and fabricate (you get the idea) a few additional choices. Find the activities that correctly reflect David's thoughts on what God does.
(four answers)
A. Builds up Jerusalem
B. Gives sight to the blind
C. Saves the righteous woman in childbirth
D. Heals the brokenhearted
E. Allows the wicked to prosper for a short season
F. Gives snow like wool
G. Makes the wind blow, and water flow

34. This is it! Psalm 150 tells us to praise God with all of the following EXCEPT:
A. The trumpet
B. A loud cry
C. The dance
D. The lute and harp
E. Loud cymbals

It's actually a little known fact that David sat down by the river with his harp, and sang (to the tune of Swanee River, of course!) this song:

Way down upon the Swanee River, far, far away,
I removed the king of Zobah's liver
Far from the Hebrews at home
It's a life of war and mayhem
Everywhere we roam—
We seek our enemies and slay them
Far from the Hebrews at home.

ANSWERS TO PSALMS QUESTIONS

#	ANS	REF	#	ANS	REF
1.	D	1:3	22.	A,C,D	91:5, 10, 13
2.	B	3	23.	B	94:4–6
3.	A	10:15	24.	B,C,	99:4, 6
4.	C	14:1		F,H	
5.	C	18:3	25.	D	104:6–9
6.	D	22:14	26.	A	108:8–9
7.	B,C,	23:2, 3, 5	27.	A	112:3
	E,F		28.	C	116:15
8.	A	24:1	29.	B	122:1
9.	B	32:1	30.	C	133:1
10.	D	37:4	31.	A	137:1
11.	B	42:1	32.	D	144:12–14
12.	C	47	33.	A,D,	147:2, 3, 16,
13.	C	51		F,G	18
14.	D	57	34.	B	150:3–5
15.	B	62:9			
16.	A	68:17			
17.	B,D,F	72:10, 15, 16	Super Challenges:		
18.	C	74:14	#1: The dedication of		
19.	A	78:5, 13, 24	David's house (30)		
		43–51	#2: "eat my bread"		
20.	D	84:10	(102:4)		
21.	C	89			

~PROVERBS~

(c. 950–700 B.C.)

1. **According to Chapter 1, what did Solomon say was the beginning of knowledge?**
   A. To listen to your father
   B. The fear of the Lord
   C. Kindergarten
   D. The desire to learn
   E. To search your own heart

2. **Solomon said in Chapter 2 that wisdom should be sought after like:**
   (two answers)
   A. Fine jewels
   B. A pure wife
   C. Silver
   D. Godiva chocolates
   E. Fine silk
   F. Hidden treasures

3. **Mercy and truth should be:**
   (two answers)
   A. Bound around your neck
   B. Inscribed on your soul
   C. Written on the tablet of your heart
   D. Always at your side
   E. Your watchwords

4. **What was the "path of the just" compared to in Chapter 4?**
   A. The road to Paradise, the eternal City of God
   B. The journey of Moses, who knew God

C. The life of a prophet, always seeing what is good in the eyes of the Lord

D. The shining sun, illuminating the perfect day

5. **Solomon described an "immoral woman" in Chapter 5. All of these were attributed to her EXCEPT:**

A. She cares not who she destroys.

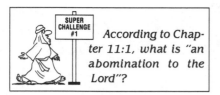

SUPER CHALLENGE #1

According to Chapter 11:1, what is "an abomination to the Lord"?

B. Her lips drip honey.

C. Her feet go down to death.

D. In the end, she is as bitter as wormwood.

E. Her steps lay hold of hell.

6. **Which of the following were part of Solomon's list of things the Lord hates?**
(four answers)

A. A proud look

B. The man who covets what is not his own

C. One who would steal from his neighbor

D. A false witness who speaks lies

E. Alarm clocks

F. Despising one's father and mother

G. A heart that devises wicked plans

H. Hands that shed innocent blood

7. **According to Chapter 8, what did Solomon say has been established "from everlasting, from the beginning, before there was ever an earth"?**

A. Righteousness

B. The Law of God

C. Understanding/wisdom

D. Truth

E. Perfect order

8. **"Wisdom has built her house . . ." said Solomon in Chapter 9. Name THREE more things that "she" (wisdom) had done:**
   A. She had sent for her cupbearer.
   B. She had acknowledged her Maker.
   C. She had slaughtered her meat.
   D. She had funded her IRA.
   E. She had dined with kings.
   F. She had furnished her table.
   G. She had sent out her maidens.

9. **Select the correct Solomonic response to this statement: "The rich man's wealth is his strong city."**
   A. "But if the Lord doesn't build the house, he who builds it labors in vain."
   B. "The destruction of the poor is their poverty."
   C. "But the gates of the evil open toward wickedness."
   D. "But the foolish shall die in destitution."
   E. "The simple man shall live in a box behind the 7-Eleven."

10. **What does the "soul of the unfaithful" feed on?**
    A. Evil
    B. Violence
    C. Lechery (lust)
    D. Mostly fruits and vegetables
    E. Pride

DID YOU KNOW that Solomon wrote most of the book of Proverbs? Chapters 30 and 31, however, are ascribed to two other authors—Agur and Lemuel, respectively. Generally, people believe that Song of Solomon was written in Solomon's early years; Proverbs was written in his mature, middle-age years; Ecclesiastes was written in his old age, as he reflected on life.

11. **"In all labor there is profit, but . . ."**
    A. "Laziness leads to the grave."
    B. "The sluggard shall be found wanting."
    C. "Honor lies in helping the poor."

D. "It's tough to get by on minimum wage."
E. "Idle chatter leads only to poverty."

12. **According to 15:1, what turns away wrath?**
    A. The peace of the Lord
    B. Wise words
    C. An immoral woman
    D. A soft answer
    E. The king's honor

Rome founded by Romulus and Remus!
(*c.* 753 B.C.)

13. **What goes before (leads to) destruction?**
    A. A jealous heart
    B. Anger
    C. Pride
    D. Foolishness

14. **What "does good, like medicine"?**
    A. A merry heart
    B. A kind word
    C. Skipping work to play golf
    D. Wise instruction
    E. Trusting in the Lord

15. **Complete this proverb: "Houses and riches are an inheritance from fathers, . . ."**
    A. "But wisdom comes from God alone."
    B. "And grace and peace are gleaned from a righteous mother."
    C. "But a prudent wife is from the Lord."
    D. "But a foolish son shall squander his wealth."

16. **According to Proverbs 20:1, whoever is led astray by this is "not wise." What does "this" refer to?**
    A. The media
    B. Wine/intoxicating drink
    C. Sexual desire/lust

D. Idol worship

E. Selfish ambition

17. **"It is better to dwell in a corner of a housetop than . . ."**
    A. "in a house with a contentious woman."
    B. "in the trunk of a '64 Impala."
    C. "in the finery of a harlot."
    D. "in great houses of evil men."
    E. "in the palace of a foolish king."

18. **In Chapter 22, what does Solomon say about borrowing?**
    A. "Never a borrower, nor a lender be."
    B. "The borrower is servant to the lender."
    C. "Borrowing is the curse of the impoverished."
    D. "Do not turn away him that would borrow."
    E. "The poor man will sit and watch the big wheel barrow."

    If your enemy is hungry and thirsty, and you give him bread and water, what will be the result?
    SUPER CHALLENGE #2

19. **"When you sit down to eat with a ruler," what should you do if you are "a man given to (strong) appetite"?**
    (Author's note: In this question, ruler is intended to mean king or leader. I know some of you are thinking, "Why in the world would you eat with a ruler? It's much easier to use a fork . . . especially if you're eating peas." And of course, you would be correct.)
    A. Do not expose your gluttony, lest you be slain.
    B. Do not drink wine in excess.
    C. Ask for a doggie bag.
    D. Put a knife to your throat.
    E. Show moderation, which is godliness.

20. In Proverbs 24, where does Solomon say there is safety?
A. Only in the wisdom of God
B. In the fortress of the Lord
C. In the stronghold of Zion
D. In a multitude of counselors
E. Only if you land on "Free Parking"

21. "A word fitly spoken," says Solomon, "is . . ." all of the following EXCEPT:
A. Like apples of gold, in settings of silver.
B. A wise reprover to an obedient ear.
C. Like an earring of gold.
D. Like the cold of snow in time of harvest.
E. Like a delicacy after a feast.

22. There is more hope for a fool than for:
A. A sluggard (lazy person)
B. Most TV sitcoms
C. A man who is wise in his own eyes
D. An unbeliever
E. An immoral woman

23. According to Proverbs 27:21, how is a man valued?
  A. By what others say about him
  B. By his diligence in important things
  C. According to his honesty
  D. By his measure of possessions
  E. Usually, so much per pound

24. What happens when the righteous are in authority?
  A. There is prosperity in the land.
  B. Justice prevails to every man.
  C. The people rejoice.
  D. The Lord blesses His people.

25. Proverbs 31 is the last of the book and discusses the "virtuous wife." All of the following are attributable to her EXCEPT:
  A. She does no evil to her husband.
  B. She teaches her daughters the ways of the Lord.
  C. She buys a field, and plants a vineyard.
  D. She makes linen garments and sells them.
  E. She reaches out her hands to the needy.

Q. How do we know that Job went to a chiropractor?

A. Because Job 16:12 says, "I was at ease, but He has shattered me; He has also taken me by the neck, and shaken me to pieces."

ANSWERS TO PROVERBS QUESTIONS

#	ANS	REF	#	ANS	REF
1.	B	1:7	18.	B	22:7
2.	C,F	2:4	19.	D	23:1
3.	A,C	3:3	20.	D	24:6
4.	D	4:18	21.	E	25:11–13
5.	A	5:3–5	22.	C	26:12
6.	A,D,	6:17–19	23.	A	27:21
	G,H		24.	C	29:2
7.	C	8:14–23	25.	B	31:12, 16, 20,
8.	C,F,G	9:2–3			24
9.	B	10:15			
10.	B	13:2			
11.	D	14:23		Super Challenges:	
12.	D	15:1		#1: Dishonest scales	
13.	C	16:18		(11:1)	
14.	A	17:22		#2: You will heap coals	
15.	C	19:14		of fire on his head.	
16.	B	20:1		(25:21–22)	
17.	A	21:9			

~ECCLESIASTES~
(c. 1000–900 B.C.)

1. Solomon began Ecclesiastes by saying "all is vanity."
He closed the first chapter by concluding:
   A. Lustful desires are the destruction of youth.
   B. As knowledge increases, so does sorrow.
   C. Life is like a box of chocolates.
   D. Things that seem good for a season, disappear like a vapor.
   E. God's plan is always unknown to mortal man.

2. Solomon stated in Chapter 2 that he did great works and secured many people and things to gratify himself. Which of these were on that list?
(four answers)
   A. Vineyards
   B. Grand sculptures
   C. Jesters and courtiers
   D. Male and female servants
   E. Musical instruments
   F. Horses and chariots
   G. Male and female singers
   H. The entire video series of Rocky and Bullwinkle cartoons

3. In Chapter 2, "the preacher" concluded that there was nothing better to do than:
   A. Share all that he had with the poor.
   B. Thank the Lord for all of His bountiful blessings.
   C. Eat, drink and enjoy the fruit of his labor.
   D. Strive to acquire as much wisdom as possible before death.

4. **Solomon's soliloquy at the beginning of Chapter 3 tells us that there is a time for every purpose EXCEPT:**
   A. Planting
   B. Praying
   C. Dancing
   D. Sewing
   E. War
   F. Keeping silent

5. **Why did "the preacher" say that he who never existed was better than he who lived or he who had lived and died?**

SUPER CHALLENGE #1

Solomon said that "when goods increase, they increase who eat them." Therefore, what did Solomon say was the only benefit of having an "additional goods"?

   A. He who had never lived would not be judged.
   B. He would never have to look at a disgusting picture of himself on his driver's license.
   C. He did not have to give all of his labor under the sun to an unknown beneficiary.
   D. He had never seen the evil work that is done under the sun.
   E. He who had not lived never experienced life's futility.

6. **According to Solomon, how is a fool's voice known?**
   A. By his many words
   B. By its simplicity
   C. According to its emptiness
   D. By its ignorance

7. **"All the labor of man is for his mouth, and yet . . ."**
   A. "Each day he begins his work anew."
   B. "His stomach is never full."
   C. "The soul is not satisfied."
   D. "His hands are callused and swollen."

E. "His mouth also condemns him."

F. "He can't swing a hammer with his teeth."

8. In Chapter 7, Solomon discussed moderation. Which of these statements were mentioned in his discussion?

(three answers)

A. "Do not be overly righteous."

B. "Do not drink wine in excess."

C. "Temper your speech with wisdom."

D. "Do not be overly wicked."

E. "Don't be overly wise."

F. "Satisfy your hunger, but don't be gluttonous."

9. What did Solomon say no one has the power to do?

A. Increase their stature

B. Eat just one Lay's potato chip

C. Alter the plan of God

Top Ten Old Testament Songs & Respective Recording Artist

10. "Stairway to Heaven," by Jacob

9. "How Do You Talk to an Angel?" by Gideon

8. "You're the Devil in Disguise," a duet by Adam & Eve

7. "War," a duet by Saul and David

6. "Girls Just Wanna Have Fun," by Solomon's Harem

5. "Dream," by Daniel

4. "I Got Friends in Low Places," by Lot

3. "Beat It," by Samson

2. "Some Guys Have All the Luck," by Solomon

1. "I Can't Get No Satisfaction," by Moses

D. Know the king's motives

E. Retain their own spirit

10. **Solomon said "the race is not to the swift, nor the battle to the strong . . . ." What did he say determines man's fate?**

A. The will of the Lord

B. Things unknown under the sun

C. His own deeds

D. Time and chance

E. Lots cast in eternity

Who Am I?

A great preacher, very wise and passionate. Speaks freely about the things of God, has very few inhibitions. He does have quite a few wives though.

SOLOMON

11. **According to Solomon, why should you be careful not to curse the king or the rich, even in your own bedroom?**

A. "The ears of God justify the righteous."

B. "A bird of the air may carry your voice."

C. "A sophisticated listening device may be in your candlestick holder."

D. "The curses of fools will be shouted on the rooftops."

E. "The winds may blow your words to holy ears."

12. **What was the preacher's opinion of childhood and youth?**

A. They are vanity.

B. They are days to be cherished.

C. They are times of innocence and frivolity.

D. They are evil.

13. **What did Solomon decide was the "whole duty of man" as a summation of Ecclesiastes?**

A. "Serve the Lord only, all of your days under the sun."

B. "Proclaim wisdom in every place and leave a heritage of righteousness to your children."

C. "Fear God and keep HIS commandments."
D. "Walk in the ways of the wise and do not forsake the instruction of your father."
E. "Put in eight hours a day, then kick back by the pool with a Coke and a concubine."

Fabric dyes!—you can now buy purple cloth!
(*c.* 900 B.C.)

"I'm a Solomon"

(To the tune of "I'm a Soul Man")

Comin' to ya,
Up from Zion
I'm never happy,
But I keep tryin'

I'm a Solomon *(sing it, girls)*
I'm a Solomon

Got what I got
The easy way,
An I get wiser
Each and every day

I'm a Solomon *(play it, Ezra)*
I'm a Solomon

Got lots of women
I try not to scare 'em
Just bring 'em home
And toss 'em in my harem Yeah, yeah.

Lead

I'm a Solomon (He's a Solomon)
I'm a Solomon (You're a Solomon)

(Repeat and fade)

ANSWERS TO ECCLESIASTES QUESTIONS

#	ANS	REF		#	ANS	REF
1.	B	1:18		10.	D	9:11
2.	A,D, E,G	2:4, 7, 8		11.	B	10:20
				12.	A	11:10
3.	C	2:24		13.	C	12:13
4.	B	3:2, 4, 7, 8				
5.	D	4:3				
6.	A	5:3		Super Challenge:		
7.	C	6:7		#1: "seeing them"		
8.	A,D,E	7:16–17		(5:11)		
9.	E	8:8				

~THE SONG OF~ SOLOMON

(c. 980–930 B.C.)

1. **Why was the Shulamite woman (Solomon's bride-to-be) dark-skinned?**
   A. She was Ethiopian.
   B. She was covered with coal dust from working in the mine.
   C. She had been darkened (tanned) by the sun.
   D. She had been treated with oils and creams in preparation for her wedding to Solomon.
   E. She was from Nubia, in Egypt.

2. **In Chapter 2, the Shulamite woman compared her lover to what TWO animals?**
   A. A gazelle
   B. A fox
   C. A lion
   D. A young stag
   E. An opossum
   F. A skunk

3. **How many men attended Solomon's couch (carriage) in the wedding procession?**
   A. 60
   B. 300
   C. Scores
   D. 144

4. Which of these were part of Solomon's description of his bride?
   (three answers)

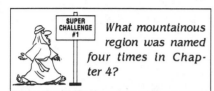

SUPER CHALLENGE #1 — What mountainous region was named four times in Chapter 4?

   A. "Your legs are as the pillars of the temple."
   B. "You have dove's eyes."
   C. "Your cheeks are as red as the new wine."
   D. "Your hair is like a flock of goats."
   E. "Your neck is like the tower of David."
   F. "Your front teeth have a gap like David Letterman's."

5. How did the bride describe her husband to the daughters of Jerusalem?
   (four answers)
   A. "His cheeks are like a bed of spices."
   B. "His voice is like the north wind."
   C. "His head is like the finest gold."
   D. "His nose is as big as a pyramid."

Top Ten Old Testament Bands

10. Haman's Hermits
 9. Count Besai's Orchestra
 8. Simeon & Garfunkel
 7. Manahath Transfer
 6. Led "My People Go" Zeppelin
 5. Debbie Gideon
 4. New Kids in the Tribe
 3. Fleetwood Malachi
 2. The Mammas and the Patriarchs
 1. Earth, Wind, Fire & Brimstone

E. "His eyes shine like sapphires."
F. "His locks are as black as a raven."
G. "His body is carved ivory."

6. **The bridegroom called out his bride from among which of the following?**
   (three answers)
   A. The beautiful women of Judah
   B. Innumerable virgins
   C. Charlie's angels
   D. The delicate maidens of the valley
   E. Ten thousand queens
   F. Eighty concubines
   G. Sixty queens

> *Fawned upon by the King of Romance, she had lovely books of poetry written about her. However, she shared her man with many other women.*
>
> THE SHULAMITE WOMAN

7. **Identify THREE kinds of fruit mentioned in Chapter 7.**
   A. Apples
   B. Peaches
   C. Cherries
   D. Pomegranates
   E. Grapes
   F. California raisins ("Yeah I heard it through the grapevine, that the Shulamite would be mine, baby!")

8. **According to Chapter 8, where was the Shulamite woman born?**
   A. In her mother's chamber
   B. Under the apple tree
   C. In the vineyard of Solomon
   D. Beside the winepresses
   E. I don't know, but Don Shula might.

> **DID YOU KNOW** that the Song of Solomon was placed, in the Hebrew Bible, in the *megilloth*? This was a collection of books that were read on the feast days of the Jews. This collection included Ruth, Esther, Ecclesiastes, and Lamentations.

ANSWERS TO SONG OF SOLOMON QUESTIONS

#	ANS	REF	#	ANS	REF
1.	C	1:6	7.	A,D,E	7:8, 12
2.	A,D	2:9, 17	8.	B	8:5
3.	A	3:7			
4.	B,D,E	4:1, 4			
5.	A,C, F,G	5:11, 13, 14	Super Challenge:		
6.	B,F,G	6:8	#1: Lebanon (4:8, 11, 15)		

~ISAIAH~

(c. 740–700 B.C.)

1. **Isaiah's first prophecy was directed toward:**
   A. Assyria
   B. Moab
   C. Judah
   D. Babylon

2. **The prophet stated that God was tired of "futile sacrifices" and instead offered a list of practical alternatives. Which THREE of the following appeared on that list?**
   A. "Destroy your idols."
   B. "Wash yourselves; make yourselves clean."
   C. "Remember the Alamo."
   D. "Plead for the widow."
   E. "Rebuke immorality and sexual impurity."
   F. "Seek justice."
   G. "Respect the Sabbath, and keep its holiness."

3. **When the Lord judges the nations "in the latter days," all of the following will apply EXCEPT:**
   A. "They shall beat their swords into plowshares."
   B. "The lion will lay down with the lamb."
   C. "Nation shall not lift up sword against nation."
   D. "They shall learn war no more."

4. **Isaiah said the "daughters of Zion" would be punished for all of the following EXCEPT:**
   A. Being haughty
   B. Abandoning their husbands
   C. Walking with outstretched necks

D. Having "wanton" (flirtatious) eyes

E. Making a jingling with their feet

5. **What did Isaiah use in Chapter 5 as an allegory to represent the people of Judah and their God?**

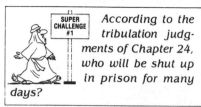

According to the tribulation judgments of Chapter 24, who will be shut up in prison for many days?

A. A wheat field

B. A palace

C. A bowling alley

D. A vineyard

E. A strong city

6. **How would God signal "the nations from afar" to come and lay siege of Judah and those who have turned from Him?**

A. He will "put it in the minds of kings."

B. He will "shout with a 'voice like thunder'."

C. He will "whistle to them from the end of the earth."

D. He will "send the prophets."

E. He will "leave a message on their voice mail."

7. **How was Isaiah's sin "purged" by the seraphim?**

A. The seraphim touched Isaiah's lips with a hot coal.

B. The seraphim touched Isaiah's forehead with the tip of his wing.

C. The seraphim cut Isaiah's right hand and put the blood across his own heart.

D. The seraphim circumcised Isaiah.

E. None of the above

8. **In Chapter 7, Isaiah made a prophecy concerning what?**

A. The final destruction of Solomon's temple

B. The scattering of the Jews

C. The Apocalypse

D. The birth of Christ

9. The Lord told Isaiah that He would be all of the following EXCEPT:
A. A mighty deliverer
B. A sanctuary
C. A stone of stumbling
D. A rock of offense
E. A trap and snare to Jerusalem

10. Which two tribes would devour each other, yet both be against Judah?
A. Reuben and Moab
B. Ephraim and Manasseh
C. Dan and Benjamin
D. Ephraim and Benjamin
E. Sioux and Cherokee

11. When God spoke against Assyria, He said that their king, Tiglath-Pileser, saw himself as conquering the earth like:
A. A child gathering stones
B. The reapers of a wheat field
C. A warrior among the infirmed
D. A person gathering eggs
E. A villain from a James Bond movie

12. Isaiah described the kingdom's restoration in Chapter 11. All of these were part of his vision EXCEPT:
A. "The wolf shall dwell with the lamb."
B. "The lion shall eat straw like the ox."
C. "The nursing child shall play by the cobra's hole."
D. "The vulture and the dove shall fly together."
E. "The leopard shall lie down with the young goat."

13. In Chapter 13, Isaiah described:
A. The overthrow of Judah by the Babylonians
B. The Toledo War
C. The conquest of Babylon by the Medes

D. The taking of Palestine by Nebuchadnezzar

E. The destruction and desolation of Assyria

14. **What three nations were prophesied against in Chapter 14?**

    A. Judah, Israel, and Babylon

    B. Babylon, Persia, and Mesopotamia

    C. Brazil, Mexico, and Canada

    D. Samaria, Damascus, and Moab

    E. Babylon, Assyria, and Philistia

15. **What would the daughters of Moab be compared to after Moab fell?**

    A. The harlots at the city gates

    B. Valley girls (like, really uncool)

    C. The ghosts of the dead

    D. A young goat abandoned by its mother

    E. A bird thrown out of the nest

16. **All of the following were part of Isaiah's description of Ethiopia and its people EXCEPT:**

    A. A dark-skinned people

    B. A tall people

    C. A people terrible from their beginning

    D. A powerful nation

    E. A land shadowed with buzzing wings

17. **Which were true concerning the judgment on Egypt? (three answers)**

    A. Fire shall fall from the sky as in Sodom.

    B. Egyptian shall fight against Egyptian.

    C. The Sphinx will come to life and eat people.

    D. The rivers will dry up or become foul.

    E. The Egyptians will be like fearful women.

    F. God will imprison their king.

18. In his prophecy against Jerusalem, Isaiah referred to it as:
   A. The rose of Sharon
   B. The Holy Mount
   C. The city of Zion
   D. A "one-camel" town
   E. The Valley of Vision

19. Which city (also prophesied against) was referred to as "a marketplace for the nations"?
   A. Ashdod
   B. Tyre
   C. Gaza
   D. Dor
   E. Taiwan

HIGH FIBER DIET

20. **Isaiah looked forward to a day when God will do all of the following "in this mountain" EXCEPT:**
   A. Cast "the evil one" into the pit
   B. Create a feast of meat and wine
   C. Swallow up death forever
   D. Wipe away all tears
   E. Take away the rebuke of His people

21. **In the day of victory, who will the Lord slay?**
   A. Lucifer, the enemy of Heaven
   B. Behemoth, the great beast
   C. Nessie, the Loch Ness monster
   D. Those whose feet are swift to shed innocent blood
   E. Leviathan, the sea serpent

22. **What seemed to be the main fault of the Ephraimites?**

A radical leader. In fact, a little on the fringe! He claims to have seen angels in church. He has slight trouble controlling his language. However, he is certainly an effective leader, and he is passionate about God.

ISAIAH

   A. They were drunkards.
   B. They were sexually perverse.
   C. They were sluggards (lazy).
   D. They were idolaters.
   E. They had bad credit reports.

23. **In what ways would destruction come upon Ariel (Jerusalem)?**
   (three answers)
   A. Earthquake
   B. Rap music from giant car speakers
   C. Whirlwinds (tornadoes)
   D. Floods of water
   E. Storm and tempest
   F. Devouring fire

24. **Where did Isaiah say the rebellious children of God had gone for help rather than to Him?**

A. Sheol (the grave)
B. Asherah (Canaanite goddess)
C. "The gods of bitterness"
D. The pharaoh of Egypt
E. Dr. Laura

25. **In Chapter 32, what did Isaiah say would take place before "the Spirit is poured upon us from on high"? (three answers)**
    A. Temples and holy places would be filled with fowls of the air.
    B. Fruit vines would be replaced by thorns.
    C. Weeds would be growing in the streets.
    D. Cities would be deserted.
    E. Towers and forts would be homes for wild animals.
    F. Gas stations would be closed.

> SUPER CHALLENGE #2
>
> Where did God say (49:16) he has inscribed the name of His people?

26. **When Jerusalem was plundered by the Assyrians, all of these were listed as results EXCEPT:**
    A. The highways lay in waste.
    B. The pool of Solomon was defiled (polluted).
    C. There were no travelers.
    D. Lebanon was shamed and shriveled.
    E. Sharon was like a wilderness.

27. **God's judgment on Edom included a prophecy that its courtyards and palaces would become inhabited by animals. Which FOUR are included here?**
    A. Jackals
    B. Badgers
    C. Wild goats
    D. Ostriches
    E. Wolves

F. Creeping things

G. Hawks

28. After being told by Isaiah to "set his house in order" and prepare for death, King Hezekiah wept and cried out to God. What was the result?

A. God turned His face from him, and he died.

B. Isaiah intervened on his behalf, and God allowed him to live five more years.

C. His health was restored, but he was killed in battle shortly thereafter.

D. God granted him an additional fifteen years.

E. After finding out that he had been misdiagnosed, Hezekiah had his doctor stoned to death, and he lived another thirty years.

29. What did Isaiah say would be Hezekiah's punishment for showing all of his treasures to the Babylonian messengers?
(two answers)

A. He would live to be mocked by his own people.

B. He had to sit in a chair for fifteen minutes and would not get a cookie after supper.

C. Some of his sons would be eunuchs in the Babylonian palace.

D. His daughters would be the concubines of Baladin (the Babylonian king).

E. The Babylonians would carry away everything in his house.

30. In Chapter 42, Isaiah's prophecy mentioned Jacob three times. Which THREE words were associated with his name?

A. Servant

B. Wellspring

C. Desert

D. Worm

E. King

F. Fox

31. **According to Chapter 43, from what TWO things would God protect Israel?**

 A. Evil enemies

 B. Fire

Top Ten Proverbs Solomon Edited Out

10. Bravery cries out in the streets, but the coward calls 9-1-1.

9. Your mother's wisdom is like an ornament around your neck; your Uncle Louie, however, still wears a ball and chain.

8. Knowledge is pleasant to the soul; even so, smart people still get test anxiety.

7. There is a way that seems right to a man; and he just refuses to stop and ask for directions.

6. The righteous shall live many days on the earth, and stay in the better nursing homes.

5. Spare the rod and spoil the child; but use the rod only if no social services people are around.

4. The evil eat the bread of wickedness—and it's not whole wheat either.

3. There are three kinds of people in this world: Those who can count, and those who can't.

2. Wisdom furnishes her table with fine silver; but the table of fools is set with paper plates and plastic forks.

1. A wise man follows instructions—but a fool ends up with parts left over.

C. The "repo" man

D. Water

E. Poverty

32. **In Chapter 44, God called Israel to see the foolishness of trusting in:**

A. Idols

B. Their own wisdom

C. Their own wealth

D. Big corporations

E. Alliances with idol-worshiping nations

Halstatts invent "spoked wheel!"
(c. 730 B.C.)

33. **"Come down and sit in the dust . . . for you shall no more be called tender and delicate." This prophecy concerned the impending destruction of:**

A. Jerusalem

B. Iceland

C. Babylon

D. Persia

E. Assyria

34. **What THREE benefits did God say the Israelites would have enjoyed, had they heeded His commandments?**

A. Their holy city would have stood strong against the enemies of God.

B. Their kings would have always been victorious.

C. Their children would have never learned to fear.

D. Their peace would have been like a river.

E. Their righteousness would have been like the waves of the sea.

F. Their descendants would have been like the sand.

35. **All of these were Isaiah's prophesies of Christ in Chapter 53 EXCEPT:**

A. "He has no form or comeliness."
B. "To the blind, He gave sight, and to the deaf, hearing."
C. "A Man of sorrows, acquainted with grief."
D. "By His stripes we are healed."
E. "He was led as a lamb to the slaughter."

36. **What TWO things did God say were required by "foreigners and eunuchs" in order to be brought to "My holy mountain"?**
A. Circumcision
B. Honoring the Sabbath
C. Not despising "My chosen ones"
D. Serving "My princes"
E. Maintaining a 2.5 (or higher) GPA
F. Keeping God's covenant

37. **Isaiah wrote that fasting that is acceptable to God includes all of these EXCEPT:**
A. To let the oppressed go free
B. To share your bread with the hungry
C. To bow down your head
D. To loosen the bonds of wickedness
E. To cover the naked

DID YOU KNOW that *Isaiah* literally means "Yahweh is salvation."

38. **From the following, select the THREE rewards that God's people would see when their "light has come."**
A. "The abundance of the sea shall be turned to you."
B. "The spices of the East will be yours."
C. "Electricity rates will be substantially lower."
D. "Your father Abraham shall lead his people again."
E. "The people from Sheba shall bring gold."
F. "The multitude of camels shall cover your land."

39. Isaiah cried out in Chapter 64, "Oh, that you would rend [tear open] the heavens! That You would come down!" If God were to "come down" what TWO things did Isaiah say would happen?
A. "The winds would cry out Your name."
B. "The clouds would part forever."
C. "The 'two-party' system would be over once and for all."
D. "The nations may tremble at Your presence."
E. "The mountains might shake."

40. The book of Isaiah ends with a description of:
A. The new earth as a paradise
B. His mother-in-law
C. The Levites crowning Jesus
D. The corpses of transgressors
E. Satan being cast into the lake of fire

ANSWERS TO ISAIAH QUESTIONS

#	ANS	REF	#	ANS	REF
1.	C	1:1	25.	B,D,E	32:12–14
2.	B,D,F	1:16–17	26.	B	33:8–9
3.	B	2:4	27.	A,C,	34:13–15
4.	B	3:16		D,G	
5.	D	5:1–7	28.	D	38:1–9
6.	C	5:26	29.	C,E	39:6–7
7.	A	6:6–7	30.	A,D,E	41:8, 14, 21
8.	D	7:14–16	31.	B,D	43:1–2
9.	A	8:14	32.	A	44:9–20
10.	B	9:21	33.	C	47:1
11.	D	10:14	34.	D,E,F	48:18–19
12.	D	11:6–8	35.	B	53:2
13.	C	13:17–19	36.	B,F	56:4–7
14.	E	14:4, 25, 29	37.	C	58:5–7
15.	E	16:2	38.	A,E,F	60:5, 6
16.	A	18:1–2	39.	D,E	64:1–2
17.	B,D,E	19:2, 5–6, 16	40.	D	66:24
18.	E	22:1, 5			
19.	B	23:1, 3			
20.	A	25:6–8	Super Challenges:		
21.	E	27:1	#1: The kings of the		
22.	A	28:1–8	earth (24:21–22)		
23.	A,E,F	29:6	#2: the palms of His		
24.	D	30:2–3	hands (49:16)		

~JEREMIAH~
(c. 740–700 B.C.)

1. **Jeremiah was the son of:**
   A. King Josiah
   B. A priest named Hilkiah
   C. A peasant farmer
   D. Isaiah

2. **All of these were signs given to Jeremiah, regarding his calling as a prophet, EXCEPT:**
   A. The Lord speaking to him during a vision, in which he was "asleep" for three days and nights
   B. The Lord touching Jeremiah's mouth with His hand
   C. A vision of an almond tree
   D. A vision of a boiling pot

3. **The house of Israel looked to whom/what as their mothers and fathers?**
   A. The pagan gods and goddesses
   B. The trees and stones
   C. The earth and the sea
   D. Their birth parents only
   E. The stars and constellations

4. **According to Jeremiah, what did the Lord say His people would no longer need to remember after He rewarded them?**
   A. Burnt offerings
   B. The commandments of the law
   C. Their social security number
   D. The ark of the covenant
   E. The temple sacrifices

5. **What THREE examples of vanity did Jeremiah say Zion would display in the day of desolation?**
   A. Clothing itself in crimson
   B. Putting on sweet-smelling fragrances
   C. Wearing Calvin Klein sweaters
   D. Adorning itself in gold
   E. Enlarging its eyes with paint
   F. Embellishing its beds with flowers

6. **From what direction did Jeremiah say the enemy would come?**

In Chapter 10, upon what group of people did Jeremiah ask God to "pour out His fury"?

   A. North
   B. South
   C. East
   D. West
   E. Above

7. **Jeremiah said that in the cities of Judah and the streets of Jerusalem cakes were being baked for:**
   A. Gods made of bronze
   B. The priests of Baal
   C. Sara Lee
   D. Immoral men
   E. The queen of heaven

8. **The judgment of God's people in Chapter 9 included: (three answers)**
   A. Driving away birds and animals from the land
   B. Turning Jerusalem into a heap of ruins
   C. Scattering the people among the Gentiles
   D. Sending a serious computer glitch at the year zero
   E. Bringing famine and starvation
   F. Sending great pestilence and sickness

9. **Which statement most accurately reflects God's analysis of idol worship in Judah and Jerusalem?**

A. Only a handful of Judah's cities worshiped the true God, and Jerusalem was a poor example of holiness.

B. Although many still worshiped the Lord, the gods and goddesses of the pagans were being sacrificed to in Jerusalem and the cities of Judah.

C. Dagon, the idol of the Philistines, had ensnared Jerusalem, and Baal had captivated the people of Judah's main cities.

D. There seemed to be as many gods as there were cities of Judah, and Jerusalem had an altar for Baal on every street.

10. **In Chapter 13, God gave Jeremiah instructions to do all of the following things EXCEPT:**
A. Go and get a linen sash
B. Dip the sash in the Jordan River
C. Bury the sash in the rocks by the river
E. Go and dig up the sash

11. **God said that He would not be favorable toward these (evil) people even if which two men stood before Him?**
A. Jacob and Joseph
B. Barnum and Bailey
C. Abraham and David
D. Joshua and Caleb
E. Moses and Samuel

12. **What instructions did God give to Jeremiah concerning marriage?**
A. He was to marry a harlot in order to symbolize the relationship of God's people to Him.
B. He was to marry the daughter of a priest.
C. He was not to marry or have children in Judah.

D. He could marry only after three years of warning the people of the upcoming Babylonian captivity.

E. He told Jeremiah, "Marriage is a good institution, but who wants to live in an institution?"

13. **Where did God sent Jeremiah to learn a lesson about His ability to remake a nation?**
A. The potter's house
B. The Mid-Atlantic Ridge
C. The blacksmith's shop
D. The altar of Baal by the temple in Jerusalem
E. The miller's house

14. **What did Pashur, the head priest, do when he heard about Jeremiah's prophecies?**
A. Asked Jeremiah to speak to an assembly at the temple
B. Put out an order to have Jeremiah killed
C. Had Jeremiah whipped and put in prison
D. Had Jeremiah beaten and put in stocks

15. **Which of the following were part of Jeremiah's prophecies concerning Jehoiakim, king of Judah? (three answers)**
A. He would soon see the end of his reign.
B. No one would mourn for him at his death.
C. He would receive the burial of a donkey.
D. His family would die with him.
E. He would be dragged out of Jerusalem's gates.
F. He would be beheaded, and his head would be placed on a pole.
G. When his life was over, he would die.

16. **What did the Lord show Jeremiah in Chapter 24 to represent the portion of people He would protect and the portion that was accursed?**

A. An angel and a serpent

B. A skin of new (less-desirable) wine, and a skin of old (fine) wine

C. A chocolate cake and broccoli

D. A new vessel (jug) and a broken vessel

E. Two baskets of figs

17. **Jeremiah prophesied that the Israelite captivity under Babylon would last:**

A. 70 years

B. Until they could all spell "Nebuchadnezzar" backwards

C. "Until God saw the repentance of their hearts"

D. "For a season"

E. 40 years

18. **Who threatened to kill Jeremiah for prophesying in the house of the Lord about the fall of Judah?**
   A. The priests
   B. The prophets
   C. The people
   D. All the above

19. **In Chapter 27, God told Jeremiah to make yokes and deliver them by servant to the kings of the surrounding countries. What did this symbolize?**
   A. Through their idolatry, they had come under the yoke of sin.
   B. Because of their perversions, they were no better than the beasts.
   C. If they thought they could escape, the *yoke* was on them.
   D. God was about to bring them into bondage.
   E. If they agreed to come under the yoke of Babylon, they could save themselves from ruin.

20. **Who was Hananiah, and why did he die shortly after Jeremiah said he would?**
   A. He was the king of Judah who was allowing the practice of idolatry.
   B. He was a false prophet who disputed Jeremiah's prediction about the captivity in Babylon.
   C. He was a priest who was cursed by God for attempting to kill Jeremiah.
   D. He was a prince from Babylon who was coming to scout the territory for Nebuchadnezzar.
   E. He was the Hebrew precursor to Bob Dylan, except he couldn't sing quite as well.

21. **Which of the following did God tell Jeremiah to do in Chapter 30?**

A. Go to Babylon and prophesy to the captives
B. Try to keep his head down and his left arm straight
C. Offer no prophecy for one year
D. Approach Zedekiah, the king of Judah, to encourage him to rebel against Nebuchadnezzar
E. Write down all of the words God had spoken to him

22. **In Chapter 32, what did God tell Jeremiah to buy?**
    A. His freedom from the prison of Zedekiah
    B. Food and clothing for a widow named Hananeel
    C. Pork belly futures
    D. A field, which was owned by his cousin
    E. A ruby, which was to symbolize God's love for His people

King Sennacherib goes mountain climbing!
(c. 720 B.C.)

23. **What did Jeremiah tell King Zedekiah about his death?**
    A. "Being in captivity at the time of death will nullify the double indemnity clause in his life insurance policy."
    B. "The king will be pierced by a sword in a foreign land."
    C. "Zedekiah's death will be brutal and humiliating."
    D. "He will not taste death until all of my prophecies are fulfilled."
    E. "The king will die in peace."

24. **After one of Babylon's early sieges, the Israelites in Jerusalem agreed to a covenant; later they renegotiated, which upset Jeremiah and God. This covenant was about what?**

A. Destroying the remaining idols and altars to Baal
B. Fasting for God's protection of the uncaptured portions of Judah
C. Releasing all Hebrew slaves
D. Offering all of their gold and silver items to Nebuchadnezzar's ambassador as a symbol of peace

25. **In Chapter 36, Jeremiah dictated his prophetic words to a scribe who wrote them on a scroll. On Jeremiah's orders, he read it at the temple, and it was later delivered to King Jehoiakim. What was the king's reaction?**
A. He had the scribe severely beaten and imprisoned.
B. He had both the scribe and Jeremiah put in stocks and publicly humiliated for ten days.
C. He thought it was somewhat repetitive but appreciated the voice and good narrative quality.
D. He tore his clothes and fell on his face before God.
E. He cut up the scroll and burned it in the fire.

26. **Why did the tribe of Benjamin put Jeremiah in prison?**
A. Their princes found his prophesies bothersome.
B. One of his enemies there accused him of stealing.
C. He had not gotten permission to enter their gates.
D. He was accused of defecting to the Chaldeans.
E. He was caught jaywalking.

27. **Where had Jeremiah been placed when he was rescued by a eunuch named Ebed-Melech?**
A. In a large wooden box where Jeremiah could barely sit up
B. In a small cave with the entrance blocked
C. On a rooftop where he was exposed to the elements and nearly died
D. In a cistern with a mud floor

28. **Which of the following were true concerning the treatment of Jeremiah by the Babylonians after the conquest of Jerusalem?**
(three answers)
   A. He was put in chains and taken to Babylon.
   B. He was given freedom by the captain of the Babylonian guard.
   C. He was wounded by a sword but recovered.
   D. He was told he could stay in Jerusalem as long as he didn't go around lamenting.
   E. He hid from Nebuchadnezzar's guard because they had put out an order to kill him.
   F. He was given the option of a fairly good life in Babylon, staying in Judah, or essentially going wherever he wished.

   SUPER CHALLENGE #2

   Who was Jeremiah's scribe/secretary?

29. **What did Ishmael (an Ammonite) and his ten men do before they were stopped by the remaining forces?**
(three answers)
   A. Captured Jeremiah and five men who were with him
   B. Stole the remaining temple treasures which Nebuchadnezzar had ordered to be left there
   C. Killed the appointed governor of Judah
   D. Killed seventy men who were coming to the temple
   E. Carried away the king's daughters and several other captives
   F. Stole much of the remaining livestock in Jerusalem

30. **Where did Jeremiah warn the remnant of people who remained in Judah NOT to go?**
   A. Babylon
   B. Egypt

C. Samaria
D. The Bronx
E. Ammon

31. **When Jeremiah later confronted those who had gone to the place he warned them not to go (see previous question), they told him they had experienced trouble ever since they:**
    A. Made prunes a regular feature of their diet
    B. Started following Jeremiah's instructions
    C. Saw their friends and families carried off to Babylon
    D. Found themselves under a Gentile ruler
    E. Stopped sacrificing to the queen of heaven

32. **Chapter 46 begins a series of closing prophecies against various nations. The first was against Egypt and mentioned which THREE Egyptian allies?**
    A. The Nubians
    B. The Libyans

Top Ten Things Solomon Knew Nothing About

10. Laundry detergent
 9. Farm machinery (with exception of "concubines")
 8. Titanium drivers
 7. Stereo equipment
 6. Cooking
 5. Poverty
 4. "The Clapper"
 3. Typing
 2. Conquering level four on "Super Mario Brothers 3"
 1. The Blues

C. The Arabians
D. The Ethiopians
E. The Jordanians
F. The Lydians

33. Of what country did Jeremiah say "[he] has been at ease from his youth . . . nor has he gone into captivity . . . he is exceedingly proud."
A. Philistia
B. Moab
C. Samaria
D. Hamath

34. Which of the following THREE statements were part of Jeremiah's prophecy against Esau (Edom)?
A. "There shall not be one house left standing."
B. "No one shall remain there."
C. "Everyone who goes by it will be astonished and will hiss at its plagues."
D. "I will make you small among nations."
E. "Your wives and daughters will be ravished by strangers."
F. "Your cable TV will be down indefinitely."

35. According to Jeremiah's final prophecy, which nation was "a golden cup in the Lord's hand, that made all the earth drunk"?
A. Persia
B. Babylon
C. Egypt
D. Assyria
E. Margaritaville

36. When Jeremiah finished these last prognostications, he wrote them down and sent them with a man named Seraiah to be read publicly. Jeremiah told him

that after they were read, he should do what with the book?

A. "Return it to Jeremiah so that it could be preserved."

B. "Bury it in a potter's vessel at the gates of the city where it was read."

C. "Tie a stone to it and toss it in the Euphrates River."

D. "Send it to a few publishers to see if he could get a deal."

E. "Deliver them to Ezra as a part of the compilation of the Jews' history."

37. **Jeremiah 52 says that Nebuzaradan, the captain of the Babylonian guard, and his men did what THREE things?**

A. Burned the house of the Lord

B. Destroyed the Baal altars in the streets of Jerusalem

C. Broke down all the walls of Jerusalem

D. Assaulted many of the women

E. Looted the temple and took the utensils used by the priests

F. Stood on Solomon's porch and performed a scene from *Les Miserables*

Use tune from "Joy to the World" (Three Dog Night version)

Jeremiah was a prophet,
With a sad tale to tell:
"There's gonna be a really awful price to pay,
Does 'captivity' ring a bell?
Yeah, it seems like it should ring a bell!"

(Chorus)
Singin' boy, what a town,
Judah's goin' down
Listen to your prophet telling of your loss,
I got it straight from The Boss!

Now no one wants to hear it,
Their logic is all gone.
Every time I tell 'em that the end is near,
They just say, "babble on!'
Yeah, they tell me to babble on.

Chorus

ANSWERS TO JEREMIAH QUESTIONS

#	ANS	REF	#	ANS	REF
1.	B	1:1	25.	E	36:23
2.	A	1:9–13	26.	D	37:11–15
3.	B	2:27	27.	D	38:1–13
4.	D	3:16	28.	A,B,D	40:1–6
5.	A,D,E	4:30	29.	C,D,E	41:1–15
6.	A	6:1, 22	30.	B	42:14–22
7.	E	7:18	31.	E	44:17–18
8.	A,B,D	9:10, 11, 16	32.	B,D,F	46:9
9.	D	11:13	33.	B	46:11, 29
10.	B	13:1–11	34.	B,C,D	49:15, 17, 18
11.	E	15:1	35.	B	51:7
12.	C	16:1–3	36.	C	51:63
13.	A	18:2	37.	A,C,E	52:13, 14, 18
14.	D	20:1–2			
15.	B,C,E	22:18–19			
16.	E	24:1–10	Super Challenges:		
17.	A	25:11	#1: the Gentiles (10:25)		
18.	D	26:7–8	#2: Baruch (45:1)		
19.	E	27:1–15			
20.	B	28:1–17			
21.	E	30:2			
22.	D	32:6–9			
23.	E	34:5–6			
24.	C	34:8–22			

~LAMENTATIONS~

(c. 590–520 B.C.)

1. **In Jeremiah's opening stanza, he referred to Jerusalem as being which THREE things?**
   A. Sinful
   B. Lonely
   C. Evil
   D. A widow
   E. A slave
   F. Really boring

2. **Jeremiah said that the people who remained in Jerusalem were doing what?**
   A. Crying out for forgiveness
   B. Packing their belongings
   C. Visiting their lake homes
   D. Sacrificing to Nebuchadnezzar
   E. Trading their valuables for food in order to survive

3. **In Chapter 2, who did Jeremiah say destroyed the city?**
   A. The Babylonians
   B. The Israelites
   C. Satan
   D. The Lord
   E. None of the above

4. **Who did Jeremiah say sat in silence, wearing sackcloth and ashes?**

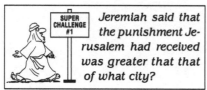

SUPER CHALLENGE #1 *Jeremiah said that the punishment Jerusalem had received was greater that that of what city?*

   A. The elders
   B. The priests
   C. Former Hebrew supermodels
   D. The widows
   E. The false prophets

5. **All of the following took place in Chapter 3 EXCEPT:**
   A. Jeremiah's consideration that God has allowed him to suffer exceedingly

Top Ten Old Testament Restaurants

10. Papa Job's: "We boil everything!"
9. Manna King: "Limited Locations"
8. The Ark Restaurant and Deli: "Buy one, get one free"
7. The Olive Oil Garden
6. Kosher Kavern
5. Pisgah Hut
4. Jonah's Seafood of Nineveh: "We know fish inside and out."
3. Goliath's Big Boy Restaurant
2. The Top O' the Tower: "Menus in six languages"
1. McDaniel's: "When you hear your stomach growl"

B. Jeremiah's reaffirmation of God's mercy

C. Jeremiah's desire to see his enemies punished

D. Jeremiah's vision for future restoration of Judah

6. **What had the "compassionate women" of Jerusalem done to their children in order to survive?**

A. Sold them to strangers

B. Prostituted them

C. Cooked and eaten them

D. Sent them out searching for scraps

Who Am I?

Emotionally unstable, alarmist. Has been known as the "weeping prophet." Is reported to have taken a long trip to bury his underwear on the banks of a foreign river.

JEREMIAH

7. **According to Jeremiah, which FOUR of the following were results of the fall of Jerusalem?**

A. The women in Zion were ravished.

B. The priests were burned alive.

C. Journalists became pushy.

D. Princes were hung up by their hands.

E. Young men ground at the millstones.

F. Elders were not respected.

G. The prophets were atoned.

EXTRA! EXTRA!

Siddhartha Guatama Buddha invents new religion!
(c. 521 B.C.)

ANSWERS TO LAMENTATIONS QUESTIONS

#	ANS	REF	#	ANS	REF
1.	B,D,E	1:1	7.	A,D, E,F	5:11–13
2.	C	1:11			
3.	D	2:1–8			
4.	A	2:10			
5.	D	3:1–18, 22, 35, 64	Super Challenge:		
6.	C	4:10	#1: Sodom (4:6)		

~EZEKIEL~

(c. 600–570 B.C.)

1. **Ezekiel's first vision was:**
   A. The valley of dry bones
   B. Four creatures inside a whirlwind
   C. A serpent rising up from the sea
   D. A bronze statue with clay feet
   E. Nebuchadnezzar in a kick-boxing match with Jackie Chan

2. **When God first spoke to Ezekiel, he told him to do all of the following EXCEPT:**
   A. Stand up on his feet
   B. Go to the house of Israel
   C. Eat a scroll with God's words on it
   D. Make a long staff of acacia wood
   E. To not fear the words of others

3. **God told Ezekiel that if he did not warn the people about their sin, the result would be:**
   A. Their blood on his hands
   B. Him dying alone
   C. Israel's death in captivity
   D. His raising up another prophet to take Ezekiel's place

4. **Which one of the following was NOT one of the signs found in Ezekiel 4?**
   A. Ezekiel drawing a picture of Jerusalem on a clay tablet
   B. A small child holding a ruby
   C. Ezekiel lying on his side for over a year

D. Ezekiel making bread over a fire fueled by cow manure

5. **In Chapter 5, God instructed Ezekiel to shave all of the hair off his head and beard and then divide it into equal portions. Which THREE things was he to do with the hair?**
(three answers)
   A. Bury some of it near the River Chebar
   B. Deliver it to Nebuchadnezzar
   C. Eat some of it
   D. Race it against a tortoise
   E. Strike around some of it with his sword
   F. Scatter it in the wind
   G. Burn it in the middle of the city

6. **Which of these were included in God's judgment of Israel, subsequent to Ezekiel's shaving?**
(four answers)
   A. A third of them would die of pestilence.
   B. The Babylonians would work thousands of them to death.

C. Wild beasts would attack them.

D. A plague of disease would fall upon them.

E. Fathers would eat sons, and sons would eat fathers.

F. Many would drown trying to flee across the river.

G. One third would fall by the sword.

7. **In Chapter 7, who/what did God say would possess the houses which formerly belonged to the Jews?**
   A. Jackals
   B. The wind
   C. The worst of the Gentiles
   D. No one
   E. Persian punkers

8. **Who/what were the people worshiping in the vision Ezekiel experienced in Chapter 8?**
   A. Tammuz (a Sumerian god)
   B. Asherah (female counterpart to Baal)
   C. The ground their wives walked on
   D. The sun
   E. An ox made of gold (named Isned)

9. **Who was spared from slaughter by the six men with battle-axes according to Ezekiel's next vision?**
   A. Only widows and young children
   B. Just one guy who was carrying an UZI
   C. Those with a mark on their forehead
   D. No one
   E. Gentiles

10. **The "wheels" that Ezekiel saw each had four different faces. Which of these was NOT one of the faces?**
    A. The face of a ram
    B. the face of a man
    C. The face of a cherub
    D. The face of a lion
    E. The face of an eagle

11. **Which THREE of the following were the punishments for the false prophets?**
    A. They were not allowed to lead sacrifices.
    B. They all had to put bumper stickers on the back of their chariots which read: "Don't follow me, I'm a false prophet."
    C. They were not to be in the records of Israel.
    D. They were not to enter into the land of Israel.
    E. Their heads were to be shaved.
    F. They were not to be in the Lord's assembly.

12. **The false prophetesses likewise came under God's scrutiny. They were doing all of the following EXCEPT:**
    A. Sewing magic charms on their sleeves
    B. Making veils of various sizes
    C. Causing the death of the innocent through deception
    D. Placing curses on the true prophets of the Lord

13. **God told Ezekiel that which three men delivered themselves by their righteousness?**
    A. Noah, Abraham, and Lot
    B. Noah, Daniel, and Job
    C. Moses, Aaron, and Joshua
    D. Aaron, Caleb, and David
    E. Larry, Curly, and Moe

14. **In Chapter 16, God compares Jerusalem to:**
    A. A vineyard that He created and maintained
    B. An abandoned infant that He rescued
    C. A field of wheat that had been overrun by wild beasts
    D. A golden bracelet that has been buried in the mud
    E. A grocery cart with a front wheel that keeps sticking.

15. **Which TWO cities did God say through Ezekiel were the sisters of the "harlot" (Israel)?**
   A. Tyre
   B. Gary, Indiana
   C. Sodom
   D. Samaria
   E. Ashdod

16. **Each of the following statements were included in Ezekiel's Chapter 18 description of a just man EXCEPT:**
   A. He has not "eaten on the mountains."
   B. He has not "approached a woman during her impurity."
   C. He "offers sacrifices at the appointed times."

Top Ten Visions Ezekiel Never Predicted

10. The Blizzard of '78
9. A man in a dark mask with a light saber
8. Indoor plumbing
7. How everyone would be wearing silver suits and driving their spaceships to work.
6. The Beatles first appearance on Ed Sullivan
5. Seeing an ice skater popped on the knee with a tire iron
4. Eurodollars
3. The final episode of M*A*S*H
2. Dollywood
1. His own—he was always so embarrassed about wearing glasses.

D. He has "given bread to the hungry."

E. He has not "exacted usury."

17. **According to Chapter 21, when the king of Babylon stood at the "fork in the road" trying to decide whether to go to Jerusalem or Rabbah (in Ammon), he used three types of divining. I've added a fourth. Can you find it?**

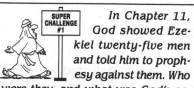

In Chapter 11, God showed Ezekiel twenty-five men and told him to prophesy against them. Who were they, and what was God's accusation against them?

A. Viewing constellations

B. Shaking arrows (casting lots)

C. Consulting images (idols)

D. Looking at the liver (probably of a slaughtered animal)

18. **Ezekiel 23 is about two sisters, Oholah and Oholibah, who were harlots. Who did they symbolize?**

A. Jerusalem and Samaria

B. Egypt and Babylon

C. Babylon and Assyria

D. Ammon and Moab

19. **What FOUR things from this list did Ezekiel say her enemies will remove from Oholibah?**

A. Her seductive smile

B. Her beautiful jewelry

C. Her ears

D. Her plantar's warts

E. Her perfumes and fragrances

F. Her clothes

G. Her nose

H. Her idols of bronze

20. **After the parable of the boiling pot in Chapter 24, Ezekiel suffered the loss of his:**

A. Son

B. Driver's license

C. Sight
D. Wife
E. Hearing

21. God referred to what city as the "gateway of the peoples"?
   A. Damascus
   B. Jerusalem
   C. Sidon
   D. St. Louis
   E. Joppa

22. God said through Ezekiel that the prince of Tyre was wiser than:
   A. David
   B. Solomon
   C. Most Jerry Springer fans
   D. The angels
   E. Daniel

23. Who was referred to as "the great monster who lies in the midst of his rivers"?
   A. Nebuchadnezzar of Babylon
   B. Sennacherib of Assyria
   C. Pharaoh of Egypt
   D. King Cyrus of Persia
   E. Mr. Legs, the octopus

24. When Ezekiel discussed the nations in "the Pit" (Chapter 32), all of these appeared EXCEPT:
   A. Egypt
   B. Babylon
   C. Assyria
   D. Edom
   E. Elam
   F. Tubal

25. God said that the false shepherds had neglected feeding the sheep and would be punished. The shepherd that He will establish over the people is:
    A. The Messiah
    B. Daniel
    C. Abraham
    D. Alan Shephard
    E. David

26. When God returns the nation of Israel from among the nations and restores the land, Ezekiel said God would do all of the following EXCEPT:
    A. Restore the sacrifices
    B. Cleanse the people from their filthiness
    C. Multiply the grain
    D. Increase the fruit of the trees
    E. Give them a new heart and spirit

27. What THREE things happened just before the bones "came together" in Ezekiel's vision of the dry bones?
    A. There was a noise.
    B. A bright light shown from the heavens.
    C. Ezekiel was suddenly weakened.
    D. There was a rattling.
    E. Ezekiel prophesied.

28. What THREE elements will be part of God's judgment on Gog for attacking Israel "in the latter days"?
    A. Violent winds
    B. Great hailstones
    C. Extensive dental work without *freezing*
    D. Attacks by wild beasts
    E. Starvation
    F. Fire
    G. Flooding rain

29. Which of the following were true concerning the aftermath of the destruction of Gog's forces? (two answers)

A. Their money would no longer carry the inscription: "In Gog We Trust."

B. The enemies' weapons of war would be burned as a heat source for seven years.

C. Twelve thousand captured soldiers of Gog would serve as Israel's slaves "for a generation."

D. It would take Israel seven months to bury all of the enemy dead.

E. It would take seventy months for the destroyed lands of Israel to rejuvenate.

30. When Ezekiel viewed the new city, what did he see on the gateposts of the outer court?

A. Lambs

B. Palm trees

C. Crosses

D. The Star of David

E. Bird droppings

SUPER CHALLENGE #2

As Ezekiel was looking through one of the gates, and the glory of God shone upon them. From which direction did God's glory come?

31. What were the two faces of the cherubs in the temple?

A. The face of an eagle

B. The face of a lamb

C. The face of a lion

D. The face of a man

E. The face of a mountain

32. Three types of offerings were to be made by the priests in the holy chambers. Which of these was NOT among them:

A. The grain offering

B. The peace offering

C. The sin offering
D. The trespass offering

Greek doctor discovers "veins" and "arteries!"
(*c.* 600 B.C.)

33. **Which of the following were rules applying to the Levites who were again to serve as priests in this new temple? (three answers)**
   A. They were not to marry.
   B. They were not to wear wool in the inner courts.
   C. They were to keep their hair well-trimmed.
   D. They were to wait at least an hour after eating before going swimming.
   E. They were to appoint judges from each tribe to serve the people in controversies.
   F. They were not to drink wine in the inner court.

34. **On what TWO days were the people to worship at the east gate of the temple?**
   A. The Sabbaths
   B. Passover (14th day of first month)
   C. Christmas
   D. Days of the New Moons
   E. Unleavened Bread Feast (the next day)

35. **Which of the following are true concerning the river that flowed from the temple? (three answers)**
   A. When Ezekiel first stood in it, it came only to his ankles.
   B. It was to serve as a natural boundary between lands occupied by the Israelites and lands occupied by Gentiles.

C. The river flowed around the city and returned to itself.
D. The river had healing powers.
E. There was a "no wake" rule in effect.
F. It held a multitude of fish.

36. **Ezekiel closes with the city being divided among the tribes of Israel, and he tells us its name. For your final Ezekiel question: Name that city!**
A. The New Jerusalem
B. Jehovah Junction
C. THE LORD IS THERE
D. Holiness and Peace
E. YAHWEH IS OUR GOD

ANSWERS TO EZEKIEL QUESTIONS

#	ANS	REF	#	ANS	REF
1.	B	1:4–14	21.	B	26:2
2.	D	2:1, 3, 6; 3:1	22.	E	28:3
3.	A	3:18–21	23.	C	29:3
4.	B	4:1–17	24.	B	32:22–32
5.	E,F,G	5:1–4	25.	D	34:23
6.	A,C, E,G	5:10–17	26.	A	36:23–30
			27.	A,D,E	37:7
7.	C	7:24	28.	B,F,G	38:22
8.	A,D	8:14, 16	29.	B,D	39:9–10, 12
9.	C	9:4–7	30.	B	40:26
10.	A	10:14	31.	C,D	41:19
11.	C,D,F	13:9	32.	B	42:13
12.	D	13:17–23	33.	B,C,G	44:15–31
13.	B	14:14	34.	A,D	46:1–3
14.	B	16:1–14	35.	A,D,F	47:1–12
15.	C,D	16:45–48	36.	C	48:35
16.	C	18:5–9			
17.	A	21:21			
18.	A	23:4	Super Challenges:		
19.	B,C, F,G	23:25, 26	#1: the princes (evil counselors) (11:1–4)		
20.	D	24:18	#2: east (43:1, 4)		

∾DANIEL∾
(c. 600–530 B.C.)

1. **Daniel was one of the Israelites carried into Babylonian captivity. He was among those being groomed for:**
   A. Leadership in the Babylonian army
   B. Service in the king's palace
   C. Teaching in the Babylonian cities
   D. A judgeship
   E. A position as lion tamer in the Babylonian Circus

2. **Since they didn't want to defile themselves by eating what the king was serving, Daniel convinced the chief eunuch to bring him and his friends what substitute?**
   A. Meat from non-split-hooved animals
   B. Strictly fruits and water
   C. Spaghetti-O's
   D. Vegetables
   E. Water only

3. **When Nebuchadnezzar summoned his astrologers, magicians, and sorcerers concerning his dream, what did he order them to do?**
   A. Interpret the dream
   B. Tell him what he had dreamed and give an interpretation
   C. Sing him an old Chaldean lullaby
   D. Cure him of his insomnia
   E. Find someone who could properly explain the dream

4. **What did Nebuchadnezzar decree when his assistants didn't offer satisfactory results?**
   A. That all magicians and astrologers were to be banished from the land
   B. That any man who could fulfill the king's edict would be made a prince and be given the king's daughter as a wife
   C. That all the wise men of Babylon should be killed
   D. That the sorcerers and their families were to be beheaded

5. **What was Daniel's reward for explaining the king's dream?**
   (three answers)
   A. He was given many great gifts.
   B. He married Nebuchadnezzar's daughter.
   C. He was made ruler over the whole province of Babylon.
   D. He was given the king's gold signet ring.

E. He was made chief administrator over all of the wise men.

F. He got to stay up an hour later at night.

6. **Why did Nebuchadnezzar have Daniel's friends and fellow administrators, Shadrach, Meshach, and Abed-Nego, cast into the fiery furnace?**

A. They would not worship his golden idol.

B. They were part of a conspiracy to overthrow him.

C. He was just in a bad mood.

D. They refused to carry out his order to kill Daniel.

E. They wanted to leave Babylon and re-establish Jerusalem.

7. **Nebuchadnezzar's next dream was about a tree which grew up into the heavens and then was cut down. Daniel told the king that the tree symbolized:**

A. Israel

B. Babylon

C. Communism

D. Nebuchadnezzar

E. Assyria

> *By what river was Daniel standing when he saw a man "clothed in linen, whose waist was girded in gold"?*
>
> SUPER CHALLENGE #1

8. **What punishment did God dole out to the king in order to humble him?**

A. He became leprous for one year.

B. His entire kingdom was given to Daniel.

C. His wife, the queen, died.

D. He was made like a beast for a period of time.

9. **Who was king of Babylon when the "handwriting on the wall" incident occurred?**

A. Nebuchadnezzar

B. Belshazzar

C. Darius

D. Cyrus

E. Don

Persian coins bear likeness of King!
(*c.* 550 B.C.)

10. **Why was Daniel cast into the lions' den?**
    A. He spoke against King Darius.
    B. The queen falsely accused him of making improper advances toward her.
    C. He forgot to floss one morning.
    D. He refused to bow to the idols of the Medes.
    E. He violated an ordinance against prayer.

11. **Daniel's vision from Chapter 7 involved four beasts. Which of these was NOT a beast Daniel described?**
    A. A lion with eagle's wings
    B. A bear with three ribs in its mouth
    C. A ram with eyes like fire
    D. A leopard with bird's wings
    E. A ten-horned beast with huge iron teeth

12. **Who appeared to Daniel just prior to the revelation concerning the seventy weeks?**
    A. Gabriel
    B. Helen Hunt in a whirlwind
    C. A spirit like the Son of Man
    D. Moses
    E. Michael, the archangel

13. **When the messenger told Daniel of future battles and kings, he mentioned several nations. Which of these was NOT named:**

A. Persia
B. Greece
C. Cyprus
D. Rome
E. Egypt

14. **What did the messenger tell Daniel would happen before "all these things [were] finished"?**
A. The Son of God would arrive in His glory.
B. The power of the holy people would be completely shattered.

Top Ten Things They Did to Shadrach, Meshach, and Abed-Nego After Removing Them from the Fiery Furnace

10. Looked to see if the little timer had popped up
9. Inspected their clothing to see if it was made from asbestos
8. Fired them from the railroad because they were lousy conductors
7. Asked them if they wanted to go outside and smoke
6. Told them they weren't so hot after all
5. Poked them with a fork to see if they were done
4. Asked them to go back in the furnace and change the filter
3. Accused them of not paying the gas bill
2. Told 'em: "If you can't stand the heat, stay out of the fiery furnace"
1. Asked them to sign the register

C. The evil one would assume an earthly throne.
D. There would be great signs in the heavens.
E. There would be earthquakes in various places.

Q. What happened to Daniel and his friends after they exited the fiery furnace?

A. They became flamous.

ANSWERS TO DANIEL QUESTIONS

#	ANS	REF		#	ANS	REF
1.	B	1:4		11.	C	7:3–7
2.	D	1:8–15		12.	A	9:21
3.	B	2:5		13.	D	11:2, 30, 42
4.	C	2:12		14.	B	12:7
5.	A,C,E	2:48				
6.	A	3:1–18				
7.	D	4:20–22		Super Challenge:		
8.	D	4:33		#1: The Tigris (10:4)		
9.	B	5:1–5				
10.	E	6:4–16				

~HOSEA~

(c. 760–720 B.C.)

1. **What is the first thing God told Hosea to do?**
   A. "Confront Israel about its sin of idolatry."
   B. "Marry the virgin daughter of King Jeroboam."
   C. "Choose a wife from the harlots."
   D. "Sever the little finger of your left hand."
   E. "Get outta Dodge before the curtain falls."

2. **When Hosea redeemed his property in Chapter 3, what was his medium of exchange?**
   A. Gold
   B. Silver and barley
   C. Copper and wheat
   D. Doves and wine

3. **Hosea said that the people asked counsel from:**
   A. Their wooden idols
   B. Their golden calves
   C. Their judges and magistrates
   D. Their evil rulers

4. **In Chapter 6, what TWO things did God say He desired more than sacrifices and burnt offerings?**
   A. Keeping of the commandments
   B. Fleeing idolatry
   C. Knowledge of God
   D. Mercy
   E. Honesty

5. **Hosea said that in Israel and Samaria they "sow the wind and reap _____."**

A. Much evil
B. The whirlwind
C. Fifty breezes per acre
D. Fire and damnation
E. Biting rains

He is a tender and loving man who clearly follows God's will, but his wife's occupation is quite risqué!

HOSEA

6. What city did Hosea say would bury the Israelites?
A. Tyre
B. Jerusalem
C. Heshbon
D. Damascus
E. Memphis

7. In Chapter 11, God compared Israel to:
A. A foolish lamb headed for slaughter
B. A rerun of "Green Acres"
C. A harlot who would not return to her husband

Top Ten Attractions at Old Testament Festivals

10. Isaiah's "Guess your age, weight and date of death" game
9. "Old Elijah's Wild Ride"
8. Pharaoh in dunk tank
7. David's "Name that Psalm" game
6. Bobbing for Adam's apples
5. Babylonian Bingo
4. Watching Samson knock down the grandstand
3. Behemoth harness racing
2. Nehemiah's wine-tasting seminars
1. Unleavened funnel cakes

D. A young boy that He nurtured

E. A virgin field being trampled by wild beasts

8. **Who does Hosea say "took his brother by the heel in the womb"?**
   A. Cain
   B. Achilles' brother
   C. Jacob
   D. Seth
   E. Joseph

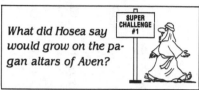

What did Hosea say would grow on the pagan altars of Aven?

SUPER CHALLENGE #1

9. **In God's anger toward His wayward people, He was like what THREE animals?**
   A. A tiger
   B. A bear
   C. A behemoth
   D. A lion
   E. A leopard
   F. A mongoose

10. **The book of Hosea closes with:**
    A. Hosea's sadness over Israel's approaching fall
    B. God's strong anger regarding His people's idolatry
    C. Hosea and Gomer singing a duet of "Happy Trails to You"
    D. God's promise of healing and restoration
    E. Hosea's resolve to separate himself from evildoers

EXTRA! EXTRA!

Dinnerware now available in iron!
(*c.* 750 B.C.)

ANSWERS TO HOSEA QUESTIONS

#	ANS	REF		#	ANS	REF
1.	C	1:2		9.	B,D,E	13:7–8
2.	B	3:2		10.	D	14:1–7
3.	A	4:12				
4.	C,D	6:6				
5.	B	8:7		Super Challenge:		
6.	E	9:6		#1: thorns and thistles		
7.	D	11:1–4		(10:8)		
8.	C	12:2–3				

Q. Why did Hosea have coal dust all over himself?

A. He was a minor prophet.

~JOEL~
(c. 800–600 B.C.)

1. **With what TWO problems was Joel initially concerned?**
   A. An attack by the Philistines
   B. The banning of "Great Goliath" golf clubs by the Hebrew PGA
   C. A locust attack
   D. A serious flooding of the Jordan that caused great loss of crops
   E. A drought
   F. A serious hailstorm

2. **Who cried out to God at the end of the first chapter? (two answers)**
   A. Motherless children
   B. Joel
   C. The priests
   D. The beasts
   E. No one

3. **Joel said "the day of the Lord is great and very terrible." Which THREE of the following were part of his description of the Lord's army?**
   A. They did not push one another.
   B. They were wounded but did not fall.
   C. They were tall like the giants of old.
   D. Their faces were fixed like wooden images.
   E. They ran like mighty men.
   F. The earth quaked before them.
   G. Their camouflage clothing made them hard to see.

4. All of these would precede the "day of the Lord" EXCEPT:

SUPER CHALLENGE #1 *Where did Joel say God would gather all of the nations for judgment?*

A. God would pour out His Spirit on all flesh.
B. The mountains would crumble.
C. The moon would be turned to blood.
D. Young men would see visions.
E. God would show wonders in the heavens and earth.

5. The Israelites had been scattered by their enemies. A boy has been exchanged for _____, and a girl for _____.
A. A horse; barley
B. A hot dog; the bun
C. Silver; a potter's vessel
D. A harlot; wine
E. Goat's milk; wheat

6. What TWO cities did God warn concerning His retaliation?

A. Tyre
B. Ashdod
C. Sidon
D. Gath
E. Samaria

7. **Joel closed by telling us that the Lord dwells in:**
   A. Zion
   B. The souls of His people
   C. His temple
   D. Judah
   E. The heavens
   F. Noah's Ark

Greeks settle in Spain!
(c. 850 B.C.)

ANSWERS TO JOEL QUESTIONS

#	ANS	REF	#	ANS	REF
1.	C,E	1:3–4, 16–18	Super Challenge:		
2.	B,D	1:19, 20	#1: The Valley of		
3.	A,E,F	2:7–10	Jehoshaphat (3:2)		
4.	B	2:28–31			
5.	D	3:3			
6.	A,C	3:4			
7.	A	3:21			

~AMOS~
(c. 760–700 B.C.)

1. **What was Amos' occupation?**
   A. Herdsman
   B. Potter
   C. Priest
   D. Coppersmith
   E. Air-traffic controller

2. **What major event took place two years after Amos' ministry?**
   A. An earthquake
   B. A deadly windstorm (probably a cyclone)
   C. An extensive famine
   D. The overthrow of King Jeroboam
   E. The siege of the Assyrians

3. **Israel was prophesied against for several reasons. Find THREE of them in this list:**
   A. They worshiped gods of stone.
   B. They sold the righteous for silver.
   C. They perverted the way of the humble.
   D. They constantly slammed the refrigerator door.
   E. They lay down by the altar on clothes taken in pledge.
   F. Their tongues were quick to lie.

4. **Where was it to be proclaimed to "assemble on the mountains of Samaria"?**
   (two answers)
   A. The hills of Zion
   B. The palaces of Ashdod
   C. The forests of Lebanon

D. The pool halls of Chicago

E. The palaces of Egypt

5. **In Chapter 4, God mentioned several things He had done in an effort to call His people back to Him. Find THREE of them in this list:**

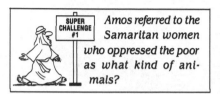

SUPER CHALLENGE #1 *Amos referred to the Samaritan women who oppressed the poor as what kind of animals?*

A. Took away bread and food in various places

B. Allowed their children to die of disease

C. Put sugar in their gas tanks

D. Withheld rain

E. Infected their cattle with sickness

F. Killed men and horses

G. Caused barrenness among their women

6. **Amos said that those who desired "the day of the Lord" were misguided. All of these are descriptions of it EXCEPT:**

DID YOU KNOW that Amos worked as a sheepbreeder, and he had a seasonal job tending sycamore fruit? He would slit these "poor man's figs" to make them sweeter and softer for market. He did all this in Tekoa, a city in Judah, approximately ten miles south of Jerusalem.

A. It will be darkness rather than light.

B. It will be like fleeing from a lion and meeting a bear.

C. There will be much screaming and wailing and no laughter.

D. It will be like leaning against a wall, only to have your hand bitten by a serpent.

7. **After Amos pleaded with God (in Chapter 7), God relented from serving two potential disasters upon Israel. What were they?**

A. A locust attack

B. A plague of leprosy

C. A recall of all sport utility vehicles

D. A conflict of fire

E. An attack by the army of Gath

8. **God said that the famine He sent would be a famine of:**

   A. Bread and water

   B. Hearing the Lord's words

   C. Righteousness

   D. Freedom

Quite backward and unpolished. With some seminary training he might have promise, but he has a bit of a hang-up with the wealthy.

AMOS

9. **What TWO events did Amos say would be a part of Israel's restoration?**

   A. The enemies of God's people would be cut asunder.

   B. The spirit of David would reign in Jerusalem.

   C. The temple ruins would be raised up.

   D. The captives would be brought back to Israel.

   E. The "Idols 'R' Us" store would be demolished.

Etruscans invent horse-drawn chariots!
(c. 750 B.C.)

ANSWERS TO AMOS QUESTIONS

#	ANS	REF	#	ANS	REF
1.	A	1:1	8.	B	8:11
2.	A	1:1	9.	C,D	9:11, 14
3.	B,C,E	2:6–8			
4.	B,E	3:9			
5.	A,D,F	4:6, 7, 10	Super Challenge:		
6.	C	5:18–19	#1: Cows (4:1)		
7.	A,D	7:1–6			

~OBADIAH~

(c. 590–550 B.C.)

1. **Obadiah's short book was a judgment on:**
   A. Ammon
   B. Judah
   C. Edom
   D. Moab
   E. Philistia

2. **Where did Obadiah say the people of this land dwelt?**
   A. In the clefts of the rock
   B. In the great fields of wheat
   C. In the shade of the old apple tree

D. In the Land of Lot

E. By the Jordan

3. **Obadiah was ostensibly upset at this nation because:**

First theatre performance!
(c. 570 B.C.)

   A. They had made an extensive business of dealing in idols.
   B. They had sold their own people into slavery.
   C. They had consistently ignored God's call to repentance.
   D. They had been an enemy to Jerusalem and Judah.
   E. They never did their chores, and he had to do them instead.

4. **In the final verse, Obadiah said the kingdom would be:**

Top Ten Reasons Solomon Grew So Bored

10. Figured out early on how to get Mario to the last screen and rescue the princess
9. No instant replay
8. Only people who were intellectually capable of arguing with him decided against it
7. No good movies without Spielberg
6. Couldn't find a way to make Proverbs funny
5. Shulamite woman needed some space
4. Ran out of colors to paint the palace
3. Couldn't get gas for his yacht
2. Bowling tournament was cancelled
1. If you've seen one Riverdance, you've seen 'em all

A. "hotels and condos"
B. "conquered by its enemies"
C. "the LORD's"
D. "held until the last days"
E. "desolate and barren"

ANSWERS TO OBADIAH QUESTIONS

#	ANS	REF	#	ANS	REF
1.	C	1:1	3.	D	1:10–14
2.	A	1:3	4.	C	1:21

～JONAH～

(c. 800–750 B.C.)

1. **Although God called Jonah to go to _____, he instead set out for _____.**
   A. Babylon; Jerusalem
   B. Nineveh; Tarshish
   C. Canada; Disney World
   D. Egypt; Lebanon
   E. Antioch; Ephesus

2. **The ship on which Jonah was a passenger encountered a "mighty tempest." When the captain came to Jonah, what was Jonah doing?**

A. Suffering from seasickness
B. Helping the sailors throw ballast overboard
C. Sleeping
D. Crying from fear
E. Praying that God would spare his life

3. **How did the crew find out that Jonah was responsible for their current trouble?**
   A. Jonah told them.
   B. They cast lots.
   C. One of the crew members recognized him.
   D. A voice from heaven told them.
   E. A raven landed on Jonah's shoulder.

4. **What happened in Nineveh when Jonah preached judgment upon the city?**

Top Ten Reasons Why Jonah Spent Three Days in a Fish

10. It was a weekend package.
9. The fish mistook him for a large herring.
8. Submarines hadn't been invented yet.
7. He was hoping to get on *Oprah*.
6. He wanted to one-up Jacques Cousteau.
5. He couldn't afford a Carnival cruise.
4. The fish considered it poetic justice since Jonah ate a lot of fish-sticks.
3. He was caught from behind while chasing the Little Mermaid.
2. He hoped to see the tropics, then realized there weren't any windows.
1. His Navy commander told him it was part of basic training.

A. The people repented.
B. He got his own Sunday morning radio show.
C. They put Jonah in the stocks and humiliated him.
D. The king had him imprisoned.
E. They laughed Jonah to scorn.

5. **What did God provide for Jonah, then take away?**
   A. Food and water
   B. Another prophet named Shirla, as a companion
   B. A bed at an inn
   B. A plant for shade
   C. A subscription to *Marine Biology* magazine

6. **Why did God say He was interested in Nineveh?**
   A. The people there followed His laws better than the Hebrews.
   B. Three great prophets were to come from that city.
   C. There were many people and much livestock.
   D. He was going to bring that city against Israel as a witness to His power.

Delphians worship Apollo!
(*c.* 770 B.C.)

ANSWERS TO JONAH QUESTIONS

#	ANS	REF	#	ANS	REF
1.	B	1:2–3	4.	A	3:1–10
2.	C	1:5–6	5.	D	4:6–7
3.	B	1:7	6.	C	4:11

~MICAH~

(c. 750–715 B.C.)

1. **Micah said that when the Lord came down to Samaria, which THREE of these things would happen?**
   A. The mountains would melt under Him.
   B. The valleys would split like wax by the fire.
   C. The waters of the Great Sea would surround the city.
   D. He would make Samaria a "heap of ruins."
   E. Men's hearts would pound with fear.

2. **What TWO things did Micah say that the evil covet and take by force?**
   A. Their neighbor's silver
   B. Fields
   C. Houses
   D. Warm-up jackets
   E. Wheat stored in barns
   F. Wives who are not their own

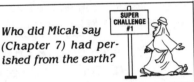

Who did Micah say (Chapter 7) had perished from the earth?

SUPER CHALLENGE #1

3. **In Chapter 3, Micah compared the evil of Israel's princes to:**
   A. Cannibalism
   B. Harlotry/prostitution
   C. The carnality of Sodom
   D. The foolishness of Pharaoh before the Exodus

4. **In the day that God rules Zion, He will call together all of these EXCEPT:**
   A. The lame
   B. The outcast
   C. The blind
   D. Those whom God had afflicted

5. What major prophecy appeared in Micah 5?
  A. The battle of Armageddon
  B. Jesus' birth in Bethlehem
  C. The seven-year tribulation period
  D. Mark McGuire's 1998 home run record
  E. The second destruction of the temple

6. What THREE things did Micah say God requires of His people?

 DID YOU KNOW that in Micah's day the prophets had been speaking lies for profit? They would proclaim peace to a nation so that another nation could prepare war against them. God hated this, and took away their prophetic gifts; this caused them great humiliation among the nations.

  A. To observe the laws of Moses
  B. To do justly
  C. To care for the widows and orphans
  D. To love mercy
  E. To flee from evil
  F. To walk humbly with God

7. According to Chapter 7, who are a man's enemies?
  A. Those who oppose his God
  B. The princes and judges
  C. His own desires
  D. The members of his own house

ANSWERS TO MICAH QUESTIONS

#	ANS	REF
1.	A,B,C	1:4–6
2.	B,C	2:2
3.	A	3:2–3
4.	C	4:6
5.	B	5:2
6.	B,D,F	6:8
7.	D	7:6

Super Challenge:
#1: The faithful man
(7:2)

Greek crafts flourish while farmers starve!
(*c.* 750 B.C.)

~NAHUM~

(c. 630–600 B.C.)

1. **Who was Nahum prophesying against?**
   A. Sennacherib and the Assyrian nation
   B. The tabloids
   C. Samaria
   D. Greece
   E. Nineveh

2. **What did Nahum say was the "dust of His [the Lord's] feet"?**
   A. The nations
   B. His enemies
   C. Clouds
   D. The deserts

3. **Which THREE pieces of advice were given as warning to the city?**

DINE HERE OFTEN?

A. "Man the fort!"
B. "Watch the road!"
C. "Hide the women and children!"
D. "Prepare to die!"
E. "Let every man come to the battle!"
F. "Strengthen your flanks!"
G. "Call out the Boy Scouts!"

4. **Nahum said the city's strongholds were weak, and compared them to:**
   A. Reeds blown by the autumn winds
   B. Clay vessels, which shatter when dropped
   C. The eggs of an ostrich
   D. A fig tree with ripened figs
   E. Ticky-tacky houses

5. **Lastly, Nahum compared the leaders of the city (commanders and captains) to what TWO things?**
   A. Locusts
   B. Flamingos
   C. Grasshoppers
   D. Mice
   E. The sloth
   F. Sparrows

ANSWERS TO NAHUM QUESTIONS

#	ANS	REF	#	ANS	REF
1.	E	1:1	4.	D	3:12
2.	C	1:3	5.	A,C	3:17
3.	A,B,F	2:1			

Pharaoh Nechos builds canal from Nile to Red Sea!
(c. 630 B.C.)

~HABAKKUK~
(c. 625–580 B.C.)

1. **Habakkuk's first question to God was essentially:**
   A. Why does my back hurt all the time?
   B. What is the meaning of life?
   C. When will You send a Redeemer?
   D. Why must the twelve tribes constantly war with one another?
   E. Why do You allow so much injustice?

2. **Who did God say He was raising up to judge Judah?**
   A. Assyria
   B. The armies of Pharaoh
   C. The Chaldeans (Babylonians)
   D. The Persians
   E. Lance Ito

3. **Which of these attributes did God ascribe to the proud man?**
   (three answers)
   A. He set himself upon a high place.
   B. He would never give you a ride in his Mercedes.
   C. He arrayed himself in splendid attire.
   D. His desire was as large as hell.
   E. He could not be satisfied.
   F. His soul was not upright.

4. **God's response to Habakkuk's question about judging one nation with another that's even more evil, ended with:**

A. "In latter days, I will destroy all evil from the earth."
B. "The Lord is in His holy temple; let all the earth keep silence before Him."
C. "And they, too, shall fall upon the sword of their own wrath and foolishness."
D. "My people have forgotten their God. My face is set against them, and with their enemies."

5. **When Habakkuk described God's wrath in Chapter 3, he asked God if He was angry at what TWO things?**

 DID YOU KNOW that *Habakkuk* is not a typical Hebrew name? It occurs only twice in the Old Testament. Some rabbis think it is related to the Hebrew word for *embrace,* and it could refer to the prophet's love for his people. Others think that the same word may refer to the prophet as one who wrestled with God. In either case, nothing is recorded about the prophet and his personal life.

A. The hills
B. The rivers
C. The sea
D. The creatures of the earth
E. The cities of Jacob

ANSWERS TO HABAKKUK QUESTIONS

#	ANS	REF	#	ANS	REF
1.	E	1:3–4	4.	B	2:20
2.	C	1:6	5.	B,C	3:8
3.	D,E,F	2:4–5			

Women's civil rights decline in Greece!
(c. 590 B.C.)

~ZEPHANIAH~

(c. 630–600 B.C.)

1. At the beginning of Chapter 1, God says He will utterly consume what from the land?
   A. Evil
   B. The idols
   C. The enemies of His people
   D. All things

2. Zephaniah said that in the "day of the Lord" the sounds of trouble will be heard in all of those places EXCEPT:

A. Maktesh (the marketplace)
B. The temples of Baal
C. The Fish Gate
D. The Second Quarter
E. The hills

3. **Moab and Ammon were to be judged like Sodom and Gomorrah. They will be overrun with:**
   (two answers)
   A. Weeds
   B. Door-to-door salesman
   C. Locusts and flies
   D. Salt pits
   E. Wild beasts

4. **This city shall become "a place for beasts to lie down, [and] everyone who passes by her will hiss and shake his fist."**
   A. Jerusalem
   B. Gilgal
   C. Damascus
   D. Terre Haute
   E. Nineveh

5. **Following the day of the Lord, who did Zephaniah say "shall do no unrighteousness"?**

   A. The Messiah
   B. The princes of Judah
   C. Politicians
   D. The new priests of the people
   E. The remnant of Israel

SUPER CHALLENGE #1 *What region of the country did God say He was setting aside for the shepherds with flocks, and the remnant of Judah?*

ANSWERS TO ZEPHANIAH QUESTIONS

#	ANS	REF	#	ANS REF
1.	D	1:2	Super Challenge:	
2.	B	1:10–11	#1: the seacoast (2:6–7)	
3.	A,D	2:9		
4.	E	2:13–15		
5.	E	3:13		

Nineveh destroyed by Babylonians and others!
(*c.* 620 B.C.)

～HAGGAI～
(c. 520–500 B.C.)

1. Haggai was upset at his people because:
   A. They were content to remain in Babylon while Jerusalem lay in ruins.
   B. They were building their own homes and ignoring the temple.
   C. They wanted him to cut his sermons down a little.
   D. They were talking about appointing a king.
   E. They were beginning to surround themselves with the trappings of idolatry.

2. All of the following were Haggai's examples of the people's frustrations EXCEPT:
   A. You have sown much but bring in little.
   B. You eat but do not have enough.
   C. You clothe yourself, but no one is warm.
   D. You run to and fro and yet stand still.
   E. The wage-earner puts his wages into a bag filled with holes.

3. Regarding the new temple, Haggai said:
   A. The glory of it would be greater than that of the former one.
   B. They would probably have to sue the architect for faulty design.
   C. Never again would God allow His dwelling place to be desecrated.
   D. It would represent God's renewed covenant with His people.
   E. God would dwell in it regardless of its size.

4. The question that God told Haggai to ask the priests concerned:
   A. Sexual immorality
   B. The Feast of Unleavened Bread
   C. Ceremonially unclean meat
   D. The duties of the temple
   E. Tithes

5. Whom did God say He had chosen as His "signet ring"?
   A. David
   B. Zerubbabel
   C. Haggai
   E. King Darius
   E. Jacob

Athlete of the Epoch— Milo of Crotona, six crowns at Olympic Games!
(c. 536 B.C.)

ANSWERS TO HAGGAI QUESTIONS

#	ANS	REF	#	ANS	REF
1.	B	1:4	4.	C	2:11–14
2.	D	1:6	5.	B	2:23
3.	A	2:9			

~ZECHARIAH~

(c. 520–510 B.C.)

1. **Whom did God tell Zechariah not to be like?**
   A. His fathers who rejected the prophets
   B. People who "slept in" on Sunday mornings
   C. The Israelites who put their own comfort ahead of the desires of the Lord
   D. The slothful men who remained in Babylon
   E. The false prophets who led the nation astray

2. **Zechariah's first "night vision" involved:**
   A. A two-headed creature rising from the sea
   B. A tower reaching into the heavens
   C. A man on a red horse, with other horses nearby
   D. A ram, a lion, an eagle and an owl
   E. A bowl of ice cream and a box of animal crackers

3. **In Chapter 2, what was the man with the measuring line going to do?**
   A. Measure the foundation for the new temple
   B. Measure the distance from Jerusalem to Samaria
   C. Destroy the second angel who sat in the golden chariot
   D. Measure the length and width of the city of Jerusalem

4. **A vision in Chapter 3 featured whom?**
   (three answers)
   A. Elijah
   B. Satan
   C. Abraham
   D. The Angel of the Lord

E. A priest named Joshua

F. King Hezekiah

G. The Mormon Tabernacle Choir

5. **What TWO types of "evildoers" were condemned by the curse of the flying scroll?**

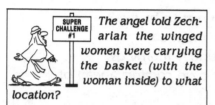
SUPER CHALLENGE #1 *The angel told Zechariah the winged women were carrying the basket (with the woman inside) to what location?*

A. Thieves

B. Idolaters

C. Perjurers

D. People who illegally park in handicap spaces

E. Adulterers

6. **When Zechariah asked the angel to explain the four chariots, each with a different colored team of horses, what did the angel say?**

A. They are the four winds, that blow across the earth.

B. They are four curses, which man must endure in the latter day.

C. They are just something we had left over from Ben-Hur.

D. They are four rulers, three of them evil, and one righteous.

E. They are the four spirits of heaven, who go before the Lord of the earth.

7. **In the days of Israel's restoration, who would approach a Jewish man for friendship, because of his affiliation with God?**

A. The Gentiles of many nations

B. Ten men from every language

C. His enemies, from past days, who sought his life

D. Foreign kings and princes

8. **This coastal city has "built herself a tower," and heaped up silver and gold. Zechariah said God would destroy it with fire.**

A. Ashdod
B. Tyre
C. Seattle
D. Sidon
E. Gaza

9. **God chose two staffs and named them "Beauty" and "Bonds." What became of the two staffs?**
   A. "Beauty" went off and made a Disney movie (with the beast), and Bonds signed a huge baseball contract.
   B. One was handed to Zechariah, and God kept the other.
   C. They were both placed in the front of the temple.
   D. They were both cut in two.
   E. One was burned in the fire; the other was given to Satan.

10. **In the day that God offered protection for Israel and Judah, He would perform all of the following against their enemies EXCEPT:**

A. Cause their sword tips to be like silk
B. Strike every horse with confusion
C. All who attempt to heave away (Jerusalem) will be cut in pieces
D. Strike every rider with madness
E. Strike the horses with blindness

11. **Which THREE from the following list were true, concerning Zechariah's prediction of the aftermath of Judah's salvation?**
    A. A fountain would cleanse the inhabitants of Jerusalem of their sins.
    B. The children would again be taught the ways of Jehovah God.
    C. Those artisans who crafted idols would be stoned to death.
    D. Violent video games would not be tolerated.
    E. The Feasting Days and Sacrifices would once again have holy meaning to the House of David.

Top Ten Things Not Predicted by Old Testament Prophets

10. E.T. would make it home.
 9. The Detroit Lions would win a Super Bowl.
 8. "The Never Ending Story" would really end.
 7. The hula-hoop
 6. Edsel would be a big hit.
 5. The Stock-Market Crash of '29
 4. Richard Simmons
 3. The return of Mr. Whipple
 2. Break up of the Beatles
 1. The resurgence of swing dancing

F. Anyone who prophesied would be killed by his parents.

G. The unclean spirit would be driven from the land.

12. Zechariah closed his book discussing the final attack on Jerusalem and a plague on its enemies. THREE aspects of the plague are included here:

A. The winds shall beat against their houses.

B. Their tongues shall dissolve in their mouths.

C. Their legs will go lame, and sores shall cover their feet.

D. They will constantly drop their hymnals while trying to sing in church, and everyone will make fun of them.

E. The horses, mules and livestock of the enemy will receive plagues as well.

F. Those who do not worship God at Jerusalem will suffer drought.

Rome is a republic!
(c. 520 B.C.)

ANSWERS TO ZECHARIAH QUESTIONS

#	ANS	REF		#	ANS	REF
1.	A	1:4		10.	A	12:3–4
2.	C	1:8		11.	A,F,G	13:1–3
3.	D	2:2		12.	B,E,F	14:12–19
4.	B,D,E	3:1				
5.	A,C	5:3				
6.	E	6:5		Super Challenge:		
7.	B	8:23		#1: Land of Shinar		
8.	B	9:3–4		(Babylon) (5:7–11)		
9.	D	11:7–14				

~MALACHI~
(c. 450–400 B.C.)

1. Whom did Malachi say God hated?
  A. Satan
  B. Guys who lied about their golf scores
  C. Cain
  D. Esau
  E. Pharaoh

2. What was disappointing the Lord about the sacrifices of the people?
  A. They were only sacrificing on an occasional basis.
  B. They were offering lame, sick and blind animals for sacrifice.

C. They were charging and accepting money to sacrifice for others.

D. Their sacrifice festivals were turning into drunken riots.

3. **With whom did God say He had made a covenant, who "walked with (Him) in peace and equity . . ."?**

   A. Moses
   B. Levi
   C. Abraham
   D. Jacob
   E. Adam

ANTIGONE— now available!
(c. 443 B.C.)

4. **According to Chapter 2, God hated this because it, "covers one's garment with violence"?**

   A. Divorce
   B. Murder
   C. False witness (lying)
   D. Greed
   E. Tie-dying

5. **Who did the Lord say He would be a "swift witness" against, in the day of His coming?**
   (three answers)

   A. Idolaters
   B. Slothful men
   C. Tailgaters
   D. Adulterers
   E. Perjurers
   F. Sorcerers

6. **What THREE things did God say He would do to reward the people for bringing all the tithes into the storehouse?**

   A. Pour out more blessings than the people can hold
   B. Give everyone a receipt for IRS purposes
   C. Bring rain and sunshine each in their season

D. Keep their sons and daughters from danger

E. Bring peace among the descendants of Adam

F. Give them a "blessed" name among the nations

G. Rebuke the insects that devour crops

7. **Whom did God say He would send prior to the "great and dreadful day of the Lord"?**

   A. A comforter

   B. the Messiah

   C. Elijah, the prophet

   D. Michael, the archangel

   E. None of the above

ANSWERS TO MALACHI QUESTIONS

#	ANS	REF	#	ANS	REF
1.	D	1:3	5.	D,E,F	3:5
2.	B	1:8, 13	6.	A,F,G	3:10–12
3.	B	2:4–6	7.	C	4:5
4.	A	2:16			

Top Ten Aphorisms Not Found in the Old Testament (or the New one either, for the matter!)

10. "I am the walrus."
 9. "Love means never having to say you're sorry."
 8. "Live to ride."
 7. "Today is the first day of the rest of your life."
 6. "Always run when there's two outs."
 5. "Have a nice day."
 4. "I love ya, tomorrow, you're only a day away"
 3. "Life is like a box of chocolates."
 2. "I'd like to teach the world to sing in perfect harmony."
 1. "Image is everything."

THE
NEW
TESTAMENT

~MATTHEW~

(c. A.D. 50–85)

1. **Matthew began with a genealogy of Christ. He stated that the number of generations from Abraham to David was equal to the number from David to the Babylonian captivity, which was ALSO the same amount as from the captivity to Christ. In each case, it was:**
   A. Ten generations
   B. Fourteen generations
   C. Eight generations
   D. Twelve generations
   E. Sixteen generations, many moons, three days, a little while, two jerks of a lamb's tail, and a New York minute

2. **Where were Joseph, Mary, and Jesus when king Herod died?**
   A. Galilee
   B. Samaria
   C. Jerusalem
   D. Egypt
   E. At his house eating "Ball Park" franks

3. **What did Matthew say John the Baptist's diet consisted of?**
   A. Fish and unleavened bread
   B. Locusts and wild honey
   C. Goat's milk and cheese
   D. Bread and wine
   E. Leftovers

4. **John the Baptist compared himself to Christ with the following analogy:**
   A. "I am not worthy to carry his sandals."
   B. "His burden shall be greater than mine."
   C. "I am but a messenger of God; He is God's son."
   D. "I call you to repentance, but He shall call you to everlasting life."

5. **What TWO things happened prior to Jesus calling his twelve disciples?**
   A. He attended a wedding at Cana.
   B. He was tempted in the wilderness by Satan.
   C. He was baptized by John.
   D. He preached the Sermon on the Mount.
   E. He descended into the depths of the earth (the grave).

6. **According to the Sermon on the Mount, what did Jesus say would be the reward for those who are pure in heart?**
   A. "Theirs is the kingdom of Heaven."
   B. "They shall be called sons of God."
   C. "They shall see God."
   D. "They shall rule over the angels."
   E. "They shall run and not faint."

7. **Why did Jesus say you should not "swear . . . by the earth"?**
   A. Because it is a part of God's creation
   B. Because it is your home
   C. Because it is not yours to pledge
   D. Because it is God's footstool

8. **What TWO things did Jesus tell the people to do when they fasted?**
   A. Anoint their head
   B. Go into a secret place

C. Wash their face
D. Lie in their beds
E. Fast for themselves

9. **"Solomon in all his glory was not arrayed like one of these." To what was Jesus referring?**
   A. A butterfly
   B. A lily
   C. A dogwood tree
   D. A dove
   E. A purple-throated, yellow-bellied sap-sucker

10. **Jesus said that not everyone who called him "Lord" would enter the kingdom of heaven. However, many would try by saying they had done what THREE things in His name?**

ZACCHAEUS

A. Healed the sick
B. Cast out demons
C. Fed the hungry
D. Prophesied
E. Baptized
F. Done many wonders

11. **Whom did Jesus commend for having the greatest faith in Israel?**
    A. A leper whom He healed
    B. Peter's mother-in-law
    C. Matthew
    D. A centurion in Capernaum
    E. A man who had cancelled his health insurance

12. **What question did the disciples of John the Baptist pose to Jesus?**

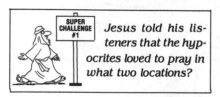

SUPER CHALLENGE #1 *Jesus told his listeners that the hypocrites loved to pray in what two locations?*

A. "Why don't your disciples fast like we do?"
B. "Is it right to pay taxes to Caesar?"
C. "Why do you associate with publicans and sinners?"
D. "Who will be greater in the kingdom of heaven, your disciples or John's?"
E. "If a Pharisee trips over a trash can while walking down the street, and no one is around to hear it, does he make a noise?"

13. **When Jesus sent out His twelve disciples, he challenged them to be as wise as _____ yet harmless as _____.**
    A. Foxes; sheep
    B. Owls; doves
    C. Solomon; children

D. Serpents; doves

E. English majors; computer nerds

14. **Jesus told his disciples they were worth more than:**
    A. The Gentiles
    B. All of Solomon's gold
    C. Many sparrows
    D. The things of this world

15. **When the scribes and Pharisees asked Jesus for a sign, He told them the only sign they would see was the sign of this prophet:**
    A. Ezekiel
    B. Elijah
    C. Jonah
    D. Micah
    E. Nostradamus

These women were sisters and opposites, but they made good roommates and worked together for the cause of Jesus. They were close friends with the disciples and were well-respected.

MARY AND MARTHA

16. **In Chapter 13, Jesus got into a boat and spoke several parables to his audience. Which of the following was NOT one of the parables?**
    A. Parable of the Loaves and Fishes
    B. Parable of the Sower
    C. Parable of the Wheat and Tares
    D. Parable of the Mustard Seed
    E. Parable of the Hidden Treasure

17. **Why did Herod the tetrarch have John the Baptist put to death?**
    A. John's disciples had threatened Herod.
    B. The people had demanded John's death.
    C. The emperor requested his death.
    D. Herod's niece requested his death.
    E. John was bootlegging wild honey.

18. **Jesus told Peter that Peter was the rock on which He would build His church. He then said He would give Peter the keys to:**
    A. Eternal life
    B. The kingdom of heaven
    C. Peace and happiness
    D. All knowledge
    E. A new Ford Taurus

19. **Which TWO Old Testament figures appeared with Jesus after his transfiguration on the mountain?**
    A. Abraham
    B. Jacob
    C. Elijah
    D. Moses
    E. David
    F. Job's wife

Germans introduce Romans to soap!
(c. A.D. 50)

20. **Jesus told his followers they could move mountains if they had faith the size of:**
    A. A grain of sand
    B. A mustard seed
    C. Their heart
    D. The temple
    E. A golf ball

21. **When Peter asked Jesus how many times he should forgive someone who sinned against him, what was Jesus' reply?**
    A. "As many times as he asks your forgiveness"
    B. "Seven times"
    C. "Seventy times seven"
    D. "Until you stop sinning against others"

22. **Jesus told Peter that the twelve disciples would receive TWO rewards. What are they?**

A. They will each have a throne.

B. They will each rule a kingdom.

C. They will judge the twelve tribes of Israel.

D. They will sit at the left hand of God.

E. A Big Mac and fries

23. **In Matthew 21, Jesus sent two of His disciples into the village for what purpose?**

    A. To bring back a donkey and a colt

    B. To secure food for the disciples

    C. To see if it was safe to enter the village

    D. To find someone for them to stay with

    E. To retrieve a copy of *The Jerusalem Times*

24. **Jesus was approached (Chapter 22) by a group of people known as Sadducees. What point did Matthew mention about their beliefs?**

    A. They believed that only Jews could attain righteousness.

    B. They accepted the Hindu tenet of reincarnation.

    C. They did not believe there would be a Messiah.

    D. They did not believe in the resurrection.

    E. They believed that when you died, your soul went to a garage in Cleveland.

> **DID YOU KNOW** that the book of Matthew was written especially for the Jewish people? These were people who knew the Old Testament and its prophecies. The promised kingdom was first offered to them, and they were foremost among those responsible for spreading the Good News.

25. **Which THREE of the following are part of Jesus' discourse regarding the tribulation of the latter days?**

    A. There will be great floods.

    B. The sun will be darkened.

    C. Violent winds will destroy cities.

D. The stars will fall from heaven.
E. The powers of the heavens will be shaken.
F. Dreadful diseases shall kill many.

26. **In the parable of the talents, what had the "wicked" servant done with the money entrusted to him?**

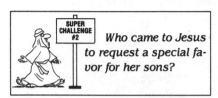

SUPER CHALLENGE #2 *Who came to Jesus to request a special favor for her sons?*

   A. Purchased something for himself
   B. Buried it in the ground
   C. Spent it on harlots and drink
   D. Bought a worthless field
   E. Bought into a "used camel" dealership

27. **To what reward did Judas agree, for betraying Jesus to the chief priests?**
   A. Two talents of gold
   B. A high position in the temple treasury
   C. Thirty pieces of silver
   D. Appointment as personal attendant to Caiaphas, the high priest
   E. A book deal and possibly a movie

28. **Whose ear was severed when the chief priests came to apprehend Jesus?**
   A. One of the chief priests'
   B. Peter's
   C. The servant of the high priest
   D. A Roman soldier's

29. **Which of these did Matthew say occurred upon Jesus' death?**
   (three answers)
   A. The earth quaked.
   B. A fierce wind blew across the land.
   C. The veil of the temple was torn in two.
   D. Lightning flashed across the sky.

E. A voice, like thunder, echoed from the heavens.

F. Graves were opened, and many of the dead came to life.

30. **Who told Mary Magdalene and the other Mary that Jesus was not in the tomb?**
    A. Peter
    B. An angel of the Lord
    C. The guards
    D. Jesus

ANSWERS TO MATTHEW QUESTIONS

#	ANS	REF	#	ANS	REF
1.	B	1:17	22.	A,C	19:28
2.	D	2:19	23.	A	21:1–2
3.	B	3:4	24.	D	22:23
4.	A	3:11	25.	B,D,E	24:29
5.	B,C	3:13; 4:1	26.	B	25:14–30
6.	C	5:8	27.	C	26:15
7.	D	5:35	28.	C	26:51
8.	A,C	6:17	29.	A,C,F	27:51–53
9.	B	6:28–29	30.	B	28:5
10.	B,D,F	7:22			
11.	D	8:5–10			
12.	A	9:14		Super Challenges:
13.	D	10:16		#1: standing in syna-
14.	C	10:31		gogues and on the
15.	C	12:39		corners of streets
16.	A	13:1–44		(6:5)
17.	D	14:1–12		#2: the mother of Zebe-
18.	B	16:19		dee's sons (21:20–
19.	C,D	17:3		28)
20.	B	17:20			
21.	C	18:22			

~MARK~

(C. A.D. 65–70)

1. **Unlike his colleague Matthew, Mark did not mention:**
   A. The tempting of Jesus in the wilderness
   B. The baptism of Jesus by John
   C. The story of Jesus' birth
   D. The calling of the disciples

2. **What was the first miracle of Jesus that Mark mentioned?**
   A. Exorcising an unclean spirit
   B. Healing Peter's wife's mother
   C. Turning water into wine at Cana
   D. Healing a leper
   E. Getting the Pharisees to agree on something

3. **In Chapter 2, the disciples did something on the Sabbath that the Pharisees said was unlawful. What was it?**
   A. Carried water to Jesus
   B. Built a small tabernacle
   C. Distributed food
   D. Plucked grain in the fields
   E. Went to the mall

4. **Jesus gave the name "Boanerges" to James and John, the sons of Zebedee. What did it mean?**
   A. "After God's Heart"
   B. "Sons of Thunder"
   C. "Men of Strength"

D. "Thirsting for Righteousness"
E. "Dukes of Hazzard"

5. **When their boat began to sink during a storm, which disciple(s) awakened Jesus?**
   A. Peter
   B. Thomas and Thaddaeus
   C. James and John
   D. Andrew
   E. The Bible doesn't say.

6. **About how many swine drowned when Jesus allowed the demons to enter them, causing the swine to run down a hill into the sea?**
   A. Five hundred
   B. Five thousand
   C. Two thousand
   D. One hundred
   E. Sow many they couldn't be counted

Top Ten Friends of John the Baptist

10. Harold the Presbyterian
 9. Ishni the Hindu
 8. Lex Lutheran
 7. Methodist Marv
 6. Abu the Muslim
 5. Big Fred the Catholic
 4. Jennifer the Unitarian
 3. Joe Episcopal
 2. Buddhist Bob
 1. Harry Krishna

7. **When the disciples were sent out, they were forbidden to take any of these EXCEPT:**
   A. Bread
   B. A little copper in their money belts
   C. A staff
   D. An extra tunic

8. **Who/what did the disciples think Jesus was when He walked across the water to their boat?**
   A. An angel
   B. A ghost
   C. A sea creature
   D. Himself
   E. Someone who had swallowed way too much helium

   > **SUPER CHALLENGE #1**
   > In Chapter 9, Jesus asked his disciples what they had been discussing while traveling on the road to Capernaum, but they refused to answer. Why?

9. **When Jesus asked His disciples, "Who do men say that I am?," they responded with all of the following EXCEPT:**
   A. John the Baptist
   B. Elijah
   C. One of the prophets
   D. The Son of God

10. **Which disciple(s) accompanied Jesus to the top of the mountain where the transfiguration occurred?**
    A. John, Phillip, and Andrew
    B. Peter, James, and John
    C. Only Peter
    D. All twelve
    E. None

11. **When the rich young ruler told Jesus he had always observed the commandments, Jesus told him to do which THREE things from this list?**

A. Sell whatever he had
B. Pay back double to anyone he had cheated
C. Repent from all evil
D. Take up his cross, and follow Him
E. Give to the poor
F. Stop trying to measure everything (he was a ruler)

12. **What tree did Jesus curse in Mark 11 for having no fruit for Him to eat?**

DID YOU KNOW that some people have considered Mark, the author of the gospel bearing that name, to have been an interpreter for Peter? Peter's preaching and testimony are sources for Mark's gospel, and Peter called Mark, "my son."

A. A fig tree
B. A "prickly" pear tree
C. An apple tree
D. A dogwood tree
E. A shoe tree

13. **When the Pharisees and Herodians tried to trick Jesus by asking him about paying taxes to Caesar, what did Jesus tell them to bring him?**
A. A wine skin
B. A mite
C. A denarius
D. A handful of grain
E. A pizza and a Coke

14. **In Chapter 13, what did Jesus tell his disciples about the temple?**
A. It would forever stand as a symbol of God's holiness.
B. The true temple is of the heart.
C. It was filled with hypocrites.
D. It would be thrown down, stone by stone.
E. The asbestos roof would one day get them all in a lot of trouble.

15. When Jesus was at the house of Simon the leper, what did He allow to happen that was criticized by some who observed it?

A. A woman washed His feet with a bottle of her tears and dried them with her hair.

B. A woman anointed His head with very expensive oil.

C. He allowed the leper to serve the food.

D. The food was offered without being blessed.

E. He permitted Simon the leper to tell several "blonde" jokes.

16. **According to Mark, what did Jesus and the aposties do in the interval between the Lord's Supper and going to the Mount of Olives?**
    A. Prayed
    B. Discussed the upcoming crucifixion of Jesus
    C. Fell asleep
    D. Sang a hymn

17. **Jesus had told Peter that he would deny Him three times before the rooster crowed. After Jesus was betrayed, who was the first to confront Peter about his affiliation with Jesus?**
    A. Caiaphas, the high priest
    B. A group of people standing by
    C. A servant girl
    D. A soldier
    E. His caddy

18. **When Jesus refused to answer questions posed by Pilate, Mark's account said Pilate:**
    A. Marveled
    B. Became extremely angry
    C. Was amused
    D. Was greatly saddened
    E. None of the above

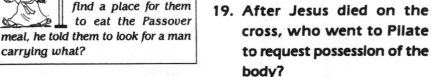

SUPER CHALLENGE #2 *When Jesus sent two of His disciples into the city to find a place for them to eat the Passover meal, he told them to look for a man carrying what?*

19. **After Jesus died on the cross, who went to Pilate to request possession of the body?**
    A. Joseph of Arimathea
    B. Mary Magdalene
    C. Jesus' brothers
    D. Peter

E. No one

F. A centurion

20. **Before Jesus was received into heaven, He told His disciples that they would do all of the following EX-CEPT:**

    A. Cast out demons

    B. Pick up serpents

    C. Raise the dead

    D. Lay hands on the sick who will re-cover

Nero orders Seneca to commit suicide!
(c. A.D. 65)

ANSWERS TO MARK QUESTIONS

#	ANS	REF	#	ANS	REF
1.	C	1	16.	D	14:26
2.	A	1:23–26	17.	C	14:66
3.	D	2:23–28	18.	A	15:5
4.	B	3:17	19.	A	15:43
5.	E	4:38	20.	C	16:17–18
6.	C	5:13			
7.	C	6:8–9			
8.	B	6:49	Super Challenges:		
9.	D	8:28	#1: They were discussing who would be the greatest. (9:33–34)		
10.	B	9:2			
11.	A,D,E	10:21			
12.	A	11:13–14	#2: a pitcher of water (14:13)		
13.	C	12:15			
14.	D	13:2			
15.	B	14:3–9			

~LUKE~

(C. A.D. 60-70)

1. **What was Zacharias' (John the Baptist's father) punishment for not believing the angel Gabriel concerning the birth of John?**
   A. He would be blind until the child was born.
   B. He would be mute until the child was born.
   C. He would be deaf for three days.
   D. He would not live to see the birth of his son.
   E. The Jerusalem dunghill would be named after him.

2. **Who blessed the infant Jesus when Mary and Joseph took Him to the temple to be circumcised?**
   A. Phanuel, a priest
   B. Anna, a prophetess
   C. Elizabeth, the mother of John the Baptist
   D. A devout man named Simeon
   E. The Pope

3. **In the fourth chapter of Luke, Jesus went into the synagogue on the Sabbath and was handed the book of which prophet?**
   A. Ezekiel
   B. Isaiah
   C. Daniel
   D. Jeremiah
   E. Habakkuk

4. **What did Jesus do to attract the attention of Peter, James, and John prior to calling them to follow Him?**

A. Healed Peter's mother
B. Cast a demon from Zebedee (James and John's father)
C. Suggested a successful location for fishing
D. Taught in the temple
E. Juggled four chain saws, while reciting the book of Leviticus from memory

5. **Each of the disciples in this list, EXCEPT ONE, had a fellow disciple with the same name. Find the one who didn't have to share his name!**
   A. Andrew
   B. Simon
   C. James
   D. Judas

Nero kills wife Octavia!
(c. A.D. 62)

6. **According to Mark 6, who had seven demons cast out of him or her?**
   A. Two men who lived in the tombs
   B. Joanna, the wife of Herod's steward
   C. Mary Magdalene
   D. Judas Iscariot
   E. A certain Pharisee

7. **After Jesus raised Jairus' daughter from the dead, what advice did He give those attending her?**
(two answers)
A. "Tell no one what has happened."
B. "Take the girl to the temple, and worship your Heavenly Father."
C. "Send the mourners away."
D. "Give her something to eat."
E. "Give her two aspirin, and call me in the morning."

8. **What did James and John ask Jesus after He was rejected in Samaria?**

A. If they should curse their land
B. If they should command fire from the heavens
C. If they should shake off the dust from their feet
D. If they should pray for their salvation
E. If they should contact the Better Business Bureau

9. In the parable of the good father, Jesus says that if a child asks for something reasonable, the good father would surely not respond by supplying a bad thing. All of these are part of the parable EXCEPT:
(If the child asks for _____, surely you would not give him _____.)
A. Water; poison
B. Bread; stone
C. A fish; a serpent
D. An egg; a scorpion

10. Which of the following were part of Jesus' criticism of the lawyers?
(three answers)

> According to Luke's gospel, certain elders of the Jews came to importune Jesus to come and heal the centurion's servant. What two things did they say about the centurion as examples of his goodness?
>
> SUPER CHALLENGE #1

A. "They load men with great burdens, which they themselves do not touch."
B. "They steal from widows and orphans."
C. "They have taken away the key of knowledge."
D. "Their fathers killed the prophets."
E. "They strain on a gnat, and swallow a camel."
F. "They spin webs like a spider."
G. "They make Judas look like a fairly decent human being."

11. Who became upset when Jesus healed a woman on the Sabbath who had been bent over for eighteen years?
A. The ruler of the synagogue
B. A group of Pharisees

C. The Sadducees

D. Caiaphas, the high priest

E. Her chiropractor

12. **In Jesus' Parable of the Great Supper, a man invited many people to a banquet, then they began making excuses as to why they could not attend. Find THREE of them in this list:**

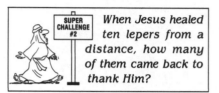

When Jesus healed ten lepers from a distance, how many of them came back to thank Him?

A. "My wife has fallen ill, and I cannot come."

B. "I have bought some land, and I must go see it."

C. "My son is home from battle, and we therefore cannot attend."

D. "I have bought some oxen, and I must test them."

E. "I am harvesting wheat, and therefore wish to be excused."

F. "I have married a wife, and therefore cannot come."

G. "I broke my leg while water skiing, and therefore I will not attend."

H. "I've fallen and I can't get up. If you will send someone to get me up, I will try to attend. By the way, what are you having?"

13. **When the prodigal son wasted all of his inheritance, what did he end up doing?**
    A. Working in a blacksmith's shop
    B. Gleaning wheat
    C. Feeding swine
    D. Grinding at the mill
    E. Bussing tables at Denny's

14. **Which of the following was NOT TRUE concerning the parable of the rich man and Lazarus:**
    A. Lazarus had terrible sores all over his body.
    B. Lazarus, a beggar, died and was carried to the bosom of Moses.
    C. The rich man had five brothers.
    D. The rich man died and went to Hades.

> **DID YOU KNOW** that Luke was the author of both the gospel of Luke and the book of Acts? He was a medical doctor, and most likely wrote these books in Rome during Paul's imprisonment there. However, it may have been during Paul's imprisonment in Caesarea that he began these books.

15. **Which of these were true concerning Zacchaeus: (three answers)**
    A. He was trying to avoid being seen by Jesus.
    B. He served as a treasurer to the chief priests.
    C. He was healed of leprosy by Jesus.
    D. He climbed up into a sycamore tree.
    E. He agreed to give half of his worldly goods to the poor.
    F. He hosted Jesus as a guest at his house.
    G. He was a center for the Jerusalem Jaguars basketball team.

16. The question posed to Jesus by the Sadducees (in Chapter 20) concerned:
    A. Marriage in the resurrection
    B. Who would hold the highest places in heaven
    C. His doctrine of salvation for Gentiles
    D. The inability of the disciples to cast out certain kinds of demons
    E. The trinity

17. What reason did Luke give for Judas's betrayal of Jesus?
    A. Judas was angry when he realized Jesus was not going to establish a "physical" kingdom at that time.
    B. He stated that Judas betrayed Jesus "out of greed."
    C. Judas hoped to gain favor with the chief priests.
    D. Luke said that "Satan entered Judas."
    E. He stated that Judas was jealous of Jesus' power.

18. Before Jesus was arrested, He went to the Mount of Olives to pray. Which TWO of the following selections were true regarding the events that took place at that time?

> **SUPER CHALLENGE #3** On the day of Jesus' resurrection, He appeared to two men who were on their way to a certain village "about seven miles from Jerusalem." What was the name of the village?

    A. His disciples all sat near Jesus and prayed with Him.
    B. An angel appeared to Jesus as He prayed.
    C. Peter saw Judas leading the group coming to arrest Jesus, drew his sword, and severed Judas's ear.
    D. Jesus sweat drops of blood while praying.
    E. Judas fired two shots into the air to signal the arrest of Jesus.

19. **According to Luke 23, when Jesus was taken to Pilate, He was initially charged by His accusers with THREE crimes. Select them from this list.**
    A. Perverting the nation
    B. Breaking the laws of the Sabbath
    C. Threatening to destroy the temple
    D. Forbidding to pay taxes to Caesar
    E. Refusing to acknowledge the gods of Rome
    F. Calling Himself Christ, a King
    G. Parking in a loading zone

20. **When Jesus was taken to Herod, what was Herod's attitude toward Him?**
    A. He was disgusted with the matter and didn't want to be bothered with it.
    B. He found it amusing that Jesus had troubled the religious leaders to such a great degree.
    C. He was glad to see Jesus and had, for a long time, hoped to see Him.
    D. He was saddened to see what Pilate had allowed to be done to Jesus.

    Says he's a Baptist, but he definitely doesn't dress like one. He has slept outdoors for months on end, and he has an unusual diet. He tends to provoke denominational leaders, and generally he seems to be right. JOHN THE BAPTIST.

21. **Who was appointed to carry the cross upon which Jesus was to be crucified?**
    A. Barabbas
    B. Simon the Cyrenian
    C. Peter
    D. A certain soldier

22. **What was the first reaction of the disciples and those with them, when Jesus appeared to them after the resurrection?**

A. They doubted that it was really Him.

B. They were terrified, thinking they had seen a spirit.

C. They immediately fell down and worshiped Him.

D. They were humbled because they had not understood what He had previously told them about rising from the dead.

23. **In Luke's gospel, Jesus' last instruction to His followers was:**

   A. "Go into the whole world and make disciples."

   B. "Remember all of the things God has shown you."

   C. "Stay in Jerusalem until you receive power from on high."

   D. "In the days to come, your Heavenly Father will show you what you are to do."

ANSWERS TO LUKE QUESTIONS

#	ANS	REF	#	ANS	REF
1.	B	1:20	19.	A,D,F	23:2
2.	D	2:25–35	20.	C	23:8
3.	B	4:17	21.	B	23:26
4.	C	5:1–11	22.	B	24:37
5.	A	6:14–16	23.	C	24:49
6.	C	8:2			
7.	A,D	8:55–56			
8.	B	9:54			
9.	A	11:11–13			
10.	A,C,D	11:46–52			
11.	A	13:11–17			
12.	B,D,F	14:16–20			
13.	C	15:15			
14.	B	16:19–31			
15.	D,E,F	19:1–8			
16.	A	20:27–33			
17.	B,D	22:3			
18.	B,D	22:39–46			

Super Challenges:
- #1: "He loves our nation, and built us a synagogue." (7:5)
- #2: one (17:15)
- #3: Emmaus (24:13)

~JOHN~
(C. A.D. 80–95)

1. **This reference to Jesus appeared three times in the first sentence of the book of John:**
   A. King
   B. Word
   C. Christ
   D. Name
   E. Messiah

2. **John said that the law came through Moses, but what TWO things came through Jesus Christ?**
   A. Mercy
   B. Compassion
   C. Grace
   D. Joy
   E. Truth

3. **According to John, Jesus nicknamed Peter "Cephas." The translation for this is:**
   A. A bull
   B. One who hears and understands
   C. Friend
   D. A stone
   E. Overweight fisherman

4. **At the wedding in Cana, what request did Jesus' mother give to the servants regarding Him?**
   A. "Please do not bother Him."
   B. "Whatever He says to you, do it."
   C. "Make certain you seat Him in a high place."

D. "Tell no one that you saw Jesus."

E. "Make no requests of Him until after the celebration."

5. **What THREE birds/animals were being sold in the temple when Jesus drove out the vendors?**
   A. Donkeys
   B. Pigeons
   C. Doves
   D. Sheep
   E. Rams
   F. Oxen
   G. Elephants

6. **To whom did Jesus say, "God is Spirit, and those who worship Him must worship in spirit and truth"?**
   A. Mary, His mother
   B. James and John
   C. A Samaritan woman

D. Nicodemus

E. The multitudes

7. **Which of the following were part of the procedure for being healed at the pool of Bethesda? (two answers)**

   A. An angel came at a certain time and stirred the waters.

   B. The waters were sanctified each year during Passover.

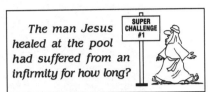

The man Jesus healed at the pool had suffered from an infirmity for how long?

SUPER CHALLENGE #1

   C. Anyone who drank the water at the proper time would be healed.

   D. Only the first person into the water at the appropriate time would be healed.

   E. A person who stayed under the water long enough would never feel pain again.

8. **Who did Jesus say accuses the Jews?**

   A. Moses, in whom they trust

   B. Jehovah

   C. Abraham

   D. Caesar

   E. The Jews themselves

9. **In John's account of the feeding of the five thousand, which two disciples were involved in Jesus' discussion of how to proceed?**

   A. Peter and John

   B. Matthew and Thomas

   C. James and John

   D. Phillip and Andrew

   E. Simon and Garfunkle

10. **What happened after Jesus taught that His flesh and blood were to be eaten and drunk in order to obtain eternal life?**

 DID YOU KNOW that in Bible times, the period of engagement for a couple to be married was spent in preparation—the groom prepared a home, and the wife, herself and her trousseau? When the time came for the marriage to be consummated, the groom went to the bride's home, often unannounced, and accompanied her to a place where they met friends and family. The groom made all these plans, not the bride. The wedding celebration generally lasted a week! This is the type of event that Jesus was at when He turned the water into wine.

A. Many of His followers deserted Him.
B. The Pharisees began plotting to have Him arrested.
C. His twelve disciples began to question His intentions.
D. Judas left to talk with the priests about betraying Jesus.

11. **On the last day of the Feast of Tabernacles, Jesus spoke in the temple, and there was confusion among the crowd. All of these are part of the account EXCEPT:**
A. Some said no prophet had arisen out of Galilee.
B. Some said the Messiah would surely not be a carpenter.
C. Some said Jesus was the Christ.
D. Some of them wanted to take Him.
E. Nicodemus questioned their judging Jesus without a hearing.

12. **The Jews attempted to stone Jesus for saying that He preceded:**
A. Abraham
B. God
C. Moses
D. Adam
E. Jacob

13. The parents of the blind man that Jesus healed feared the Jews who questioned them about their son. John's gospel said they knew that anyone who confessed that Jesus was Christ would be punished in what way?
A. By being stoned to death
B. By being sent out of the country
C. By being put out of the synagogue
D. By getting a physical beating and a fine
E. Having to set pictures of all the chief priests on their pianos

14. In Chapter 11, Jesus raised Lazarus from the dead. Who were Lazarus' TWO sisters?
A. Phoebe
B. Martha

Top Ten Questions Jesus Was Never Asked

10. "What's your favorite animal, and why?"
9. "Does your chewing gum lose its flavor on the bedpost overnight?"
8. "Are those little pink fabric softener sheets better than a liquid?"
7. "What's the best restaurant in Jerusalem?"
6. "Whatever happened to the three wise men?"
5. "What do you say to God when He sneezes?"
4. "If there are no tears in Heaven, does that mean there aren't any onions there?"
3. "Do you have a *disciple of the month?*"
2. "How do you feel about technology stocks?"
1. "When snow melts, where does the white go?"

C. Mary

D. Anna, the prophetess

E. Priscilla

F. Mulan

15. **What did Jesus tell Peter that he must do in order to be part of Him?**

Domitian is emperor! (*c.* A.D. 81–96)

    A. Be willing to die for the kingdom of heaven

    B. Love others as Jesus had loved him

    C. Forgive the trespasses of all men

    D. Allow Jesus to wash his feet

    E. Become a "fisher of men"

16. **Who said to Jesus, "Lord, show us the Father, and it will be sufficient for us"?**

    A. John

    B. Peter

    C. Thomas

    D. Phillip

17. **John's account stated that Judas came with a detachment of troops and officers to arrest Jesus. He asked them who they were seeking, and they answered, "Jesus of Nazareth." After He replied, "I am He," what happened?**

    A. Judas kissed Jesus on the cheek.

    B. The troops drew back and fell to the ground.

    C. A soldier quickly grabbed Jesus and shackled His hands.

    D. His disciples ran away in various directions.

    E. Jesus was read His Miranda rights.

18. **Who asked Jesus, "What is truth?"**

    A. Judas Iscariot

    B. Annas

    C. Pilate

D. Caiaphas

E. Herod

19. What happened to Jesus' tunic?

A. Four soldiers cast lots for it.

B. Joseph of Arimathea retrieved it to clothe Jesus' body.

C. Mary Magdalene purchased it from a soldier.

D. The gospel of John did not say.

20. Who followed Peter into the tomb?

A. Mary Magdalene

B. Martha

C. The other disciple

D. Lazarus

E. Prince, his German shepherd

> **SUPER CHALLENGE #2**
>
> *According to John's account, how did Jesus signify who would betray Him after He had washed His disciples' feet?*

21. The last chapter of John tells of:

A. Jesus ascending into heaven

B. Jesus appearing to the eleven disciples at the upper room

C. Mary telling seven of the disciples about seeing Jesus

D. The disciples receiving the Holy Spirit

E. Jesus and several of His disciples having a fish barbecue

ANSWERS TO JOHN QUESTIONS

#	ANS	REF	#	ANS	REF
1.	B	1:1	17.	B	18:6
2.	C,E	1:17	18.	C	18:38
3.	D	1:42	19.	A	19:23–24
4.	B	2:5	20.	C	20:8
5.	C,D,F	2:14	21.	E	21:5–13
6.	C	4:7–24			
7.	A,D	5:4			
8.	A	5:45	Super Challenges:		
9.	D	6:5–11	#1: 38 years (5:5)		
10.	A	6:66	#2: Dipped bread and		
11.	B	7:40–53	handed it to him		
12.	A	8:58–59	(13:26)		
13.	C	9:22			
14.	B,C	11:1–2, 19			
15.	D	13:8			
16.	D	14:8			

~ACTS~
(c. A.D. 60–64)

1. **The Book of Acts is generally credited to Luke and is written to:**
   A. "All believers of Jesus Christ"
   B. Theophilus
   C. "The leaders of the temple"
   D. ". . . all who must learn and understand the truth"
   E. His great aunt, Minnie

2. **At the end of Chapter 1, what did the group of Jesus' disciples and followers decide by casting lots?**
   A. Who would replace Judas Iscariot as an apostle
   B. Who the spiritual leader of the disciples would be
   C. Where each disciple would go to begin establishing churches
   D. Who would go to the temple to continue Jesus' teaching there
   E. Who would take out the garbage

3. **Which of these accompanied the Holy Spirit's "visit" on the Day of Pentecost?**
   (three answers)
   A. Nearly 10,000 new believers were baptized.
   B. The pool by the Sheep Gate at Bethesda was stirred by an angel, and dozens were healed.
   C. The sound of a mighty, rushing wind came from heaven.
   D. Jesus appeared in their midst.
   E. The apostles began to speak in foreign tongues, so that those from other nations each heard in their own language.

F. Peter stood and gave an explanation of what was occurring.

G. Some of the disciples were captured and beaten.

4. **According to Chapter Four, who were the first TWO apostles to be taken into custody?**
   A. Andrew
   B. Peter
   C. John
   D. James
   E. Judas, the son of James
   F. Al

5. **Why were Ananias and his wife, Sapphira, struck dead?**
   A. They were telling the Christians that Peter was stealing from them.
   B. They took money from the treasury.
   C. They were caught committing adultery.
   D. They lied about the price they had received for some land.
   E. They refused to teach Sunday school.

6. **When Stephen was brought before the council, he presented a history of God's involvement with the Jews, beginning with _____ and ending with _____.**
   A. Adam; David
   B. Abraham; Solomon
   C. Jacob; Zechariah
   D. Moses; Hezekiah
   E. Noah; Nehemiah

7. **Where did Philip begin a successful ministry, doing many miracles, and converting a former sorcerer named Simon?**

A. Samaria
B. Jericho
C. Capernaum
D. Philippi
E. Down in Monterey

8. **All of the following were true concerning Saul's encounter with Jesus near Damascus EXCEPT:**
A. Saul was blind for three days.
B. He ate nothing for three days.
C. His skin became leprous.

The Top Ten Things Jesus <u>Might</u> Have Said to His Disciples After They Feared He Was a Ghost

10. "Don't be afraid, I'm Casper, the *friendly* ghost!"
9. "Well then, I guess I can see why you were a little spooked."
8. "Remember, I'm Jesus, not Boooo-dah."
7. "No wonder this wind feels like it's blowing right through me!"
6. "I am the ghost of Christmas past, present, and future."
5. "I'll bet you were having a rather spirited conversation."
4. "I brought you some chicken from those poultry guys."
3. "Hi, I'm the ghost of a surgeon. Does anyone here need an apparition?"
2. "I just saw a big pike beneath my feet. I think I'll spear it."
1. "Excuse me, is this the Interghostal Waterway?"

D. He drank nothing for three days.

E. The men traveling with Saul also heard a voice but saw nothing.

9. **What was Peter's connection with Tabitha (Dorcas)?**
   A. Peter and Tabitha had been engaged to be married.
   B. Tabitha made clothes for Peter and some of the other disciples.
   C. Peter raised Tabitha from the dead.
   D. Tabitha was a cousin to Mary Magdalene.
   E. Tabitha ran a diner where Peter liked to stop for breakfast.

Who Am I?

Powerful CEO-type leader and a fascinating preacher. Had quite an amazing testimony. He's a bit short on tact, however, and can be unforgiving with the younger leaders. He demands excellence from Christians. He has also been known to preach all night.

PAUL

10. **While Peter was on a housetop praying, he fell into a trance and saw the same vision three times. What was it?**
    A. Four beasts, three great and one small, rising from the sea
    B. A man being lowered in a basket, beside a jasper wall
    C. Jesus sitting at the right hand of God, wearing a golden crown
    D. A large sheet descending from heaven, filled with all kinds of animals and birds

11. **When Peter went up to Caesarea, he stayed at the home of a man named Cornelius. When the Holy Spirit fell upon the group there, some of those who came with Peter were astonished. Why?**
    A. Because Peter had originally not wanted to go there
    B. Because the people receiving the Holy Spirit were Gentiles

C. Because none of the people spoke in tongues

D. Because the people had been extremely critical of Peter

E. Because Peter hadn't mispronounced any words

12. **Which of these were true concerning Antioch? (three answers)**

   A. Barnabas took Paul there.

   B. Paul was imprisoned there for a short time.

   C. The disciples were first called Christians there.

   D. Barnabas owned a small business there.

   E. There were no prophets there.

   F. Paul and Barnabas stayed there for a year and taught many people.

   G. The only stop light in town went out every time it rained.

13. **According to Chapter 12, who was the first apostle to be killed as a martyr?**

   A. John, brother of James

   B. James, brother of John

   C. Phillip

   D. Bartholomew

   E. Andrew

What Pharisee cautioned the council regarding the treatment of the apostles saying, ". . . if this is of God, you cannot overthrow it"?

SUPER CHALLENGE #1

14. **What happened to Bar-Jesus (Elymas the sorcerer) when he attempted to turn the proconsul away from faith in Jesus?**

   A. He was struck blind by Paul.

   B. He was trampled by horses.

   C. He fell dead into a river at Salamis.

   D. The proconsul (Sergius Paulus) ordered him to prison.

   E. He tripped over a rock and fell into a patch of poison ivy.

15. When Paul and Barnabas came to Lystra, Paul healed a lame man. Because of this, by what names did the people of the city call the two men? (two answers)

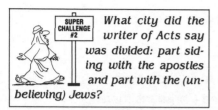

SUPER CHALLENGE #2 *What city did the writer of Acts say was divided: part siding with the apostles and part with the (un-believing) Jews?*

A. Thor
B. Achilles
C. Hermes
D. Mars
E. Zeus
F. Doctor

16. In Chapter 15, a controversy arose, which resulted in an official letter being taken to the new converts at Antioch. What topic was being debated?
A. Circumcision
B. Things defiled by idols
C. Sexual immorality
D. Dietary laws
E. Susan Lucci's Emmy

17. What was the response of the Philippian jailer, when he realized that an earthquake had opened the doors of the prison where Paul and Silas were being held?
A. He came to the cell with his sword drawn, intending to kill anyone who tried to escape.
B. He ran outside, hoping to catch anyone who may have gotten past him.
C. Thinking everyone had escaped, he drew his sword to kill himself.
D. He laid on the ground and placed a rock by his head, hoping to convince his superior that he had been injured in the earthquake.
E. He got out his work contract to see if he received hazard pay for earthquakes.

18. When Paul spoke to the Athenians at Mars' Hill, he mentioned an inscription he had read on an altar. What was it?
    A. "To all the gods of Rome"
    B. "The altar of Remus and Romulus"
    C. "To the gods of the universe"
    D. "To the unknown god"
    E. "Class of 40 A.D."

19. What TWO items were said to have merely touched Paul's body, then carried the capacity to heal others?
    A. Aprons
    B. Handkerchiefs

HOLY SPIRIT

C. Tunics
D. Scarves
E. Sandals
F. "Old Navy" sweatshirts

20. **What happened at Troas to a young man named Eutychus?**
   A. He was burned at the stake for preaching Christ.
   B. He was baptized by Paul and prophesied of Peter's approaching death.
   C. He attacked Timothy, severely injuring him.
   D. He saved Paul's life.
   E. He fell asleep while Paul was preaching and fell out of a window.

21. **When Paul went back to Jerusalem, he was attacked by the people. When he finally got a chance to speak, the crowd listened until he:**
   A. Mentioned his vision on the road to Damascus
   B. Told them about his blindness and subsequent healing
   C. Referred to Jesus as the "Just One"
   D. Said that the Lord told him He was sending him to the Gentiles
   E. Pulled out his banjo

22. **When a group of about forty Jews formed a conspiracy to kill Paul, who caught wind of it and saved Paul?**
   A. Ananias, the high priest
   B. Paul's nephew
   C. Peter
   D. A slave girl whom Paul had healed
   E. The Lone Ranger

23. In Chapters 23–26, Paul was tried before three different leaders. Which of the following was NOT one of the men who heard Paul's case?
   A. Felix
   B. Caesar
   C. Festus
   D. Agrippa

24. When the ship ran aground, where did Paul and his fellow sailors find themselves?
   A. The island of Malta
   B. Syracuse, on the island of Sicilia
   C. Crete
   D. The southern tip of Italy (Italia)

Where was Paul headed when he was involved in a shipwreck?

SUPER CHALLENGE #3

   E. An uncertain location where an older couple came to meet them and identified themselves as Mr. and Mrs. Howell

25. Which of the following occurred at the place where Paul shipwrecked?
(three answers)
   A. The natives of that place attacked Paul and the others.
   B. Paul was bitten by a viper.
   C. Paul healed many people of their illnesses.
   D. The natives drove them from their village, believing Paul to be a demon.
   E. Paul and the men stayed at that place for about a year.
   F. One of the leading citizens there courteously hosted Paul and his friends for three days.
   G. While there, Paul took a cameo role in a local theater production of "Joseph and the Amazing Technicolor Dreamcoat."

26. At the close of the book of Acts, Paul was:
   A. Dead, having been martyred for his belief
   B. In prison, awaiting trial before Caesar
   C. Living in a rented house in Rome with little or no persecution
   D. On a ship headed back to Jerusalem
   E. Talking to his life insurance agent, trying to find out why they cancelled his policy

ANSWERS TO ACTS QUESTIONS

#	ANS	REF	#	ANS	REF
1.	B	1:1	20.	E	20:9
2.	A	1:15–26	21.	D	22:21–23
3.	C,E,F	2:1–41	22.	B	23:12–16
4.	B,C	3:1; 4:3	23.	B	23:34–26:32
5.	D	5:1–10	24.	A	28:1
6.	B	7:2, 47	25.	B,C,F	28:1–11
7.	A	8:5–13	26.	C	28:16–31
8.	C	9:7–9			
9.	C	9:36–41			
10.	D	10:9–16	Super Challenges:		
11.	B	10:45	#1: Gamaliel (5:34–39)		
12.	A,C,F	11:25–27	#2: Iconium (14:1–4)		
13.	B	12:2	#3: Italy (27:1)		
14.	A	13:6–11			
15.	C,E	14:11–13			
16.	A	15:1–31			
17.	C	16:27			
18.	D	17:23			
19.	A,B	19:12			

~ROMANS~
(c. A.D. 57)

1. **Paul said in Chapter 1 that the gospel is the power of God to salvation to which TWO peoples?**
   A. The Romans
   B. The Gentiles
   C. The Greeks
   D. The Jews
   E. The Slaves
   F. The Canadians

2. **To Paul's rhetorical questions, "What advantage has the Jew?" and "What is the profit of circumcision?," his initial response essentially was:**
   A. None, unless he truly believes
   B. Much in every way
   C. That it is a poor substitute for righteousness
   D. With circumcision comes much responsibility
   E. Very little, since the resurrection of Christ

3. **In Chapter 4, Paul discusses the "righteousness apart from circumcision" of this Old Testament patriarch:**
   A. Noah
   B. Jacob
   C. Moses
   D. Abraham
   E. Pharaoh

4. **Paul said that "we glory in tribulation" because:**
   A. Tribulation produces perseverance, which then creates character, then hope.
   B. Christ suffered much, and as we also suffer, we become like Him.

C. Tribulation reminds us that God is our only Healer in suffering.

D. From tribulation comes submission, from submission faith, from faith, joy and peace which passes understanding.

E. From tribulation comes anger and frustration, leading to cynicism, and finally isolation, meaning at last everyone will leave you alone.

> **?** **DID YOU KNOW** that Paul had neither founded nor visited the church at Rome when he wrote them his letter?

5. What relationship does Paul use to symbolize the law's authority over the people?
   A. A king over his subjects
   B. A wife to her husband
   C. A son to his father

Top Ten Things the Prodigal Son Spent His Money on Besides "Riotous Living"

10. A complete collection of Beanie Babies
9. Video games
8. All of Pink Floyd's stuff on eight track tapes
7. Fifteen cases of "Silly Putty"
6. Wiped out several shelves at the "Dollar Store"
5. Had pictures taken with all of his friends in a photo booth
4. Spent several weeks at Disney World
3. Hired Julio Iglasias to sing at one of his parties
2. Joined the Kathy Lee Gifford Fan Club
1. Every Wednesday was "Chucky Cheese" day

D. A student to his teacher

E. A slave to his owner

6. **At the end of Chapter 8, Paul listed several things which he was convinced cannot separate God's people from His love. Which THREE of the following were included in that list?**

   A. Sins of the fathers

   B. Angels

   C. The enemies of God

   D. Things to come

   E. This earthly flesh

   F. Death

   G. Bullet-proof glass

   Paul tells the Roman Christians they should NOT present their members (parts of their bodies) as what?

   SUPER CHALLENGE #1

7. **Paul said that God shows mercy to some people, and others He:**

   A. Gives over to much suffering

   B. Destroys

   C. Hardens

   D. Prospers for His own purposes

   E. Finds rather annoying

8. **In Chapter 11, Paul said that he was from which tribe?**

   A. The tribe of Dan

   B. The tribe of Judah

   C. The tribe of Benjamin

   D. The tribe of Manasseh

   E. The tribe of Cherokee (actually Paul's title was "Grand Cherokee")

9. **What illustration did Paul use in Chapter 11 to symbolize God's acceptance of Gentiles in place of Jews?**

   A. The branches of a wild olive tree

   B. A potter and damaged vessels

   C. A crown being taken from a king and given to slaves

D. A metalsmith making a perfect tool from imperfect material

E. Something he got from Yogi Berra

10. **Paul's list of gifts Christians receive according to (God's) grace includes all of the following EXCEPT:**

   A. Prophecy

   B. Ministry/serving

   C. Giving

   D. Healing

   E. Leadership

11. **Paul said that we should owe no one anything EXCEPT:**

A. Respect
B. To love one another
C. The sharing of our joy in Christ
D. What is rightfully due him
E. An RSVP when requested

12. **In Paul's Chapter 14 example, the man who is weak in faith eats only:**
    A. Fruits
    B. Vegetables
    C. Meat
    D. Unleavened bread
    E. What his mommy tells him to eat

13. **Jesus has been established on earth to confirm the promises made to the fathers, said Paul. He then refers to Isaiah's prophecy of Jesus as being:**
    A. "The root of Jesse"
    B. "The Great Deliverer"
    C. "The Rose of Sharon"
    D. "A Cornerstone"

Ming-Ti introduces Buddhism to China!
(*c*. A.D. 58)

14. **Paul said it was always his goal to preach the gospel:**
    A. Outside the "holy city"
    B. To the Greeks
    C. Wherever he was welcomed
    D. Where people had not heard of Christ
    E. In a warm church with padded pews and air conditioning

15. **Where did Paul plan to go BEFORE he could visit the Romans?**
    A. Philippi
    B. Ephesus
    C. Jerusalem

D. Tarsus
E. Chicago

16. **What advice did Paul give to the Roman Christians regarding people who caused divisions among them?**
   A. Rebuke them.
   B. Avoid them.
   C. Turn them over to Satan.
   D. Do not let them be named among your members.
   E. Use them for fill.

SUPER CHALLENGE #2 *Paul said he would visit the Romans on his way to what country?*

ANSWERS TO ROMANS QUESTIONS

#	ANS	REF		#	ANS	REF
1.	C,D	1:16		13.	A	15:12
2.	B	3:2		14.	D	15:20–21
3.	D	4:9–25		15.	C	15:25
4.	A	5:3–4		16.	B	16:17
5.	B	7:2–5				
6.	B,D,F	8:38–39				
7.	C	9:18		**Super Challenges:**		
8.	C	11:1		#1: Instruments of un-		
9.	A	11:17–24		righteousness (6:13)		
10.	D	12:6–8		#2: Spain (15:24)		
11.	B	13:8				
12.	B	14:2				

FIRST CORINTHIANS

(c. A.D. 55–56)

1. **Paul told the "divided" Corinthians that he was sent to preach rather than:**
   A. Settle childish disputes
   B. Baptize
   C. Distribute offerings
   D. Undermine the law
   E. Coach the Corinthian Church Softball team

2. **Regarding the work of Apollos (an Alexandrian Jew who preached Christ to the Corinthians), Paul and God, Paul said:**
   A. "Apollos taught, I preached, and the Spirit brought you to faith."
   B. "God calls all to Him; Apollos and I share in your salvation."
   C. "Apollos has misled you. Take my instruction and let God do a great work within you."
   D. "I planted, Apollos watered, but God gave the increase."

3. **How did Paul refer to himself and the apostles?**
   A. As the "first stronghold" of the faith
   B. As "servants who cannot be served"
   C. As "messengers without an earthly home"
   D. As "fools for Christ's sake"
   E. As "men who will never again have a regular job"

4. The Corinthian Christians were instructed not to associate with those who referred to themselves as brothers yet were:
(three answers)
A. Fornicators (sexually immoral)
B. Arrogant/proud
C. Drunkards
D. Liars
E. Prone to violence
F. Idolaters
G. Tailgaters

5. All of the following were part of Paul's Chapter 7 Instructions for marriage EXCEPT:
A. A man should have no more wives than he can care for.
B. Husbands and wives should give each other the affection they are due.
C. The husband has authority over his wife's body.
D. The wife has authority over her husband's body.
E. If one spouse is not a believer and yet is willing to remain with a believing spouse, the believing spouse should allow them to stay.

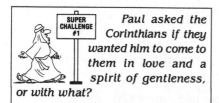

SUPER CHALLENGE #1 *Paul asked the Corinthians if they wanted him to come to them in love and a spirit of gentleness, or with what?*

6. Paul said that he had become all things that he might save some. Find THREE examples he cited from this list:
A. Though he was free, he became a servant.
B. He became as the weak, to win the weak.
C. He gave up much wealth, that he might win the poor.
D. To win those without the law, he became as one without law.

E. To share with the Stoics, he became a Stoic of Christ.

F. To win the trekkies, he put on pointed ears.

7. In Chapter 11, Paul referred to a woman's hair as:

A. A crown of glory

B. A halo

C. A symbol of authority

D. A sign of holiness

E. The standard excuse for her always being late

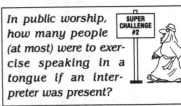

In public worship, how many people (at most) were to exercise speaking in a tongue if an interpreter was present?

SUPER CHALLENGE #2

Top Ten Issues the People Debated Before Jesus Came Along

10. Why didn't the water in the Mediterranean Sea run off the edge of the earth?

9. Should there be a background check on anyone who wanted to buy a spear?

8. How many stone tablets should be loaded in a Xerox machine?

7. Should "Y" be a consonant or a vowel?

6. Who should have a mailbox in the temple?

5. Which is the more optimum transportation, camel or donkey?

4. Did Solomon make his wives and concubines wear nametags?

3. Does aspirin really reduce the risk of a heart attack?

2. How many weeks of paid vacation should the chief priests get each year?

1. If demons enter animals which are then slaughtered and packaged, should there be a warning label?

8. **The list of "gifts of the Spirit" in Chapter 12, included all of the following EXCEPT:**
   A. The word of wisdom
   B. The gift of leadership
   C. The gift of healing
   D. Interpretation of tongues
   E. The working of miracles

9. **What gift did Paul state that the Corinthians should especially desire?**
   A. Speaking in foreign tongues
   B. The gift of healing
   C. Discerning of spirits
   D. The gift of prophecy
   E. An expensive birthday gift

10. **The last enemy that Christ will destroy is:**
    A. Satan
    B. Hatred
    C. Death
    D. Pride
    E. Static cling

 DID YOU KNOW that there were actually four letters written by Paul to the Corinthians? The first and third letter have been lost. He mentions these letters in 1 Corinthians 5:9 and 2 Corinthians 2:3.

11. **In closing his letter, Paul mentioned that he wanted to come and visit the Corinthians but planned to stay in what city until Pentecost, because "a . . . door has been opened to me"?**
    A. Ephesus
    B. Rome
    C. Philippi
    D. Thessalonica
    E. Gotham City (it was the door to the "Bat Cave")

ANSWERS TO FIRST CORINTHIANS QUESTIONS

#	ANS	REF	#	ANS	REF
1.	B	1:17	10.	C	15:26
2.	D	3:6	11.	A	16:8–9
3.	D	4:10			
4.	A,C,F	5:11			
5.	A	7:1–16	Super Challenges:		
6.	A,B,D	9:19–22	#1: A rod (4:21)		
7.	C	11:10	#2: three (14:27)		
8.	B	12:4–10			
9.	D	14:1–6			

Q. Who played baseball in the Bible?

A. In the Big Inning, Eve stole first, Adam stole second, and the Prodigal Son ran home. The Giants and the Angels were rained out.

SECOND CORINTHIANS

(C. A.D. 56)

1. **Paul reported to the Corinthians that, while in Asia, he and his companions endured such burdens that:**
   A. They were tempted to give up.
   B. They despaired of life itself.
   C. It seemed they had been abandoned.
   D. The Corinthian issues seemed meaningless by comparison.
   E. He changed his name to Job.

2. **Paul figuratively used what image to illustrate the difference between the Old Testament (covenant) of Moses and the new covenant of Jesus Christ?**
   A. A veil
   B. A lamb
   C. A lantern
   D. A vineyard

3. **The Corinthians were warned not to be "unequally yoked together" with:**
   A. False teachers
   B. Gnostics
   C. The uncertain masses
   D. Unbelievers
   E. Fried eggs

4. **Paul mentioned this helper of his, calling him his "partner and fellow worker concerning you," and reminding the Corinthians that they had refreshed this man's spirit. Name him.**

A. Timothy
B. Silas
C. Luke
D. Titus
E. Agrippa

5. **Second Corinthians Chapter 9 offers guidelines for giving. All of these are included EXCEPT:**
A. Each person should give as he has decided in his heart.
B. God loves a cheerful giver.

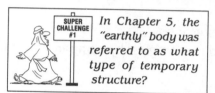

SUPER CHALLENGE #1

In Chapter 5, the "earthly" body was referred to as what type of temporary structure?

C. The collecting of an offering should be a part of every worship meeting.
D. Do not give grudgingly or under compulsion.

6. **Paul offered a fairly comprehensive list of his tribulations as a minister. Which THREE of these were included?**

SUPER CHALLENGE #2

In what city did Paul say he escaped danger by being let down in a basket through a window?

A. He was stabbed.
B. He was beaten with rods three times.
C. He was dragged behind oxen for two miles.
D. He suffered broken limbs.
E. He was shipwrecked three times.
F. He received thirty-nine lashes on five separate occasions.
G. He had his Reeboks stolen.

7. **Paul said that he was given a "thorn in the flesh." What was it?**
A. A large scar on the side of his face
B. A severe limp

C. A speech impediment

D. An irremovable tattoo that said "Live to circumcise"

E. The Bible doesn't say.

8. **In Paul's closing, he instructed the Corinthian Christians to do which THREE of the following:**

A. "Be of one mind."

B. "Pray without ceasing."

Top Ten Most Questionable Legends Regarding Unusual People That Paul and/or the Disciples Supposedly Encountered

10. A man with no eyes who could beat anyone at ping-pong

9. A very large person with an animal-like body who claimed to have been the model for the Sphinx

8. A young girl, traveling with a scarecrow, a tin man, and a cowardly lion

7. Little Richard

6. Beowulf

5. The Golden Girls

4. "The Four Pharisees," a popular adult-contemporary singing group, whose best-selling song was called "Listen to the Rhythm of the Falling Hail and Brimstone"

3. A troll who lived under a bridge

2. Jake and the fat man

1. Yoda

C. "Live in peace."

D. "Greet one another with a holy kiss."

E. "Begin the collecting of the offering for the saints."

F. "Look both ways before crossing the street."

She was involved with the fashion industry—selling purple cloth. She also held church meetings at her home. Paul is the one who mentions her name.

LYDIA

ANSWERS TO SECOND CORINTHIANS QUESTIONS

#	ANS	REF
1.	B	1:8
2.	A	3:13–18
3.	D	6:14
4.	D	7:13; 8:23
5.	C	9:6–7
6.	B,E,F	11:23–27
7.	E	12:7–10
8.	A,C,D	13:11–12

Super Challenges:
#1: A tent (5:1)
#2: Damascus (11:32–33)

~GALATIANS~
(C. A.D. 48–57)

1. Paul explained to the Galatians that after his conversion, he did not go immediately to Jerusalem to confer with the disciples. In fact it was three years before he went to see:
   A. Peter
   B. Philip
   C. Timothy
   D. James and John, the sons of Zebedee
   E. His dentist

2. Paul said that not even Titus (a Greek) was compelled to:
   A. Observe the dietary laws
   B. Worship in the temple
   C. Be circumcised
   D. Learn the ways of our fathers
   E. Use Grecian Formula

3. About what hypocrisy did Paul confront Peter (and Barnabas)?
   A. They were eating meat that they would not allow others to eat.
   B. They were accepting money for healing the sick.
   C. They would not eat with the Gentiles when certain Jews were present.
   D. They were allowing the people to refer to them as gods.

4. How much time passed between the covenant with Abraham and the Law of Moses?

Package deal: preacher and associate. Slight ego problem regarding fellow workers and seating positions. Love rain storms at night.

JAMES AND JOHN, THE SONS OF THUNDER

A. 7 generations
B. 430 years
C. 220 years
D. 640 years
E. None

5. Who did Paul use in Chapter 4 as symbols of freedom and bondage?

A. The Egyptians and the Israelites
B. Abel and Cain

SUPER CHALLENGE #1

Paul used what word to refer to the status of Peter, James, and John?

C. Jacob and Esau
D. Isaac and Hagar

6. If the Galatians were to become circumcised, then: (three answers)

A. Christ will profit them nothing.
B. They will have no inheritance among the saints.

C. Paul sees no need to ever return to them.

D. They are obligated to keep the whole law.

E. They have fallen from grace.

F. They may want to stock up on aspirin.

7. Paul said that we should not do what while doing good?

A. Receive glory for ourselves

B. Weaken the power of the cross

C. Distort the truth of Christ

D. Grow weary

E. Avoid ice cream

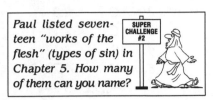

Paul listed seventeen "works of the flesh" (types of sin) in Chapter 5. How many of them can you name? SUPER CHALLENGE #2

ANSWERS TO GALATIANS QUESTIONS

#	ANS	REF
1.	A	1:18
2.	C	2:3
3.	C	2:11–14
4.	B	3:17
5.	D	4:22–31
6.	A,D,E	5:2–4
7.	D	6:9

Super Challenges:
#1: pillars (2:9)
#2: adultery, fornication, uncleanness, licentiousness, idolatry, sorcery, hatred, contentions, jealousies, outbursts of wrath, selfish ambitions, dissensions, heresies, envy, murders, drunkenness, revelries (5:19–21)

~EPHESIANS~

(C. A.D. 60–62)

1. **What did Paul say was the body of Christ?**
   A. The Bread of the Holy Communion
   B. Love and peace
   C. The fullness of the Spirit
   D. The church

2. **The Gentiles of Ephesus were formerly without God or hope. What TWO reasons were given for this?**
   A. They were worshiping the goddess Diana as pagans.
   B. They were aliens from the commonwealth of Israel.
   C. They were strangers from the covenant of promise.
   D. They believed in many gods, none of them the True God.
   E. Billy Graham had never held a crusade in Ephesus.

3. **In Chapter 3, Paul described his status by stating:**
   A. "I am equal in spiritual matters with Christ's apostles."
   B. "God has seen fit to elevate me to be a leader of men."
   C. "I am less than the least of all the saints."
   D. "I was sent to be your father in spiritual things."
   E. "No one can make me clean out my desk and be out by noon, because I have neither a desk nor a clock."

4. **Paul said there was one of all the following EXCEPT:**
   A. Body
   B. Spirit
   C. Covenant
   D. Faith
   E. Baptism

5. What THREE types of evil persons have no inheritance in "the kingdom of Christ and God" according to Chapter 5?

SUPER CHALLENGE #1

Paul told the Ephesians they should put away their anger before what natural event occurred?

A. Fornicator (sexually immoral)
B. Greedy/covetous
C. Drunkard
D. Liars
E. Impure/unclean
F. Sleazy talk-show hosts

6. **The last verse of Chapter 5 found Paul encouraging husbands to love their wives, and in return, wives should give their husbands:**

    A. Respect

    B. Love

    C. Complete obedience

    D. Spiritual adoration

    E. An apron and a dish towel

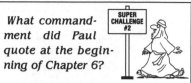

What commandment did Paul quote at the beginning of Chapter 6?

7. **In the final chapter of Ephesians, Paul dealt with all of the following EXCEPT:**

    A. The relationship between parents and children

    B. The preparations for his next visit to Ephesus

    C. The armor of God

    D. The relationship of servants and masters

    E. His ambassador, Tychicus

DID YOU KNOW that Ephesus was the most important commercial center of its day? It was located in present-day Turkey; regional trade routes intersected there, and they possessed a natural harbor. It was also a religious center for pagan worship, as the temple to Diana was located there.

ANSWERS TO EPHESIANS QUESTIONS

#	ANS	REF
1.	D	1:22–23
2.	B,C	2:12
3.	C	3:8
4.	C	4:4–6
5.	A,B,E	5:5
6.	A	5:33
7.	B	6:1–24

Super Challenges:
#1: The sun goes down (4:26)
#2: Honor your father and mother. (6:2)

~PHILIPPIANS~
(C. A.D. 60–63)

1. **Paul told the Philippians of his chains, meaning:**
   A. He was symbolically chained to Christ.
   B. It would be very difficult to leave his current work at Corinth.
   C. He was quite literally in prison.
   D. He was very ill.
   E. He was selling necklaces on the side.

2. **What associate of Paul's nearly died of an illness and then was sent to Philippi?**
   A. Epaphroditus
   B. Timothy
   C. Titus
   D. Silas
   E. Dr. Watson

3. **Paul cited several reasons why he should have confidence "in the flesh." Which of these was NOT one of the reasons?**
   A. He was a Pharisee.
   B. He was circumcised on the eighth day.
   C. He had persecuted the church.
   D. He taught often in the temple.
   E. He was blameless in the righteousness of the law.

4. **What were the names of the TWO women whom Paul urged to "be of the same mind"?**
   A. Salome
   B. Betsy
   C. Euodia

D. Lydia

E. Syntyche

5. **Paul said that his fellow workers among the Philippians:**

A. Have their names written in The Book of Life

B. Are his crown in glory

C. Outshine the angels

Top Ten Early Church Arguments Paul Never Addressed in His Letters

10. When three forks are used, should one or two be on the napkin?

9. Should people who give more than ten percent receive double Top Value Stamps?

8. Should Sunday school be before or after church?

7. If you don't have little kids, do you still have to work in the nursery?

6. If someone had offered their dentures to an idol before they were converted, should they ever smile afterward?

5. If an apostle gave a message, and there was no one there to hear it, did he really say anything?

4. Is it okay to play Monopoly on Sunday?

3. If someone speaks in tongues and there is no interpreter, should that person be given a severe tongue-lashing?

2. Should coffee and donuts be offered in the fellowship hall or in the lobby in front of the sanctuary?

1. Should Paul's letters to the IRS become part of the New Testament?

D. Could not be repaid in a hundred lifetimes

E. Probably all fell into the "Earned Income" bracket

6. **What had made the Philippians unique among the churches?**

   A. Their honesty and like-mindedness

   B. Their financial support for Paul

   C. The great number of women actively involved

   D. Their tremendous growth

   E. They have no committees

7. **The themes of Paul's letter to the Philippians are: (three answers)**

   A. Joy

   B. Unity

   C. Humility

   D. Love

   E. Patience

   F. Manliness

Paul is executed by the Romans!
(c. A.D. 60–62)

ANSWERS TO PHILIPPIANS QUESTIONS

#	ANS	REF	#	ANS	REF
1.	C	1:7–18	6.	B	4:15
2.	A	2:25–30	7.	A,B,C	1–4
3.	D	3:4–6			
4.	C,E	4:2	Super Challenge:		
5.	A	4:3	#1: their belly (3:19)		

~COLOSSIANS~
(C. A.D. 60–63)

1. **The Colossian church was apparently never visited by Paul, and it was founded instead by:**
   A. Mark and Barnabas
   B. Epaphras
   C. Luke and Demas
   D. Onesimus and Tychicus
   E. Paul's twin sister, Pauline

2. **Paul referred to Jesus as:**
   (two answers)
   A. "The firstborn over all creation"
   B. "A shelter in the time of storm"
   C. "The image of the invisible God"
   D. "The quiet voice of righteousness"
   E. "Like a rock"

3. **Paul instructed the Colossians not to be cheated out of their reward by people who practice what TWO things:**
   A. Prayers to the dead
   B. Worship of the Greek gods and goddesses
   C. False humility
   D. Worship of angels
   E. Synchronized swimming

4. **Finish this sentence: "Wives, submit to your own husbands . . ."**
   A. In whatever you do.
   B. In all things.
   C. As it is fitting to the Lord.

D. As they see fit.

E. Whether you like it or not.

5. **What TWO suggestions did Paul offer regarding speech?**

A. We should speak softly, being certain of our spirit.

B. Our speech should be tempered with grace.

C. We are defined by our words.

D. Our speech should be seasoned with salt.

E. It's your dirtiest foot that usually ends up in your mouth.

6. **Paul asked the Colossians to "remember my chains." To what did this refer?**

A. The fact that he was writing this letter while he was imprisoned.

B. The fact that they were supposed to bring him some chains when they came to visit him in Rome.

C. The fact that he had formerly been in prison.

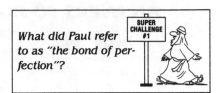

What did Paul refer to as "the bond of perfection"?

SUPER CHALLENGE #1

D. The fact that he had once been a member of a heavy-metal band.

7. Paul instructed the Colossians to share their letter with the church of:

A. Ephesus

B. Antioch

C. Laodicea

D. Miletus

E. Smyrna

DID YOU KNOW that the Gnostic heresy was popular among the people of Colosse? Gnosticism taught that Jesus never existed as a genuine human being, but rather had a phantom or angelic form. This philosophy contradicts both the idea that Jesus was divine and that He was human.

ANSWERS TO COLOSSIANS QUESTIONS

#	ANS	REF	#	ANS	REF
1.	B	1:7–8	6.	A	4:3
2.	A,C	1:15	7.	C	4:16
3.	C,D	2:18			
4.	C	3:18	Super Challenge:		
5.	B,D	4:6	#1: love (3:14)		

FIRST AND ~SECOND~ THESSALONIANS

(C. A.D. 50–52)

1. **The church at Thessalonica had turned to God from:**
   A. Sexual immorality
   B. Idols
   C. Idleness (laziness)
   D. Evil reveling
   E. Serious coffee addiction

2. **Paul said that he and his companions wanted to visit the Thessalonians, but didn't. Why?**
   A. He was imprisoned before they could arrange to come.
   B. The church at Corinth had dire need for their presence.
   C. The Spirit of God led them down a different path.
   D. Satan hindered them.
   E. There were no good restaurants there.

3. **What THREE pieces of practical advice did Paul offer to the Thessalonians so that they would "lack nothing"?**
   A. "Lead a quiet life."
   B. "Sing psalms (songs) often with the family of the faith."

C. "Work with your own hands."
D. "Understand the futility of material wealth."
E. "Mind your own business."

4. **Paul said that "the day of the Lord [would occur] like a thief in the night," and destruction will come like:**

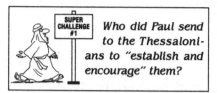

Who did Paul send to the Thessalonians to "establish and encourage" them?

    A. Swarms of locusts landing in a field before harvest
    B. God's assault on Pharaoh of old
    C. Labor pains coming upon a pregnant woman
D. The flood of Noah
E. A visit from Wyatt Earp

5. **Paul said the return of Christ will be accompanied by: (two answers)**
    A. A thousand trumpets
    B. Flaming fire
    C. His mighty angels
    D. The falling of the stars
    E. The London Philharmonic

6. **The "day of the Lord" will not come unless: (two answers)**

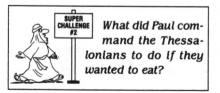

What did Paul command the Thessalonians to do if they wanted to eat?

    A. There is a great "falling away."
    B. The temple of Solomon is rebuilt.
    C. Elijah returns as a harbinger of the end.
    D. The man of sin is revealed.

7. **It had been reported to Paul that some of the Thessalonians had become:**

A. Very ill
B. Great spiritual comforters
C. Greedy
D. Busybodies
E. Accountants

> **DID YOU KNOW** that Thessalonica was the capital city of Macedonia and was a major trade city connecting Macedonia to the Roman Empire? The geographical location of this city had global ramifications for evangelism.

ANSWERS TO FIRST AND SECOND THESSALONIANS QUESTIONS

#	ANS	REF
1.	B	1:9
2.	D	2:18
3.	A,C,E	4:11
4.	C	5:3
5.	B,C	1:7–8
6.	A,D	2:3
7.	D	3:11

Super Challenges:
#1: Timothy (1 Thess. 3:2, 6)
#2: work (2 Thess. 3:10)

FIRST AND ~SECOND~ TIMOTHY

(C. A.D. 62–68)

1. **What TWO people did Paul say he "delivered to Satan"?**
   A. Chloe
   B. Alexander
   C. Judas
   D. Hymenaeus
   E. Aquila

2. **If a woman exercises faith, love and holiness with self-control, what will her reward be?**
   A. She will have safety in childbearing.
   B. She will be the joy of her husband.
   C. She shall be called righteous.
   D. Her children will be of the "holy seed."
   E. She will receive a gift certificate to WalMart.

3. **All of the following are part of Paul's list of qualifications for a bishop EXCEPT:**
   A. Must be blameless
   B. Cannot have more than one wife
   C. Must be one who has never tasted wine
   D. Must rule his own house well
   E. Must be gentle

4. **Paul said that some will appear in the latter times forbidding what TWO things?**

A. Circumcision

B. Worship of the True God

C. Marriage

D. Eating certain foods

E. Water skiing after 7:00 P.M.

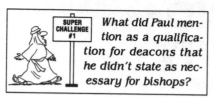

SUPER CHALLENGE #1 *What did Paul mention as a qualification for deacons that he didn't state as necessary for bishops?*

5. Who was "worse than an unbeliever"?

A. One who steals from widows

B. One who does not provide for his own family

C. One who corrupts children

D. One who undermines the grace of Christ with the law

E. One who smokes in Sunday school

6. What instruction was given by Paul regarding health?

A very young but astute leader. Highly recommended.

TIMOTHY

A. "Your sicknesses would be healed through the prayer of faith."

B. "You should drink some wine for your illnesses."

C. "You should rely on God as well as herbs and medicines for relief of your ailments."

D. "You should rest as you have need."

E. "You can't survive indefinitely on fast food."

7. How did Paul address Timothy?

A. "A fellow laborer in Christ"

B. "A fellow servant of the faith"

C. "God's chosen reaper of the harvest"

D. "A beloved son"

E. "To whom it may concern"

8. What THREE examples of endurance did Paul utilize in Chapter 2?

A. A soldier concentrating only on the affairs of battle

B. A sculptor painstakingly chipping away rock

C. A vineyard keeper carefully maintaining the vines and harvesting the fruit

D. An athlete competing according to the rules

E. A farmer first sharing in the benefits of his crops

SUPER CHALLENGE #2

Who was Paul's only companion with him by this time?

9. **Paul assured Timothy that all who desire to live godly in Christ:**

A. Will rise again in the final resurrection

B. Will be easily recognized

C. Will experience persecution

D. Will ultimately be successful

10. **Timothy was instructed to bring which TWO of the following with him when he came to visit Paul:**

A. Paul's letters proving his Roman citizenship

B. A cloak

C. Some books and parchments

D. Writing instruments

E. Paul's Rolodex

DID YOU KNOW that Paul was executed by the Roman emperor Nero? Nero committed suicide the following year in June A.D. 68. Second Timothy was the last letter Paul wrote.

ANSWERS TO FIRST AND SECOND TIMOTHY QUESTIONS

#	ANS	REF	#	ANS	REF
1.	B,D	1:13	9.	C	3:12
2.	A	2:15	10.	B,C	4:13
3.	C	3:3			
4.	C,D	4:3			
5.	B	5:8	Super Challenges:		
6.	B	5:23	#1: reverent wives		
7.	D	1:2	(1 Tim. 3:11)		
8.	A,D,E	2:3–6	#2: Luke (2 Tim. 4:11)		

~TITUS~

(C. A.D. 62–65)

1. Where did Paul leave Titus?
   A. Corinth
   B. Athens
   C. Crete
   D. Thessalonica
   E. Walla Walla, Washington

2. "One of their own prophets" claimed the people of this region were always:
(three answers)
   A. Generous
   B. Liars
   C. Greedy

ON THE SEVENTH DAY, GOD RESTED.

D. Evil beasts

E. Scoffers

F. Lazy gluttons

G. Cow tippers

3. **The *older woman* should be all of these things EXCEPT:**

   A. Reverent

   B. An admonisher of the younger woman

Top Ten Answers Supplied by Paul That Never Made It into the Bible

10. "If you don't have caller I.D., try using *54."
9. "Just because someone sticks out their tongue at you doesn't mean you have to do the same to them."
8. "You probably just need a little more nitrogen."
7. "No, I'm not going to call myself 'The Apostle formerly known as Saul.'"
6. "Of course the latex is a little less durable, but the brushes will clean up with soap and water."
5. "Yes, Cool Whip can turn boring foods into tasty treats."
4. "No, goldfish don't float on the top for several days in a row just to relax. Sorry."
3. "It sounds like the carburetor to me, but you might try changing the air filter first, and see if that helps."
2. "Maybe."
1. "I say you and your mother-in-law should split the cost of the damage and knock off the wrestling the next time you're in a jewelry store."

C. Not given to wine

D. A teacher of good things

E. An excellent mother

4. Who should be rejected after two warnings?

A. One who gossips

B. A divisive person

C. A sexually immoral brother

D. One who refuses to work

E. A choir member who sings off-key

What part of a young man's life should be "above condemnation"?

5. What was Zenas' occupation?

A. artist

B. warrior princess

C. lawyer

D. missionary

ANSWERS TO TITUS QUESTIONS

#	ANS	REF	
1.	C	1:5	Super Challenge:
2.	B,D,F	1:12	#1: speech (2:8)
3.	E	2:3–4	
4.	B	3:10	
5.	C	3:13	

~PHILEMON~

(C. A.D. 60–63)

1. Which TWO people, other than Philemon, does Paul greet in the opening verses of this book?
   A. Timothy
   B. Apphia
   C. Onesimus
   D. Archippus

2. The letter from Paul to Philemon concerned:
   A. The Colossian church
   B. A donation to impoverished Christians at Jerusalem
   C. Philemon's help in getting Paul released from prison
   D. A runaway slave that belonged to Philemon
   E. A first effort at a chain letter

3. **Paul refers to Onesimus as:**
   A. My own heart
   B. My beloved friend
   C. A true servant of the gospel
   D. A good-for-nothing
   E. One whom I admire

 DID YOU KNOW that Apphia is commonly considered to be Philemon's wife? She would have been responsible for the supervision of their slaves, such as Onesimus.

4. **Paul told Philemon to:**
   A. Send him money and medicine
   B. Get the guest room ready for his visit
   C. Tell the church that Paul assumed he would be executed soon
   D. Continue to monitor the churches of Colosse
   E. Invest in companies that make chain

Top Ten Reasons They Built the Tower of Babel

10. Tower of Pisa was about to tip over
9. Better air traffic control site
8. To draw tourists away from Ruby Falls
7. Point of entry for giant slide
6. Revenue from revolving restaurant at top
5. Didn't have instructions for a sphinx
4. Too much time on their hands
3. On a clear day, you could see Mt. Sinai
2. Press box for the Hebrew NFL
1. It was the only thing they could build which didn't require handicap accessibility.

5. Who also greets Philemon and his household in Paul's farewell?
(five answers)
A. Epaphras
B. Mark
C. Aristarchus
D. Demas
E. Luke
F. John

ANSWERS TO PHILEMON QUESTIONS

#	ANS	REF	#	ANS	REF
1.	B,D	1:2	4.	B	1:22
2.	D	1:10–16	5.	A,B,C,	1:23
3.	A	1:12		D,E	

~HEBREWS~
(C. A.D. 50–64)

1. **The first chapter of Hebrews related Jesus as being greater than:**
   A. Men
   B. Angels
   C. The prophets
   D. Satan
   E. The disciples

2. **In Chapter 3, we find Jesus being compared to:**
   A. Moses
   B. Abraham
   C. Adam
   D. Joshua
   E. Peter

3. **Why does the high priest have compassion on those who are "ignorant and going astray"?**
   A. He was chosen for his compassion.
   B. God commands that he do so.
   C. He is the model for Christ, who is the Compassionate One.
   D. He, also, is capable of weakness.
   E. He gets paid extra for it.

4. **The author of Hebrews said that God confirmed His promise to Abraham in what way?**
   A. By the rite of circumcision
   B. By giving Abraham a son in his old age

C. By swearing an oath by Himself

D. By making him a "father of many nations"

E. By giving Abraham His "Dick Tracy Secret Decoder Pen" to keep as security

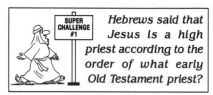

Hebrews said that Jesus is a high priest according to the order of what early Old Testament priest?

5. According to Chapter 7, what differentiates Jesus from former "high priests"?

Top Ten "Farming" Comparisons Paul Opted to Forego

10. "I planted, Apollos watered, and then you decided to buy a load of manure from the Pharisees."

9. "Your faith is becoming weedy, you need to be sprayed with the anhydrous ammonia of holy perseverance."

8. "You were growing in the Lord . . . now it appears Satan has run over you with a twelve bottom plow."

7. "Oh foolish Galatians, who has disked you up?"

6. "I have sent the apostles Matthew, Mark and John Deere."

5. "You were ripping up the fields for God, who tipped over your tractor?"

4. "I thought you understood the message of the gospel, but now it appears you don't know beans about it."

3. "Did you think that when the Lord returns you could just run to Him as if He were the Farmers Home Administration?"

2. "God will allow your sins to go unpunished when pigs fly!"

1. "What kind of *clod* do you think I am??!!"

A. Jesus is immortal.
B. He has no need to offer up sacrifices.
C. He need not collect tithes.
D. He can forgive sins.
E. None of the above

6. **According to the Law, without this, there is no remission (forgiveness) of sin.**
   A. Restitution
   B. Repentance
   C. An apology
   D. Shedding of blood
   E. "Sports star" status

Nero succeeds Claudius as Roman emperor!
(c. A.D. 54)

7. **What did the writer say followers of Christ should NOT give up?**
   A. Assembling together
   B. Daily prayers of thankfulness
   C. Reading of the scriptures
   D. Seeking the good and proper will of God
   E. Bible trivia books

8. **Chapter 11 named an Old Testament figure who did not see death. Name him.**
   A. Noah
   B. Isaac
   C. Abel
   D. Enoch
   E. Moses

SUPER CHALLENGE #2

What did the author say the Hebrews gladly accepted?

9. **The writer stated that the people had not been brought to the mountain "that burned with fire," but rather to:**
   (two answers)
   A. Beulah Land
   B. Mount Zion

C. The heavenly Jerusalem
D. Paradise
E. Blueberry Hill

10. **At the conclusion of Hebrews, we learn that one of the leaders of the early church had been "set free." Who?**
    A. Paul
    B. Timothy
    C. Peter
    D. Barnabas
    E. Silas

Who Am I?

Great experience as a priest. Has no personal history that we know of. There is no mention of his family line or birth.

MELCHIZEDEK

ANSWERS TO HEBREWS QUESTIONS

#	ANS	REF		#	ANS	REF
1.	B	1:4–14		9.	B,C	12:22
2.	A	3:2–19		10.	B	13:23
3.	D	5:2				
4.	C	6:13–17				
5.	B	7:27		Super Challenges:		
6.	D	9:22		#1: Melchizedek (5:6)		
7.	A	10:25		#2: plundering of their		
8.	D	11:5		property (10:34)		

~JAMES~

(C. A.D. 45–62)

1. **What should a person never say when they are tempted?**
   A. "I have done nothing wrong."
   B. "God is tempting me."
   C. "No one will notice a small sin."
   D. "God has abandoned me."
   E. "Oh, *piffle!*"

2. **James said that everyone should be swift to listen, but:**
   (two answers)
   A. Slow to speak
   B. Swifter to forgive
   C. Slow to act
   D. Slow to anger
   E. Swift to avoid those who are not too swift

3. **"Faith without _____ is dead."**
   A. Love
   B. Joy
   C. Works
   D. Hope
   E. Oxygen

4. **James described this as "a fire, a world of iniquity." What is it?**
   A. Sexual lust
   B. Greed for money and power

C. The Island of Crete
D. The tongue
E. Hell/Hades

5. **James said that life is:**
   A. Like the sun, which rises and sets in the same day
   B. Like a raindrop, which strikes the earth then cannot be found a little while later
   C. Like a garment, that is worn awhile, then disposed
   D. Like a vapor, that appears for a little while, then vanishes
   E. Like his sock drawer; always unorganized and discouraging

Top Ten Things Expressly Omitted from the Levitican Dietary Laws

10. Grits
9. Two all beef patties, special sauce, lettuce, cheese, pickles, onions on a sesame-seed bun
8. PBJ sandwich
7. Hershey bars
6. TV dinners
5. Spam
4. Quiche
3. Wonder bread
2. Rice Krispies
1. Sara Lee

6. Someone who turns a sinner from the error of his ways does what TWO things:
   A. Edifies the church
   B. Saves a soul from death
   C. Covers a multitude of sins
   D. Creates joy among the angels
   E. Gets a heavenly brownie point

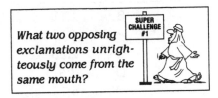

What two opposing exclamations unrighteously come from the same mouth?

SUPER CHALLENGE #1

#	ANS	REF	#	ANS	REF
1.	B	1:13	Super Challenge:		
2.	A,D	1:19	#1: blessing and cursing		
3.	C	2:26	(3:10)		
4.	D	3:6			
5.	D	4:14			
6.	B,C	5:19–20			

Romans invade Britain!
(c. A.D. 43)

FIRST AND SECOND PETER

(c. A.D. 63–67)

1. Peter stated that the prophets of old studied diligently concerning the grace of Christ and who would suffer for it. Who else did Peter say desired to look into these things?
   A. He and the other disciples
   B. The detractors of the faith
   C. Many who study the law
   D. The angels

2. In Chapter 2, Peter referred to Christ and His followers as:
   A. A flock of innocent lambs
   B. A forest of young trees
   C. Living stones
   D. A lion caring for his cubs

3. In advising how Christians should relate to their fellow human beings, Peter said the king should be _____, but God should be _____.
   A. Honored/feared
   B. Feared/honored
   C. Obeyed/worshiped
   D. Respected/obeyed
   E. Married/single

4. Peter said the time had come for judgment, to begin with:

A. The worst of the evildoers
B. The house of God
C. The father of lies
D. The chosen tribes
E. Leftover hippies

5. A final warning is issued to beware of the devil who is compared to:

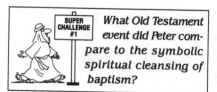

What Old Testament event did Peter compare to the symbolic spiritual cleansing of baptism?

A. A wolf in sheep's clothing
B. A roaring lion
C. A destroyer of men and door-keeper of Hell
D. A sly serpent

6. The writer said that when he (and the others) shared the power of Christ with the people, "we did not follow . . .":
A. The old law and commandments
B. The rituals of the past
C. Cleverly devised fables
D. The paths of the destroyers of the faith
E. The yellow, brick road

7. In Chapter 2, Peter discussed God's ability to judge the unrighteous while sparing His own. Three examples are given. Which of these is NOT one of them?

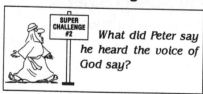

What did Peter say he heard the voice of God say?

A. Sparing Noah and his family while destroying everyone else
B. Giving Israel to David after judging Saul
C. Calling Lot out before turning Sodom and Gomorrah into ashes
D. Casting the angels who sinned into the dungeons of hell

8. **Peter reminded his readers that one day with the Lord:**
   A. Is like a hundred years
   B. Is without measure
   C. Encounters no nightfall
   D. Is like a thousand years
   E. Beats a week anywhere
      else

DID YOU KNOW that the first official persecution of the Christians was instigated by Nero? He blamed the Christians for the burning of Rome in A.D. 64. Peter wrote his epistles, 1 and 2 Peter, just before the Neronian outbreaks.

ANSWERS TO FIRST AND SECOND PETER QUESTIONS

#	ANS	REF	#	ANS	REF
1.	D	1:12	Super Challenges:		
2.	C	2:4–5	#1: The Great Flood		
3.	A	2:17	(3:20)		
4.	B	4:17	#2: "This is My beloved		
5.	B	5:8	Son, in whom I am		
6.	C	1:16	well pleased."		
7.	B	2:4–7	(1 Peter 1:17–18)		
8.	D	3:8			

FIRST, SECOND, ~AND~ THIRD JOHN

(C. A.D. 80–100)

1. **John started out by telling his readers that God is:**
   A. Light
   B. Love
   C. The beginning and the end of all things
   D. All powerful
   E. Holy

2. **John addressed THREE specific types of people in Chapter 2. Find them in this list.**
   A. False teachers
   B. Legalists and lawyers
   C. Young men
   D. Fathers
   E. Little children
   F. Mothers
   G. Donkey racers

3. **John offered TWO results for Christ's followers which will take place upon His return:**
   A. "Each one shall receive the crown of righteousness."
   B. "We shall be like Him."
   C. "All mysteries shall be revealed."
   D. "We shall see Him as He is."
   E. "Our enemies will be cut asunder."

4. **John said who has seen God?**
   A. Only Moses
   B. Moses and Enoch
   C. Adam
   D. Those prophets He chose to reveal Himself to
   E. No one

5. **What THREE elements bear witness on earth:**

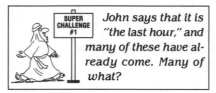
SUPER CHALLENGE #1 — *John says that it is "the last hour," and many of these have already come. Many of what?*

   A. The blood
   B. The holy scriptures
   C. The Spirit
   D. The church
   E. The water
   F. The law

6. **Second John is a very brief letter addressed to:**
   A. "My beloved friend Timothy"
   B. "All the believers at Antioch"
   C. "The elect lady and her children"
   D. "My little children in the faith"
   E. "Occupant"

7. **Three men are mentioned in Third John. Which of the following statements reflects the most accurate picture of the situation?**
   A. Diotrephes and Demetrius are faithful believers, but Gaius was causing problems within the church.
   B. Gaius and Demetrius were praised for their good testimony, but Diotrephes seemed to have an ego problem.
   C. John felt that Demetrius should be expelled from the fellowship and Gaius agreed, but Diotrephes was leaning the other way.
   D. Gaius was guilty of sexual misconduct, and John was responding to questions by Demetrius and Diotrephes as to how to pursue the matter.

E. Demetrius had been allowing his dog, "Billy-Bob" to trespass on the property of Gaius, ruining his wife Joni's flower bed. In retaliation, Gaius sent his dog "Goliath" over to Demetrius' place. Goliath went for a swim in Gaius' pool, and his shed hair plugged up the filter. Diotrephes was sent to repair the apparatus, and wrote to John requesting proper repair techniques.

> **DID YOU KNOW** that John addressed his second letter to *the elect lady?* This reference could be to a church group, as the church was often referred to in feminine terms. However, it is also possible that there was a specific woman, an esteemed friend, and her family that he was writing to.

ANSWERS TO FIRST, SECOND, AND THIRD JOHN QUESTIONS

#	ANS	REF	#	ANS	REF
1.	A	1:5		Super Challenge:	
2.	C,D,E	2:12–14		#1: antichrists (1 John	
3.	B,D	3:2		2:18)	
4.	E	4:12			
5.	A,C,E	5:8			
6.	C	1:1			
7.	B	1:1–14			

Mt. Vesuvius erupts— Pompeii destroyed!
(C. A.D. 79)

~JUDE~

(C. A.D. 50–80)

1. Who did Jude say God has reserved in chains for the judgment day?
A. The great prostitute
B. The evil men of old
C. The Nephilim (giants) of Noah's day
D. The disobedient angels
E. Some gangster rappers

2. What Old Testament cities did Jude mention in his epistle? (two answers)
A. Sodom and Gomorrah
B. Ur
C. Korah
D. Babylon
E. Jerusalem

St. Peter executed!
(c. A.D. 57)

3. Michael the archangel disputed about what?
A. His golf score-card
B. The day of judgment
C. The body of Moses
D. The ways of man

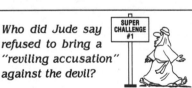

Who did Jude say refused to bring a "reviling accusation" against the devil?

SUPER CHALLENGE #1

4. Jude used some colorful metaphors to describe the false teachers and evil people of the day. All of these are part of his remarks EXCEPT:
A. They are barren fields, which never produce grain.
B. They are clouds without water, blown about by the wind.

C. They are late autumn trees without fruit.

D. They are raging waves of the sea, foaming up their own shame.

E. They are wandering stars for which the darkest blackness is reserved.

 DID YOU KNOW that Jude, the author of the book bearing his name, was the brother of Jesus? He simply refers to himself as "Jude, a bondservant of Christ, and brother of James." However, it is commonly known that James was Jesus's half-brother, so Jude felt it adequate to identify himself by that relationship. It could also be a humble awareness that he did not believe Jesus during his family life with Him (see John 7:5).

ANSWERS TO JUDE QUESTIONS

#	ANS	REF	#	ANS	REF
1.	D	1:6	Super Challenge:		
2.	A,C	1:7, 11	#1: Michael the arch-		
3.	C	1:9	angel (1:9)		
4.	A	1:12–13			

~REVELATION~

(*c*. A.D. 90–96)

1. John's greeting mentioned that Revelation was being written to the seven churches of Asia. To correspond with this, he said that around God's throne are:
   A. Seven Spirits
   B. Seven high (ranking) angels
   C. Seven servants
   D. Seven virgins
   E. Seven cases of 7-Up

2. Where was John when he received the revelation?
   A. Athens
   B. Crete
   C. Patmos
   D. Cyprus
   E. On a mountain in Tibet

3. The church at Laodicea was accused of being "lukewarm, and neither hot nor cold" therefore God would do what?
   A. Spit them out of His mouth
   B. Sentence them to the heaps of Gehenna (the city dump)
   C. Cast them into the lake of fire
   D. Cast them into outer darkness
   E. Sentence them to probation and community service

4. After the messages to the seven churches, John, again in the Spirit, sees the four beasts mentioned

in Ezekiel. All of the following are true concerning them EXCEPT:

A. The creatures had an excess of eyes.

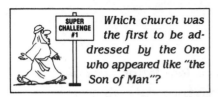
SUPER CHALLENGE #1

Which church was the first to be addressed by the One who appeared like "the Son of Man"?

B. One of the creatures had a man's face.

C. They never rest.

D. Two of the creatures had wings.

E. Twenty-four elders respond to the praise offered by the four creatures.

5. **Which of the seven seals revealed the souls of the martyrs?**
   A. The second seal
   B. The fourth seal
   C. The fifth seal
   D. None of the seals
   E. An Easter Seal

6. **After the fifth angel sounded his trumpet, the bottomless pit was opened, spewing smoke. Who/what emerged from the smoke?**
   A. The destroyer
   B. Locusts
   C. The Great Whore
   D. Poisonous serpents
   E. Firemen

7. **A woman in labor appeared, followed by a "great fiery red dragon." What did John say the dragon is preparing to do?**
   A. Kill the woman
   B. Fight with Michael and the angels
   C. Devour the child
   D. Attack the earth and its inhabitants

E. See if he can get Peter, Paul and Mary to write a song about him

8. **According to Chapter 13, which THREE of the following were true concerning the "beast from the earth"?**

A. His number is 666.

B. He destroys the beast from the sea.

C. He battles against the 144,000 undefiled men.

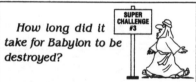
In Chapter 11, power is given to the two witnesses for 1,260 days. After that they will die. How?

SUPER CHALLENGE #2

D. He tells the people to create an image of the first beast.

E. He has the voice of a lamb and the scales of a dragon.

F. He causes everyone to get a mark on their hand or forehead.

9. **At the pouring out of the sixth bowl, a great river dries up. Which one?**

A. The Tigris

B. The Euphrates

C. The Nile

D. The Jordan

E. The Ohio

How long did it take for Babylon to be destroyed?

SUPER CHALLENGE #3

10. **All of these were attributed to Christ just prior to His second coming EXCEPT:**

A. He wore a crown of thorns on His head.

B. He sat upon a white horse.

C. His robe was red, dipped in blood.

D. His eyes were like fire.

E. Out of His mouth went a sharp sword.

11. **When the angel showed John the new "holy Jerusalem," he noticed TWO things that were visibly absent. What were they?**

A. Altars
B. Rivers and streams
C. The sun
D. A temple
E. Restrooms

12. What were the last words John heard Jesus speak?

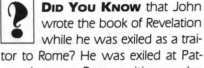 **DID YOU KNOW** that John wrote the book of Revelation while he was exiled as a traitor to Rome? He was exiled at Patmos because Roman citizens who refused to worship the emperor, Nero, as god were tortured, executed, or exiled as traitors.

A. "Seal up the book now, until the end."

B. "Write down everything you have seen, and share it with all of the churches."

C. "Know that all of these things shall come to pass."

D. "Surely I am coming quickly."

ANSWERS TO REVELATION QUESTIONS

#	ANS	REF
1.	A	1:4
2.	C	1:9
3.	A	3:16
4.	D	4:7–11
5.	C	6:9
6.	B	9:3
7.	C	12:4
8.	A,D,F	13:11–18
9.	B	16:12
10.	A	19:11–15
11.	C,D	21:22, 23
12.	D	22:20

Super Challenges:
 #1: Ephesus (2:1)
 #2: They are killed by
      the beast from the
      bottomless pit.
      (11:7)
 #3: one hour (18:17, 19)

~AFTERWORD~

Wait, we're not finished yet! You can't get away from me that easily! Yes, I've a couple more things to tell you . . . First of all thanks, and I really mean *thanks* for buying this book and spending your time with me! I'm sure I speak for Teri, my editor, and all the fine folks at Thomas Nelson Publishing when I say how much your friendship and trust mean to us. So, at the risk of being redundant, thank you!

Secondly, let's encourage one another with the knowledge that the Bible is full of practical ideas for happiness in this life, as well as promises for the next one. Our world still has problems, and God still has the answers. Join me in my attempt to become a more useful and positive person!

Finally, nurture your sense of humor. Laughter is still the best medicine, and it doesn't hurt to overdose on it occasionally. Don't overlook the fact that it's free, even if you *don't* have a prescription card!

As my parting gift, here is my list of the:

Top Ten Things You'll Have Time to Do Now That You've Finished This Book

10. Kill the tarantulas that have invaded your kitchen
9. Watch *It's a Wonderful Life* for the twenty-fourth time
8. Clean behind your refrigerator
7. Feed your boa constrictor
6. Check out some garage sales
5. Call your dentist just to chat
4. Organize your presidential campaign
3. Wolf down a "Grand Slam" breakfast at Denny's
2. Study your Sunday school lesson
1. Wait for the sequel!